D1555338

Behold the Lamb

BEHOLD THE LAMB

**AN EXPOSITION OF THE THEOLOGICAL
THEMES IN THE GOSPEL OF JOHN**

RAY SUMMERS

BROADMAN PRESS
Nashville, Tennessee

4213–74
ISBN: 0–8054–1374–X

Dewey Decimal Classification: 226.5
Subject heading: BIBLE. N. T. JOHN

Library of Congress Catalog Card Number: 78–67924
Printed in the United States of America.

Preface

Although the Gospel of John stands fourth in the New Testament arrangement of Gospels, it likely stands first in the devotion of a vast majority of Christians. While it had its challengers, its use by the earliest Christian writers demonstrates the long history of this devotion.

To date, the oldest extant portion of a New Testament book is the famous John Rylands Fragment 457. This small papyrus fragment containing a small part of the Greek text of John has been safely dated no later than the second quarter of the second Christian century, and it is most likely from the first quarter. We are fairly certain, therefore, that by A.D. 125–30 the Gospel of John was in circulation even in Egypt. Both extensive and intensive use of the Gospel have marked its history.

It would be difficult to overestimate the importance of an understanding of this Gospel for an understanding of the total message of the New Testament. In its doctrine of God's revelation of himself in Jesus Christ, it stands in the lofty company of the letter to the Hebrews. In its doctrine of the person and work of Jesus Christ, its depth challenges that of Ephesians and Colossians. In its doctrine of salvation by faith identification with Jesus Christ, it yields no ground to Galatians and Romans. Its doctrine of the Holy Spirit is foundational for an understanding of the Spirit's activity in the Acts of the Apostles and in the great sections on the Spirit in Romans 8 and 1 Corinthians 12—14. Its distinctive realized eschatology, the "now" of Christ's presence and kingdom, still leaves open the "not yet" of his coming in consummation of that kingdom. That must be a part of our working material for getting at one of the most discussed subjects in contemporary theology. Without this beautiful Gospel, how impoverished we would be in practically every area of Christian thought.

For twentieth-century thought and life, this first-century book stands to challenge us in our theology and ethics. Here is revealed Jesus Christ, God's incarnate Word, as our eternal contemporary who points for us "the way" because he is "The Way."

Contents

PART TWO
The Lamb and the New Israel
13:1 to 21:25

Introduction

The milieu of the Gospel of John is one of the first questions facing any serious study of the book. It is a perplexing milieu embracing a multiplicity of problems which have defied comfortable solution. When was the Gospel written? By whom was it written? To whom was it originally directed? Is it the most Hellenistic of the four Gospels or is it the most Hebraic? It is doubtful if opinion in these areas is more fragmented with regard to any other New Testament book. Some of the most respected New Testament scholars have despaired of finding satisfying conclusions.

Neither the scope nor the purpose of this volume permit lengthy pursuit of these questions. Brief consideration by way of suggestion for more extensive reading is in order. In 1965 Harold S. Songer published an article entitled "The Gospel of John in Recent Research." [1] He succinctly traced the lines of shifting opinion from the beginning of the twentieth century, with a major emphasis on the mid-century situation. For example, relative to the questions of authorship and date, he cites two very opposite positions: those who around 1900 held confidently to the view of an apostolic eyewitness as author (hence, well within the first century) and those who firmly denied such authorship and held the view that the Gospel was a product of mid second-century Hellenistic mysticism. As the years have passed, however, opinions have developed into three fairly well-defined categories: those who hold to apostolic authorship,[2] those who deny any form

9

of apostolic authorship,[3] and those who hold to a mediating position.[4]

Scholars who hold the mediating view vary in the details of mediation. In 1940 H. E. Dana, in the earliest effort at applying the methodology of form criticism to the Fourth Gospel, suggested that while the apostle John was the chief apostolic factor behind the Gospel, the actual writing was probably by "another John who had been a personal disciple of Jesus" and that "both Johns lived at Ephesus near the end of the first century." [5] Other scholars have held that the mediating agent was John the Elder of Papias' well-known statement without suggesting that he had been a personal follower of Jesus. A. T. Robertson, however, dismissed John the Elder as a very shadowy figure whom Eusebius erroneously found in the Papias reference.[6] Robertson held firmly to John the apostle as the author.

A growing facet of the mediating view of authorship is the idea of a school or circle of scholars in the Christian community of Asia Minor. With variations in the details of opinion as to how the work was done, these scholars are identified as the writers of all of the Johannine books of the New Testament: Fourth Gospel; First, Second, and Third Epistles; Apocalypse. Two excellent works of most recent date present fruitful reading on this phase of the subject. R. Alan Culpepper has done masterful research in surveying the entire phenomenon of schools of the New Testament world: the Pythagorean school, the Lyceum, the school of Philo, the Qumran school, and others.[7] He has established what precisely constituted a "school" and has applied these criteria to establish the validity of a "Johannine school" of producing scholars.

Making significant use of Culpepper's work but preferring the more loosely defined term *circle* to the more rigidly defined *school*, Elizabeth Schussler Fiorenza has applied the hypothesis in the production of the Johannine books.[8] Her specific area of interest is in the writing of the Gospel and the Apocalypse. She convincingly cites Barrett's proposed form of the Johannine-school hypothesis as widely influential today. Barrett acknowledged that his hypothesis was incapable of proof but expressed the hope that it would stimulate the discussion of the growth of early Christian literature.[9] It has. Here is a sketch of his proposal: John the apostle migrated from Palestine to Ephesus where he lived to old age and composed apocalyptic works. He gathered a number of pupils who grew under his commanding influence. After his death, they continued his work. One pupil wrote our Apocalypse near the end of the reign of Domitian, incorporating into it the apocalyptic writings of John himself. Another pupil produced the epistles, or possibly one pupil produced 1 John and another under the title "The Elder" produced 2 and 3 John. It remained for yet another to produce John 1—20. Barrett characterizes that one as "bolder" and "widely read both in Judaism and Hellenism." At a later date when John's views had defeated the Gnostics and "vindicated the permanent validity of the primitive Gospel," chapters 1—20 were edited with the addition of chapter 21 which was a part of the tradition of the life and experience of John, perhaps material which John himself had left. Barrett calls this final and unidentifiable editor "the evangelist" and praises him as "perhaps the greatest theologian in all the history of the Church." The early Christians identified the authority behind all of these works as John the son of Zebedee, "foe of heretics and beloved of his Lord."

In a more recent variation of the mediating idea, William E. Hull has suggested a solution to the complex problem by consideration of the persons involved in the pronouns of John 21:24–25.[10] From this viewpoint the composition of the Gospel reflects three stages. *First*, the eyewitness who brought to Asia this account of Jesus' life, death, and resurrection is reflected in the expressions, "This is the disciple" and "his testimony" in verse 24. Hull thinks that this is almost certainly the beloved disciple of verses 20–23, but he thinks that the "cumulative force of the evidence" is against identifying this beloved disciple with John the son of Zebedee.[11] *Second*, the Christian community of Asia which accepted this witness as valid and became its guarantor to others is reflected in the "we" of verse 24. *Third*, some unidentified individual within that Christian community, using materials which the beloved disciple had written to perpetuate for future generations the memories of his eyewitness experience, put those materials into the form in which we have them in our Gospel of John. That person is reflected in the "I" of verse 25. One may accept Hull's attractive view and at the same time reject his hesitancy in identifying the original witness, the beloved disciple, with John the apostle.

Historically the date of the writing of the Gospel has been linked with the matter of authorship. Scholars who have rejected any really viable link with apostolic authorship have tended to date the Gospel well into the second century. Scholars holding to apostolic origin or to a mediating view with some viable link to apostolic origin have generally dated the book in the A.D. 90–95 period. Several factors have influenced this tendency: (1) the general, though not unanimous, acceptance of an Asian location of origin of all of the traditionally Johannine writings; (2) the tradition of John's residency in Asia about that time; (3) the general, though again not unanimous, acceptance of the origin and circulation of the Synoptic Gospels several years before the appearance of the Fourth Gospel and the date of their origin in the A.D. 65–80 span.

A notable exception to this approach is the recent publication of J. A. T. Robinson's *Redating the New Testament.*[12] For 360 pages he argues exhaustively, exhaustingly, and sometimes exasperatingly that all of the twenty-seven books of the New Testament were written in the two decades before the destruction of Jerusalem in A.D. 70. His key at this point is a negative one, that is, the only New Testament references to the destruction of Jerusalem view it as a future event (Jesus' Mount of Olives discourse on Tuesday before his death on Friday, Matt. 24–25; Mark 13; Luke 21). Since Jesus predicted it as a *future* event and no book in the New Testament mentions it as an *accomplished* event, it must follow, he argues, that it had not happened when the books were written. In similar vein, he dates Acts about A.D. 62 because it mentions neither the Neronian persecution, the death of Peter, nor the death of Paul.

Robinson's history is one of stirring up his contemporaries to debate. In this book he issues the challenge that they prove him wrong. It is too early to predict how much his views will be challenged and how much they will be ignored. The initial response has been the usual early response of mixed cheers and jeers. It is not too early to predict that New Testament scholarship will not quickly give up the results of a hundred years of critical investigation. The date of about A.D. 90–95 for the Johannine books will remain secure even for many who would welcome really solid and positive evidence for an early dating, particularly of the Gospel. The question is, How solid and positive is Robinson's evidence?

With the questions of authorship and date, one must consider the identity of the initial recipients of this Gospel. To whom was it directed? What was the situation which called for such a Gospel? Were the recipients whom the author had in focus Greek or Hebrew? Were they Christian or non-Christian? With all due respect for the scholarly stature of C. K. Barrett and with tremendous appreciation for his classic commentary on this Gospel, we cannot accept at surface value his statement:

It is easy, when we read the Gospel, to believe that John, though doubtless aware of the necessity of strengthening Christians and converting the heathen, wrote primarily to satisfy himself. His gospel must be written: it was no concern of his whether it was also read.[13]

It would be a rare author with a rare brand of compulsion who could write with such depth and simplicity, with such intense concern for the ultimate importance of his message, then having completed it to say: "There. I *had* to write it. I care not whether it is read!"

Although the element of purpose stated in John 20:30–31 is sometimes discounted in contemporary studies on John, it will be considered as central in this volume. John's favorite word for the miracles of Jesus is "signs." Many fine works have been published on John as the book of signs. For him the miracles are events which, as signs, point beyond themselves to something more important than the event itself. For example, the raising of Lazarus was important, but it pointed to something of greater importance. It indicated that Jesus was "the resurrection and the life"; where he was present, the power of life over death was already working.

Up to this statement of purpose in 20:30–31, John had used seven of Jesus' miracles:

Turning water to wine, 2:1–11
Healing the son of the king's officer, 4:46–54
Healing the lame man at the pool, 5:1–9
Feeding the five thousand, 6:1–13
Walking on the water, 6:16–21
Healing the man who was born blind, 9:1–41
Raising Lazarus from the dead, 11:1–44.

Four of these are in John's Gospel alone (five, if the healing of the son of the king's officer is a different miracle from the healing of the son of a Roman centurion in Luke 7:1–10 and Matt. 8:5–13).

John used miracles which make the greatest demand on credence. In the other Gospels Jesus heals temporary blindness; in John he gives sight to a man born blind. In the other Gospels, he restores to life a little girl who had been dead only a few minutes and a young man who had probably been dead no more than a few hours; in John he raises a man who had been dead four days.

John's statement of purpose indicates his deliberate selection of these particular miracles with a twofold objective: to convince his readers: (1) that Jesus who had done these things was the Christ, the Son of God and (2) that by that faith they might have life in his name. The statement is so explicit that it is difficult to see how one can deny that it was his purpose or why one should seek to deny it.

The question remains, Who were these people whom John sought to convince and to bring to faith that Jesus was the Christ? The position of this volume will be that they were Jews, specifically the Jews of the Dispersion (non-Palestinian), starting with those of his own territory of ministry, Asia. Three cities of great Jewish concentration after the devastation of Palestine in the Jewish-Roman war of A.D. 66–70 have been suggested as the place of writing of John: Ephesus, Antioch, Alexandria. Only Ephesus has significant support. Robinson has stated it well.[14] The material of the Gospel was forged in teaching within the Christian community in Judea in controversy with the Jews of that area.[15] In its present form it is directed to winning to Christian faith the Greek-speaking Jews of what Robinson calls the greatest "dispersion" of all, one that swept both church and synagogue from Judea.

It is very generally held that Matthew was written for a Jewish-Christian constituency and is largely didactic in nature instructing its readers in the implications of Jesus as the Davidic messianic King. It might logically follow that Matthew is the most Hebraic of the Gospels. Closer examination, however, may challenge that conclusion. With the possible exception of Revelation, John may prove to be the most Hebraic book in the New Testament.

While Matthew has the term "the Jews" six times, John has it seventy. Grant Matthew's concern for showing that Jesus is the Christ of Judaism, but note that John uses the title "Christ" more often than Matthew and that he is the only New Testament writer who uses it in its Hebrew (Aramaic) form, "the Messiah." While Gentiles play a prominent role in Matthew, and to some extent in Mark and Luke, they are never mentioned in John, with the single exception of Pilate. When John uses the Greek word for *Gentiles* (translated "nations"), the reference is always to the *Jews.*

John is sometimes considered anti-Jewish. This, however, should not be used in a racial sense. He may be accurately characterized as "anti" Jewish in that he stands on the side of Jesus in all of the controversy between Jesus and the Jews. And in this sense "the Jews" most often means the Jewish religious authorities who opposed Jesus. Sometimes more specifically it refers to the Pharisees. The entire ministry of Jesus in this Gospel may be told in terms of controversy over Jewish doctrine and practice. How did Jesus' teaching and practice differ from that of the authorities? He was a Jew and considered himself within Judaism. He challenged the authorities' teaching and practice. They regarded him as a lawbreaker and disturber of the people. On one occasion John cites their agreement to dispel from the synagogue any person who confessed that Jesus was the Christ (9:22).

John struggled with this problem of the Jews' rejection of Jesus as the Messiah with the same intensity that another Jewish-Christian theologian struggled with it, the apostle Paul. Smith has some instructive paragraphs at this point.[16] Unlike Paul, however, John never found even partial solution or relief in seeing the Jews' rejection as a signal to turn to the evangelization of the Gentiles. John does reflect the concept of Christ's redemption for all, Jew and Gentile (1:12; 17:21; and perhaps 10:16, though some understand this as a reference to the Jews of the Dispersion). He knew that Christianity is for the whole world. The major thrust of his Gospel, however, deals with the Jews and Jesus. If the truth about Jesus was declared by Abraham (8:39,56), Moses (1:45; 5:39–47; 7:19–24), and Isaiah (12:41), why could the Jews not see and accept Jesus as the fulfillment of God's redemptive work? How could they reject him?

So, for the Jews beyond Judea as for the Jews of Jesus' time in Judea, he is the Way. To accept him means that everything becomes new. It is to be born again even when one is old, like Nicodemus who was a Pharisee, a teacher of Israel, and a member of the Sanhedrin (3:1–10). He remained a Jew but never a Jew as he had once been a Jew. He accepted the insults of the authorities when they were condemning Jesus without a trial (8:50–52). By implication at least, he braved the wrath of the Sanhedrin in joining a fellow member, Joseph of Arimathea, in refusing to vote for Jesus' execution and the wrath of Pilate in asking for permission to bury Jesus (Luke 23:50–53; John 19:38–42). He found Jesus to be the fulfillment of God's promise of a Redeemer. What Nicodemus had experienced, John desired for all of the Jews. To that end he framed his Gospel for the Greek-speaking Jews of the Hellenistic world.

The theme of the Gospel of John rivals authorship, date, and recipients as an area of diverse opinion. This is clear from scanning the table of contents or outline page of any book—or a shelf of them—on this very popular Gospel. It is doubtful if an analysis of this diversity would contribute significantly to the development of the theme which is proposed for this volume. Such an analysis is, therefore, omitted.

In popular opinion the Logos (the Word) is frequently expressed as the theme of the Gospel. It is extremely doubtful if the writer considered it so. It is used in the poetic structure of the prologue (1:1–18) and never appears again. It does not appear to be the theme of this Gospel any more than it does for 1 John where it appears in the prologue (1:1–4) or for Revelation where it is one of several titles or names for Christ (1:2; 19:13). It is an intriguing link between these three of the five books in the Johannine corpus and the question of their origin, but it is not their theme.

For this volume the organizing theme will be the Lamb. Recognizably that theme is open to challenge since it appears only twice in the dramatic statement, "Behold, the Lamb of God" (1:29,36). In this construction it is used for the Redeemer, Christ, who may be considered the theme of nearly every New Testament book. While the Lamb as the Redeemer who takes away the sin of the world actually is used only in these two places, a case can be made for John's developing a redemption role for the Passover Lamb in the end of the Gospel. The theme of redemption in the Passover experience was not foreign to Hebrew theology. While it was not an emphasis in the original Passover event, the entire Exodus experience came to be developed as a redemptive event; in the Passover, God redeemed Israel from Egypt.

The format is not to be that of a verse-by-verse commentary. Excellent comprehensive commentaries are abundant. They represent a very wide range of approach and opinion. Running the risk of leaving out someone's favorite commentary, let me list a few of the most used and quoted, including representatives from a wide range of approach and opinion. See the bibliography in the back of this book for full publishing data on these, as well as an extensive list of other commentaries and books. From the older traditional viewpoint see: Alvah Hovey, *John*, "An American Commentary on the New Testament"; William Hendriksen's two volume work in his *New Testament Commentary* series; R. C. H. Lenski's volume in his *"Commentary on the New Testament"*; B. F. Westcott's *Commentary on the Gospel According to St. John.* From the more contemporary publications, conservative from the viewpoint of being true to the cardinal doctrines of the Christian faith, open to truth, and using all of the tools for correct exegesis see: C. K. Barrett's monograph commentary; Raymond E. Brown's two volume work in "The Anchor Bible" series; William E. Hull's treatment in *The Broadman Bible Commentary.* From the very liberal, existential hermeneutical viewpoint see: R. Bultmann's *Gospel of John: a Commentary* and for very excellent assistance in understanding Bultmann's rearrangement or restructuring of the text of the Fourth Gospel use Dwight Moody Smith's *Composition and Order of the Fourth Gospel: Bultmann's Literary Theory.*

Linked to Christ as the Lamb, the structure of this book will develop the generally recognized division of the Gospel into two parts. In chapters 2—12 the emphasis is on Christ's relation to Israel at large. In chapters 13—21 the emphasis is on his relation to the small circle of followers whom we know as the twelve apostles. A latent but striking parallel in the two parts will be developed: Part I, The Lamb and the Old Israel—Introduced, Manifested, Rejected in relation to the raising of Lazarus from the dead; Part II, The Lamb and the New Israel—Introduced, Manifested, Accepted in relation to his own resurrection from the dead. Within this structure many of the rich metaphors, theological roles, acts, and motifs will be examined by way of exposition of the biblical text. Documentation will reflect inadequately my indebtedness to a multitude of interpreters and theologians of diverse opinions whose works I have absorbed in more than forty years of teaching this Gospel. Stand or fall, the thematic organization is my own and the exposition reflects my own understanding of this Gospel. The devout hope is that through it all the readers may better

Behold the Lamb!

Notes

1. Harold S. Songer, "The Gospel of John in Recent Research," *Review and Expositor,* Fall 1965, pp. 417–428.
2. Such as William Hendriksen, "Exposition of the Gospel According to John," 2 vols., *New Testament Commentary* (Grand Rapids: Baker Book House, 1953 and 1954).
3. Such as R. Bultmann, *The Gospel of John,* ed. R. W. N. Hoare and J. K. Riches, trans. G. R. Beasley-Murray (Philadelphia: The Westminster Press, 1971).
4. Such as C. K. Barrett, *The Gospel According to St. John* (London: S.P.C.K., 1958).
5. H. E. Dana, *The Ephesian Tradition* (Kansas City: The Kansas City Press, 1940), p. 168.

6. A. T. Robertson, *Epochs in the Life of the Apostle John* (New York: Fleming H. Revell Company, 1935), pp. 22–29.

7. R. Alan Culpepper, *The Johannine School* (Missoula, Montana: Scholars Press, 1975).

8. Elizabeth Schussler Fiorenza, "The Quest for the Johannine School: The Apocalypse and the Fourth Gospel," *New Testament Studies*, July 1977, pp. 402–427.

9. Barrett, pp. 113–114.

10. William E. Hull, "John," *The Broadman Bible Commentary*, vol. 9, ed. Clifton J. Allen (Nashville: Broadman Press, 1970). This appears to be an adaptation and simplification of Bultmann, pp. 717–718.

11. Hull, pp. 196–198 and 375–376. For defense of John the son of Zebedee as the beloved disciple and the author of the Gospel of John, read B. F. Westcott, *The Gospel According to St. John* (London: James Clarke and Co., 1958), pp. v–xxxii. In several publications, Floyd V. Filson argues for Lazarus as the beloved disciple and, hence, the writer of the Fourth Gospel. Read especially his *Gospel According to John*, "The Layman's Bible Commentary, Vol. 19" (Richmond: John Knox Press, 1963), pp. 22–25.

12. J. A. T. Robinson, *Redating the New Testament* (Philadelphia: The Westminster Press, 1976).

13. Barrett, p. 115.

14. J. A. T. Robinson, "The Destination and Purpose of St. John's Gospel," *New Testament Studies*, January 1960, p. 131. See also a response to this discerning article by J. W. Bowker, "The Origin and Purpose of St. John's Gospel," *New Testament Studies*, July 1965, pp. 398–408.

15. Compare Dana in his basic thesis that the "Ephesian Tradition," the oral account of Jesus which is reflected in John's Gospel, began in a "Judean Tradition" and spread to a "Palestinian Tradition" before coming the "Ephesian Tradition."

16. T. C. Smith, *Jesus in the Gospel of John* (Nashville: Broadman Press, 1959), pp. 14–17.

Prologue
The Lamb Anticipated
by the Logos
(1:1–18)

The poetic or hymnic nature of the prologue to the Gospel of John is generally recognized.[1] The search for a literary source which John may have used continues with no consensus as to a solution. With no indication of a source and no definition of his main term, John launches into his discussion of the Logos.

The original being and the creative activity of the Logos (vv. 1–5): "In the beginning . . . ." Read that phrase alone and Genesis 1:1 comes to mind. It is not to be read alone: "In the beginning was the Word." John's term is *Logos*. It has multiple uses—a doctrine, a teaching, a discourse. Its main meaning is "word," and that is John's meaning here. It becomes clear in the passage that he is using "Word" for Christ. A word is a means of communication. That is appropriate since Christ comes to be God's supreme "communication" to man. That, however, comes later. First, John speaks of the Word in the eternity in which there was only God. Even then the Word *was*, the Word was *with God*, the Word *was God*. The best term we have found for expressing this is *preexistence*—the original being of the Word. The Greek word which is translated "was" means being without reference to origin. There was never a time when the Word was not. So the ancient theologians could discuss the proposition, "There was never a time when the Son was not."

The Word was "with God," *(pros ton theon* in the Greek text). The expression stresses the very closest relationship. We can accurately translate it "face to face with God," but that fails really to express the idea of intimacy. How can language adequately express the intimacy involved when the very next clause states that "the Word was God"? A delicate and difficult to translate construction is in the Greek text of this clause, the Greek noun for God *(theon)* without the definite article. The stress is on nature, character. The Word was as "divine" as God was "divine." The Word was deity as God was deity. The fault is not with the idea; it is with the weakness of language in expressing the idea. Verse 2 repeats verse 1 in parallel—the Word that *was* God was *with* God in the beginning. How better can we express it than in the term "the original being" of the Word?

Verse 3 transports us again to Genesis 1:1 and introduces the creative activity of the Word. In the beginning the creative word of God went forth, "God said." Out of chaos (disorder) came cosmos (order); out of darkness came light; out of nonbeing came being, life. Once again the creative Word of God goes forth. This time it is the incarnate Word (v. 14). Out of spiritual disorder comes spiritual order; out of spiritual darkness comes spiritual light; out of spiritual death comes spiritual life.

The ancient Hebrew thought of one's words as an extension of his person. I stretch out my hand; it is an extension of me; it works, it accomplishes. In the same way I send out my words; they are an extension of my person; they work, they accomplish. By this analogy, the creative Word of God was an extension of the very person of God in creation, "All things were made through him, and without him was not anything made that was made." The preexistent Word was the active agent of the eternal God in creation. In Colossians 1:16–18 Paul stressed the role of Christ in creation. He stated that Christ was before all things (v. 17), Christ created all things (v. 16), and that all things having been created are sustained by Christ (v. 17), "in him all things hold together."

In Pauline and in Johannine theology the Christ who created is the Christ who redeems. This is in line with the Old Testament emphasis on the doctrines of creation and redemption. The God who redeems is the God who created. Correspondingly in the New Testament, the Christ who redeems is the Christ who created. In both cases the encouraging assurance is that by his very nature God is redemptive. He will not see his creation involved in sin and do nothing about it. He moves redemptively into his creation and the incarnate Word is the agent of that redeeming action.

As the Word was related to *God* in his being (vv. 1–2), and to the *world* in his creativity (v. 3), so he is related to *man* in giving life (vv. 4–5). A striking feature of the structure of the Fourth Gospel is the introduction in the prologue of many of the concepts which are developed in the remainder of the book. Among these are: life, light, darkness, witness, belief, children of God, born of God, glory, truth, grace. In verses 4–5 life, light, and darkness appear. They will reappear throughout the Gospel. In 1:4 life, which is characteristically resident in the Word, comes to be light, the illumination of the very nature of God and what God the Creator desires of man the creature. In 20:31 it becomes the possession of the one who believes that Jesus is the Christ, the Son of God. And in between is the recurring theme that the very purpose of Christ's coming into the world was that man might have life.

In the world this light through life is constantly opposed. The opposition is termed "darkness" (v. 5). Darkness is not simply a negative concept; it is not merely the absence of illumination, knowledge of God. It is in positive opposition to God and to man. Darkness speaks of evil—active rebellion, active hostility to God and to God's purposes. The encouraging word, however, is that the light just keeps on shining (present tense), and the darkness is unable to suppress it (literally, "to hold it down"). In John 1:5 the darkness is not able to hold the light down; in 1 John 2:8 the darkness is unable to hold the light back; the true, genuine light is shining and the darkness is retreating before it (literally,

"is being led away"). This is John's sense of assurance in the ultimate triumph of God's purpose for his creation. It is a prelude
to the assuring words of Christ on the very night before his execution, "I have overcome the world" (John 16:33). In history that
victory awaited realization and still does; in God's purpose it was
an accomplished fact and still is.

The incarnation of the Logos and his revelation of God (vv. 6–18):
In verses 6–8 John the Baptist appears as a messenger sent from
God to bear witness to the coming of the true light into the
world. An overpowering sense of purpose pervades the entire
passage. A man came to be; he was sent from God, even his
name meant "one whom God has graciously given"; he was sent
to bear witness to the fact that "the light of men" (v. 4) was
coming into the world; the end purpose of his witness was to
bring man to belief in that "light."

For an understanding of this role of John, one needs to review
the marvelously beautiful account of John and Jesus in Luke 1:5
to 3:38. It is a dramatic presentation paralleling John and Jesus
up to their public ministries: announcement of their coming
births; account of their births; their acceptance into the covenant
people of God through naming and circumcision; the years of
silence; the beginning of their public ministries at thirty years
of age; the end of John's ministry; the continuing ministry of
Jesus.[2]

John was of priestly lineage; both his father and mother were
of priestly families (Luke 1:5). His ministry, however, was not
that of a priest but that of a prophet. In this respect he resembled
Jeremiah of the Old Testament prophets. Verses 6–13 anticipate
elements which will be developed in the main body of the Gospel.
That he was not the anticipated Messiah but was to bear witness
to the Messiah (vv. 7–8) anticipates 1:19–28. That Jesus was the
true light and the coming Redeemer (vv. 9–13) anticipates 1:29–
42. That he would be rejected by Israel at large (vv. 10*b*–11)
but accepted by some within Israel (vv. 12–13) anticipates the

total ministry of Jesus as presented in John. Wherever Jesus taught or worked, a division resulted (John uses the word for "schism"), some accepting him, some rejecting him.

The emphasis on belief is strong in this passage as well as throughout the Gospel. John the Baptist's *witness* was that all might believe. Later Jesus' *words* will be that all may believe, and his *works* will be that all may believe. John's purpose in selecting the seven miracles in writing the Gospel was that all might believe (20:31).

The emphasis on rejection is tragic. Coming into the world, Christ brought illumination, light, to all (v. 9), but some did not recognize him as the Redeemer (v. 10). He came unto his own created world (literally, "his own things, possessions"), but those who were his own people (the Jews) rejected him (v. 11). To those who did by faith accept him, relatively few when compared with the masses who rejected him, he gave the authority to become the children of God (v. 12). These were the ones who experienced spiritual birth in relation to the desire (will) of God, not those who experienced only physical birth in relation to the desire of the flesh (v. 13). John the Baptist, Jesus, and Paul all insisted that to be born physically the descendant of Abraham did not put one into covenant relationship to God. Such relationship comes only on the basis of faith. Verse 13 anticipates Jesus' conversation with Nicodemus (3:1–21) and the Jewish religious authorities (8:33–59) contrasting physical birth with spiritual birth.

"And the Word became flesh and dwelt among us" (v. 14). The simplicity of that affirmation conveys the profundity of the entire redemptive work of God. The Word who was (being *without* reference to origin) came to be (being *with* reference to origin) flesh. While there was never a time when the Word *was not*, there was a time when the Word *was not flesh*. The Word *became* flesh. The eternal Word took upon himself the limitation of human flesh to dwell as a man among men that he might redeem men from sin and make them to become sons of

God. This calls to mind the incarnation hymn of Philippians
2:6–11: Christ existing in the form of God did not regard that
as something to be retained by force. Rather he gave that up to
accept the form of a man even when that involved humility,
suffering, and death, even the death of a cross. To become flesh
meant all of that, but it also meant redemption for man's sin.

To dwell among us means to live with us. The Greek word
means to live in a tent, commonly translated "tabernacle." In
the Exodus experience of Israel, God's tabernacle (tent) stood
in the midst of the camp with all of the people's tents around
it. This meant God's presence in the midst of his people; he was
living with them.[3] So the Word became flesh and lived among
men to reveal to them the glory of God. The glory of God is
the manifestation of his character as divine and perfect. His glory
was manifest historically in his great works among men—his presence in the Temple, his giving of the Law, his deliverance of
Israel from Egypt, his miracles. None of these, however, could
reveal his glory as his only begotten Son could reveal it. In that
Son, those who accepted him beheld the glory of God, his grace,
his truth revealed as only his Son could reveal it. His glory revealed through the giving of the Law through Moses was real,
but it was dim compared with his glory revealed in the giving
of grace and truth by his Son. This is not a confession of John
alone. It is the confession of the worshiping people of God in
the day of John's writing and through the ages which have
followed.

In verse 18 John wrote of man's longing to see God but his
inability to see God. It is part of his human limitation that he
cannot see God. Not with the limitation of physical eyes do we
see one who is Spirit (John 4:24). We cannot by human sight
reduce the invisible to the visible. Jesus Christ, the Son of God,
however, makes it possible for us to know what God is like. Remember his words to Philip, "He who has seen me has seen the
Father" (John 14:9). Through Christ the Godlike we can see God

the Christlike. Do we long to know what God is like? Let us look at Jesus Christ his Son.

To be "in the bosom of" one is to be in bliss, as was Lazarus in Abraham's bosom (Luke 16:22). It is to be in such close relation as to share the most confidential matters, as was the beloved disciple leaning on Jesus' bosom at the Last Supper (John 13:23). Such a person is the Son of God who "made God known" to us. The word which is translated "made God known" is the word for explaining precisely and clearly. No Greek student can resist the impulse to transliterate the word, "he has exegeted" God for us. It is the best of all words for the idea of explaining meaning. Just by being who he is, as well as by his teachings, Jesus makes God known to us fully and completely. With this dramatic verse, John made the transition from the Logos to the Lamb. The eternal Word (v. 1) who has become the incarnate Word (v. 14) is identified as the Son of God (v. 18) who next appears as "the Lamb of God, who takes away the sin of the world!" (v. 29).

Notes

1. Very helpful works on the prologue are: Raymond B. Brown, "The Prologue of the Gospel of John," *Review and Expositor,* Fall 1965, pp. 429–439; James L. Price, "The Search for the Theology of the Fourth Evangelist," *Journal of the American Academy of Religion,* March 1967, pp. 3–15; J. A. T. Robinson, "The Relation of the Prologue to the Gospel of St. John," *New Testament Studies,* January 1963, pp. 120–129; Barrett, pp. 125–149; Hull, pp. 209–220.

2. This is developed at length in my *Commentary on Luke* (Waco: Word Books, Publisher, 1972), pp. 23–52.

3. By a beautiful symbol in Revelation 21:3, God pitches his tent (tabernacle) to dwell eternally with his people. I have developed this idea in *Worthy Is the Lamb* (Nashville: Broadman Press, 1951), pp. 211–212 and *The Life Beyond* (Nashville: Broadman Press, 1959), pp. 201–214.

PART ONE
The Lamb
and the Old Israel
1:19 to 12:50

I. Introduction of the Lamb
(1:19–51)

The role of John the Baptist as a witness was clearly and emphatically set out in the prologue. He came "for testimony" to "bear witness" concerning the light that was to come into the world (v. 7). He was not that light but was to "bear witness" concerning that light (v. 8). His witness is anticipated in verse 15, "This was he of whom I said, 'He who comes after me ranks before me, for he was before me.' " That witness will be narrated specifically in verses 29–34, but in general it comprises all of the John the Baptist sections in this Gospel (1:19–36; 3:22–30 definitely, and 31–36 probably). One must also include at this point Jesus' reference to the witness of John in 5:30–47. He cited a fourfold witness to himself as the Son of God: John (v. 33); his own works (v. 36); the Father (v. 37); the Scripture (vv. 36–37,39).

For a total grasp of the importance of John the Baptist as the forerunner to announce the coming of Jesus as the Messiah, one's study must include the Synoptic materials (Mark 1:2–11; Matt. 3:1–17; Luke 1:5–80; 3:1–23). It is also instructive to include Jesus' appraisal of John as the greatest of the Hebrew prophets (Matt. 11:2–19; Luke 7:18–35). Josephus made note of John as a good man who was so influential among the people that Herod Antipas, fearing his popularity, put John to death lest he start a rebellion. Josephus includes in his report the view of many of the Jews that the destruction of Herod's armies by Aretas IV was God's punishment for Herod's execution of John.[1]

The first facet of John's witness in this Gospel is negative, that is, he was not the Messiah who was anticipated by the Jews (1:19–28). When Jewish religious authorities came to question him, he made that fact very clear. Born of the prayers of his parents (Luke 1:13) and of the purpose (Luke 1:16–17) and power (Luke 1:19,36–37) of God, prepared for the work of a prophet (Luke 1:80), John appeared with the dramatic proclamation: Prepare your hearts for the coming of the messianic King.[2] His appearance was in the desert country north of the Dead Sea and near the Jordan River. Most likely it was beside the highway from Jericho across the Jordan into Perea, a major route, particularly for Jews traveling between Judea and Galilee and wanting to bypass Samaria.

Verse 28 places John's baptizing at a "Bethany beyond the Jordan," not the Bethany at Jerusalem. Biblical geographers, however, have not been able to locate such a Bethany. Some manuscripts have "Bethabara" a town which Origen located early in the third century when he was trying unsuccessfully to find a Bethany beyond the Jordan. Other manuscripts have "Betharabah," a place known as one of the boundary markers for the tribe of Judah (Josh. 15:6,61; 18:22). This would have been just a few miles north of the Dead Sea.

In his strange grab and with his startling message, John attracted immediate attention. Great crowds gathered to listen; many accepted his message and submitted to his baptism (Mark 1:5; Matt. 3:5–6). According to Matthew 3:7 there were even Pharisees and Sadducees who came to request baptism. It was a new and popular messianic movement in Israel. Alarmed at the news, the Temple officials in Jerusalem sent priests and Levites as messengers to question John about himself and his message (1:19).

Their first question, "Who are you?" is emphatic in form and may well be translated, "*You*, who are you?" The question calls for John to identify himself. It may reflect their awareness of a variety of opinions which people were expressing. So their question meant, "Who are you in your own thinking?" Verse 20 seems to reflect that John sensed that their real interest was not who he was but whether he was claiming to be the Christ. He was preaching that the messianic kingdom was breaking into history. He was calling for the spiritual cleansing of confession and repentance in preparation for it. He was administering the symbolic cleansing of baptism to *Jews*, calling upon them to accept baptism as a *Gentile* who turned from his religion to accept the religion of Israel. Did he, then, think of himself as the messianic king? His denial, "I am not the Christ," was as emphatic as their question. It may be translated "*I?* I am not the Christ."

Their second question (v. 21) is in two parts, "What then? Are you Elijah?" In the first part the gender of the interrogative pronoun is changed from the masculine (who?) of verse 19 to the neuter (what?). The particle translated "then" is inferential, looking back to John's saying that he was not the Christ. The total intent of the question is simply, "If you are not the Christ, what are you?" The second part of their question carries the dialogue forward to another possibility, "Are you Elijah?" This question clearly reflects the Hebrew anticipation of the return of Elijah as an agent of God in the consummation of his purpose for his creation. In Malachi 4:5–6 was God's promise.

Behold, I will send you Elijah the prophet before the great and terrible day of the Lord comes. And he will turn the hearts of fathers to their children and the hearts of children to their fathers, lest I come and smite the land with a curse.

The day of the Lord was to be a day of weal (blessing upon the obedient) and of woe (judgment upon the disobedient). Elijah would have an important part in it.

The role of John the Baptist after the pattern of Elijah is reflected elsewhere in the New Testament. In Luke 1:17 Gabriel's announcement to Zacharias of the coming of John employed the Malachi 4:5–6 passage. Zacharias' son would go before the Lord "in the spirit and power" of Elijah. He would "make ready for the Lord" a prepared people. At the transfiguration of Jesus, Elijah appeared with Moses and talked with Jesus about his approaching death in Jerusalem (Luke 9:31). Jesus had predicted his death a week before at the confession at Caesarea Philippi (Luke 9:18–22; Mark 8:27–33; Matt. 16:13–23), and the apostles had rejected the idea. It is important to note that in that confession experience the apostles indicated that some people thought Jesus was Elijah. Now Jesus had accepted their confession that he was the Christ and had affirmed that as the Christ he would be rejected by Israel, would suffer, and die; Elijah had come to talk with him about his approaching death. The apostles were confused.

On the way down from the mountain the next day, the three who had been with Jesus at the transfiguration asked him if the appearance of Elijah was the fulfillment of the Malachi prophecy that Elijah would return in preparation for the coming of the Messiah (Matt. 17:10). Jesus responded that Elijah had already come, had been rejected and put to death, and that he too would experience similar rejection and death (v. 12). The three understood his meaning; the coming of John in his preparatory role was the fulfillment of the Malachi prophecy. If the three were acquainted with the story of John's birth, it would make clear for them Gabriel's use of that prophecy.

How, then, are we to understand John's response to the question of the Temple committee, "Are you Elijah?" His response was negative and emphatic, "I am not." From the viewpoints from which John responded to the authorities and Jesus responded to the apostles, both were true. John was not Elijah in the *literal* sense in which they anticipated Elijah's return to the world, perhaps as dramatically as he had been taken from it. John was Elijah in the *symbolic* sense of his being God's messenger to prepare a people for the coming of the Messiah.

The third question from the committee likewise drew a negative response from John. "Are you the prophet?" And he answered, "No" (v. 21). Their question brought up another element

in Hebrew messianic anticipation. Through Moses God had promised Israel that the time would come when he would raise up
in Israel a prophet like Moses (Deut. 18:15), a prophet who would
speak to Israel all which God commanded him (v. 18). God would
hold responsible in judgment anyone who refused to obey his
word through that prophet (v. 19). A prophet like Moses came
to be a fixed part of their anticipation. Again John's response
was a denial, "No." He was not that Moses-like prophet.[3] Hull
suggests an increasing emphasis on negation in John's three responses "(I am not . . . Not I . . . No!)"[4] This may be valid; the
grammatical constructions change as he moved from one phase
of denial to the other. Certainly the curt "No" of the third denial
(v. 21) could leave no question as to John's rejection of all of
their tentative attempts at identification—with Christ, Elijah, or
the Moses-like prophet.

When John had rejected all of their suggestions about his self-
identification, they changed their approach by asking him to identify himself so they could make a positive report to the Temple
authorities (v. 22, "Who are you? . . . What do you say about
yourself?"). He answered by quoting Isaiah 40:3, "I am the voice
of one crying in the wilderness, 'Make straight the way of the
Lord.' " The Synoptic Gospels which do not have this dialogue
between John and the Temple authorities have the same identification in introducing the beginning of John's preaching (Mark
1:3; Matt. 3:3; Luke 3:4–6). This beautiful song in Isaiah 40:3–5
is a call for men to make spiritual preparation for the coming
of the messianic King as men would build a road for their king
to travel as he came to visit their territory. So John understood
that his role was that of the servant who went ahead into that
roadless territory to cry out: The King is coming. Prepare your
hearts for him.

In taking up verses 24–27, we must devote some attention to
the question of the precise identity of those who were pressing
the argument with John beyond his identification of himself as

the voice in the wilderness. Verse 19 indicates that "the Jews" of Jerusalem sent "priests and Levites" to question John. Verse 24 indicates the participation of Pharisees in at least this part of the discussion with John. There is an ambiguity due to variant readings in different manuscripts of the Gospel. Some manuscripts have the definite article with the participle and verb making the reading, "Now they had been sent from the Pharisees." This suggests that "the Jews" of verse 19 were Pharisees who sent the priests and Levites to question John. Although that would be a rare situation, the Pharisees sending Sadducees on a mission, Robertson[5] so interprets it. There were of course Pharisees in the Sanhedrin. Hendriksen rejects Robertson's interpretation as being entirely unreasonable.[6] He holds rather that "from the Pharisees" means that all of those who were *sent* were priests and Levites who were also Pharisees. Negatively, he argues that there is no proof that all priests were Sadducees.

Other manuscripts, the ones having better support, omit the article leaving the translation to be something like "And some Pharisees had been sent." This would mean that among the priests and Levites of verse 19 were some who identified with the Pharisees rather than the more customary priestly alignment with the Sadducees. Among others Brown[7] and Barrett[8] note that there were priests who were Pharisees, though Barrett questions the authority of the Pharisees to send such a delegation.

Whether all of those who had been sent by the Sanhedrin (Hendriksen's view) or only some of them (Brown's preference), it is clear that the ones who continued to pursue the questioning in verse 25 were Pharisees. This might be expected since they were the most scrupulous of the Jews in desiring loyalty to the Scriptures and practices of the Hebrew faith. They were not willing to drop the matter with John's identification of himself as only a wilderness voice. By baptizing he was performing an official act. If he was not an official of some sort, why was he performing an official act (v. 25)?

On the surface their question suggests that Hebrew messianic anticipation included the practice of baptism by the Messiah or by the other eschatological figures (Elijah; the Moses-like prophet). Hendriksen accepts this view and finds the basis for such anticipation of baptism as a messianic act in the washing and cleansing in relation to God's purpose for Israel in such passages as Ezekiel 36:25; 37:23.[9] Barrett discounts it. He states that such inference should not be found here. Rather their question merely meant, "Why do you perform what appears to be an official act if you have no official status?"[10] It seems clear that the Pharisees were not so much troubled by John's message as they were by his practice. He was the son of a priest; he had not aligned himself to serve as a priest; why was he performing a priestly function in baptizing?

In his response John pointed out the great difference in what he was doing and what the Messiah would do, though what the Messiah would do is not indicated until verse 29 in an incident which took place the next day. In his present encounter with the Pharisees, John indicated first that what he was doing was a symbolic act; he was baptizing "in water," a translation better than "with water." The background, or model, for what he was doing was likely the well-known practice of proselyte baptism of Gentiles who converted to the Hebrew faith. One of the requirements for them was baptism by which was symbolized their cleansing from their old Gentile way of life. For John and for the Jews a new day was dawning; God's promised Messiah was coming (indeed was already there, though they did not recognize him, v. 26 b). John was calling his fellow Jews to confession, repentance, and baptism symbolic of cleansing. He did not regard that as serious infringement on the prerogative of the priests in official acts.

In the Synoptic examples of his preaching, John contrasted the symbolic "in water" baptizing which he was practicing with the literal, cleansing "in the Holy Spirit" baptizing which the Messiah would do (Matt. 3:11–12; Luke 3:16–17). In this Gospel John belittled the importance of himself (v. 23) and what he was doing (v. 26a) and pointed out the contrasting importance of the Messiah for whom he was preparing the way (vv. 26b–27). The Messiah was already present in their midst, but they did not recognize him as such. Borrowing from the Synoptics and looking forward in John (vv. 32–34), we know that Jesus had already come from Nazareth to identify with this new messianic movement and had asked for and received baptism at John's hands. John recognized him, but the Temple authorities did not. That one John knew to be so great and so important that he felt that he was not worthy of performing the lowest slave's service of kneeling to loose the lace of the Messiah's sandal. Appropriately the great do not recognize their own greatness. Later Jesus would describe John as the greatest of all of the Hebrew prophets because he was privileged to present the Messiah (Matt. 11:7–11; Luke 7:24–28).

The second facet of John's witness is a positive one (1:29–42). It is here that he introduces Jesus as the Lamb of God, indicating his redemptive role. In sequence this came on the day following John's dialogue with the Temple authorities. He had clearly rejected any messianic identification for himself. He had indicated that he was sent to prepare the way for the Messiah and that the Messiah had indeed appeared already. On this day as Jesus approached, John pointed him out with the dramatic words, "Behold, the Lamb of God, who takes away the sin of the world!" (v. 29). The audience to whom John spoke is not identified. It may have been only the large company mentioned in the Gospels as attending the ministry of John (Matt. 3:5; Mark 1:5; Luke 3:1–3,7,12,14,15). In this setting, however, there is a strong implication that the Temple representatives were still present and witnessed John's identification of Jesus.

In making the introduction of Jesus as the Lamb of God, John referred to a previous statement which he had made about Jesus. It is the same witness to which reference was made in the prologue

(v. 15), but nowhere before this is there in the Gospels an occasion when John made such a statement. There are places where he spoke of a greater one who was coming after him (Matt. 3:11; Mark 1:7; Luke 3:16; John 1:27). We do not know when the witness was made. Nor is it given here in the plain and simple Greek which usually characterizes this Gospel. It is almost like a Hebrew *mashal* (riddle), which is a form this writer used in other places. A literal translation of verse 30 would be something like this, "This is the one of whom I said, "Behind me comes a man who has become ahead of me because he was before me.' " All translators understand the sentence as John's reference to the preexistent Christ—he existed before John; he comes after John; he goes on ahead of John in the significance, extent, and effectiveness of his ministry. Note John's words on a future occasion in comparing Jesus' ministry and his own, "He must increase, but I must decrease" (3:30). *Today's English Version,* combining translation and paraphrase, expresses the meaning of the verse, "A man is coming after me, but he is greater than I am, because he existed before I was born" (1:30).

"I myself did not know him" (v. 31) does not likely mean that John did not know Jesus prior to Jesus' coming to him for baptism. That, of course, is possible. They could have grown up so far removed in circumstances that they had not met. With the unique situation of their conception and birth to the devoted cousins, Elizabeth and Mary, and their living no farther apart than the distance from Nazareth to Judea, it would be most unlikely that they had never met. Too, John's words when Jesus requested baptism of him seem to suggest prior knowledge of the kind of man Jesus was, "I need to be baptized by you, and do you come to me?" (Matt. 3:14).

Most likely what John meant was that he knew that the Messiah was to "be revealed to Israel" and that his own ministry was to prepare the way for that manifestation (v. 31), but he did not identify Jesus as the Messiah until the dove came upon him at his baptism (v. 32). God had revealed to John that this was the way he would recognize the one for whom he was preparing the way (v. 33). When John saw it, the identification was clear; he was convinced that Jesus was "the Son of God" (v. 34). While there is no descriptive narration of Jesus' baptism in the Fourth Gospel as there is in the Synoptics, this "Son of God" identification touches those descriptive narratives in the words of the voice from heaven, "Thou art my beloved Son; with thee I am well pleased" (Luke 3:22). Jesus as the Son of God is a consistent theme in the Gospel of John.

As noted earlier we are taking the Lamb of God as the organizing concept of Jesus in the Gospel of John. We must now consider the content of that concept. We must consider what John meant by his words "Behold, the Lamb of God, who takes away the sin of the world!" It is a dramatic expression. The word which is translated "behold" is the imperative form of the verb "to look." In Johannine writings it is always followed by something which is startling or amazing—"Look, the Lamb of God, that takes away the sin of the world!" (Compare this with 1 John 3:1; Rev. 3:1,5; John 1:47; 19:26,27.)

What was there in Hebrew religious thought which made this "Lamb of God" expression meaningful for John's listeners? What did it mean to John the Baptist himself? Of ultimate importance is the question: What did it mean to the writer of this Gospel, to his original readers, and to us today? Interpreters are in general agreement at several points: (1) It had to have some Old Testament frame of references to have meaning for John's listeners. (2) It is a fusion or amalgamation of several Old Testament concepts of sacrifice for sin. (3) It is primarily a reference to the Passover lamb, even though in the original Passover event which launched the Exodus, there was no element of the expiation of sin.[11]

Old Testament sacrificial offerings involving lambs (or rams), and worthy of mention are: the Passover Lamb (Ex. 12), the suffering servant lamb (Isa. 53); the daily burnt offering lambs (Ex. 29); the day of Atonement ram (Num. 29; Lev. 16). When all of these and lesser known ones are examined and the evidences weighed, the impression is that in John's use of the Lamb of God there is a blending of the suffering servant lamb (which is so prominent in the theology of Luke) and the Passover lamb with the latter furnishing the major emphasis.

It is true that in the original event the Passover lamb sacrifice was not related to the expiation of sin. Through the centuries of observance of the meaningful Passover supper, however, an element of redemption came in. In the Exodus event, initiated by the original Passover, God "redeemed" Israel. By the New Testament day, the sacrifice of the Passover lambs was a cultic service carried out by the priests in the Temple. At the final Passover in the life of Jesus, the week of his sacrifice on the cross, John definitely frames his account to reflect the idea of Jesus' death as a Passover sacrifice.

The concept of Jesus as a sacrificed lamb came to be very meaningful for the early Christians. Examples of this include: Acts 8:32 where, in the Philip and the eunuch event, Christ's death was explained in terms of the suffering servant lamb of Isaiah 53; 1 Corinthians 5:7 where Paul stated that Christ was our Passover sacrifice; 1 Peter 1:18–19, a sermon outline setting forth Christ's redemptive death: We are not redeemed by silver or gold we are redeemed by *blood*, a *lamb's* blood, *faultless, spotless,* and that Lamb is Christ. Every italicized word begins with the Greek letter alpha (a) giving the alliteration of a sermon outline or perhaps a hymn. The climactic presentation of Christ as a sacrificed lamb is in the book of Revelation. In Revelation 5 Christ appears as the Lamb which bears on its throat the marks of sacrifice in religious worship, but he is still alive. In Revelation 6—7 this sacrificed but living Lamb opens the sealed book to reveal God's judgment on the unredeemed and his protection for the redeemed. In chapter 14 he stands on Mount Zion surrounded by

144,000 redeemed ones who sing his praises as the end nears. In chapter 19, with garments stained by the blood of sacrifice and with sword in mouth as in chapter 1, he rides to victory over every enemy of his cause and his people. The concept of Christ as the redeeming Lamb is a fitting one for organizing the theology of the Gospel of John

John's second witness introducing Christ to the Old Israel came on the next day (v. 35) after the first one. This time it was a more restricted witness, but it set in motion those events which would ultimately lead to a New Israel. He was standing with two of his disciples when Jesus passed by. He pointed Jesus out to the two with the words which they may have heard the day before, "Behold, the Lamb of God!" The two followed Jesus and, encouraged by his question as to what they were seeking, asked where he was staying (v. 38). His invitation "Come and see" begins a come-and-see link of events in his gathering of his first disciples. They went with him and spent the remainder of the day with him.

The kind of time used in John is not always clear. If Jewish time is involved in verse 39, it was 4:00 P.M. If Roman time was involved, it was 10:00 A.M. Whatever the extent of their stay or the undisclosed nature of their conversation, they went away convinced that their leader, John the Baptist, was right; this man was indeed the Christ. Imagination suggests that they talked with Jesus about John's identification of him as the redeeming Lamb of God, about his relation to John's ministry, and about how both John and Jesus were related to the total redemptive purpose and work of God.

Here began a nucleus for the New Israel but the framing of it and the training of it would be a difficult process. One of the two disciples of John who spent those hours with Jesus was Andrew. The other is not identified. By popular tradition the name of John, the son of Zebedee, has been associated with this unidentified one. Andrew sought out his brother Simon, reported to him,

"We have found the Messiah," and brought him to Jesus. Bringing others to Jesus characterizes Andrew in this Gospel (6:8–9; 12:22). Jesus looked intently at Simon; the compound verb meant to fix one's gaze on an object. Then he addressed Simon in words which have supplied intriguing questions to interpreters of the Gospels. "So you are Simon the son of John? You will be called Cephas" (v. 42). Did Jesus have prior knowledge of Simon? Did he know enough about him to know that he was known as "Simon the son of John"? Nazareth was only about twenty miles from Capernaum, home of Simon and Andrew. They shared a fishing business there with James and John and their father, Zebedee (Mark 1:16–20). The earliest public ministry which the Synoptic Gospels record of Jesus was in Capernaum (Luke 4:23). When Jesus was rejected in Nazareth, he moved to Capernaum and established his headquarters there (Luke 4:28–31; Matt. 4:13). He may have known Simon's background so as to indicate here that in the future he would be known not as Simon, John's son, but as Simon the Rock; Cephas in Aramaic and Peter in Greek mean a rock or a stone. Or is this another Johannine instance of Jesus' "knowing" a person and the person's character without having been informed of it; such cases as Nicodemus (John 3), the Samaritan woman (John 4), or even Nathanael of this chapter (vv. 47–51)? In all of this casting about, we must not lose the main point. The main point is that Jesus was speaking of Simon's future life and character in association with him. Having come to Jesus, his life would be forever different.

Two men spent several hours with Jesus. For one of them, Andrew, life was never the same. He had found the Messiah. Likewise for his brother, Simon, life was never the same after Andrew brought him to Jesus. What can we say of the unidentified man who with Andrew spent those hours with Jesus? As far as positive demonstrable matters are concerned, we must remain silent as the New Testament remains silent. There is, however, the possibility of some knowledge at this point. It depends on the correct construction of the word which is translated "first" in verse 41. Andrew first found his brother Simon and brought him to Jesus. Some manuscripts of John have an adverbial form of the word. If that is accurate, it modifies the verb and indicates that the first action of Andrew after those hours with Jesus was to find his brother and to bring him to Jesus. Other manuscripts have the adjectival form of the word. If that is accurate, it modifies Andrew and indicates that Andrew first brought his brother to Jesus with the implication that the unidentified man then found his brother and brought him to Jesus.

For two good reviews of the entire question see Barrett who thinks that both ideas are valid but that the weight of evidence is for the adverbial form indicating Andrew's first action and implying nothing about the other man.[12] See also Hendriksen who weighs all of the textual evidence, brings in other possible evidences, and holds for the adjectival form.[13] By this, both Andrew and the other disciple of John brought their brothers to Jesus. Hendriksen extends the popular tradition that the unidentified man was John the son of Zebedee, that the brother he brought to Jesus was James, and that John is behind the eyewitness-like account of this encounter. It is most interesting to note that later on in Galilee the first men whom Jesus called to join him in his travels and works were these two pairs of brothers: Peter and Andrew, James and John (Mark 1:16–20). While there is no evidence one way or the other, from the viewpoint of probability there is strong likelihood for John as the unidentified disciple.

On the next day Jesus left the scene of John's ministry and went to Galilee (v. 43). The presence of disciples with him a bit later (2:2,11) suggests that at least Andrew, Peter, the unidentified man (John?), and perhaps that man's brother (James?) went to Galilee with him. Their home was there, and they were returning from attending the ministry of John the Baptist. They had found a new teacher whom they believed to be the Messiah. In Galilee or before leaving for Galilee, the language of verse 43 does not make it clear, Jesus found a man named Philip and called to him, "Follow me." The same word is used of Jesus' finding Philip as was used of Andrew's finding Simon. Does this mean only a chance meeting? Could it suggest that Andrew and Simon who were from Bethsaida, the same town as Philip, had talked to Jesus about him?[14] Philip's following Jesus seems to have been of a permanent nature. Later he would be named as one of the twelve apostles with the four brothers.

Continuing the pattern of seeking, finding, and bringing to Jesus, Philip found a man named Nathanael (vv. 45–51). Again, it is not clear as to whether this was in Judea or Galilee. This man is mentioned only in this Gospel. He is not named among the twelve apostles in any of the four lists of them (Matt., Mark, Luke, Acts). Efforts to identify him with Bartholomew in those four lists are not convincing.[15] The only other time he appears in John is in 21:2 where he is one of the seven who experienced the postresurrection appearance of Jesus at a fishing site on the Sea of Galilee. It may be implied that he was one of the disciples with Jesus in the next event in sequence (2:2,11), but no names are given there.

This is the most extended encounter of Jesus with early followers in this section. It is another instance of evidence of Jesus' recognition of a man's character. In it Nathanael moved from sarcastic skepticism to fervent faith. Philip's "We have found" (v. 45) probably included the other followers of verses 40–42. He reported that they had found the Messiah of whom the two major sections of their Scriptures spoke—the Law and the Prophets. His name was Jesus; he was from Nazareth; he was the son of Joseph. It would be natural to refer to Jesus as the son of Joseph in a Gospel which contains no reference to Jesus' origin other than the expression of 1:14, "the Word became flesh." John contains no indication of how that came about. Only Matthew and Luke contain that. John was reporting the words of a man who had just met Jesus and likely had no knowledge of his background

other than his Nazareth residence. Since Nathanael was from
Cana (John 21:1), which was only a few miles from Nazareth,
Philip may have thought that Nathanael would identify Jesus by
that association with the town carpenter, Joseph.

Nathanael's response was a sarcastic reference to Nazareth
which sounds like a proverb, "Can any good thing come out of
Nazareth?" Certainly there was nothing in the Hebrew Scriptures
and tradition to link Nazareth or any other site outside of Judea
with the place of origin of the Messiah. Philip's invitation "Come
and see" carries the idea that seeing is believing. If Nathanael
will come to get acquainted with Jesus, he will be convinced
that he is the Messiah. What sincere seeker, and such Nathanael
seemed to be, could reject that opportunity? He went to see,
but he was not at all prepared for what he experienced. The
passage which reports the encounter is filled with fascinating and
at times perplexing questions.

As Nathanael approached, Jesus said, "Behold, an Israelite indeed, in whom is no guile!" The word translated "indeed" means
that which is real or genuine. The word which is translated "guile"
means that which is deceitful or false. Jesus, therefore, said that
Nathanael was genuinely an Israelite in whom there was nothing
false; he was the ideal Israelite, true to all that was required of
one. Nathanael did not deny the truth of what Jesus said; he
did not even possess false humility! He was simply perplexed
that Jesus could be so accurate in his knowledge of him when
they had never met. Jesus' explanation was enigmatic. Freely
rendered it meant that before Philip had even approached Nathanael, Jesus had observed Nathanael under a fig tree and something about his presence there or what he was doing there indicated his genuineness. Whatever it was, it prompted Nathanael's
recognition that Jesus, too, was genuine; his response was a confession, "Rabbi, you are the Son of God! You are the King of Israel!"

Even when one grants Jesus' superhuman knowledge of the

character of people as cited previously, the question remains as to what there was that Jesus observed about Nathanael's presence under the fig tree which triggered Nathanael's sudden conclusion that Jesus really was the one of whom the Law and the Prophets wrote (v. 45). Was Nathanael in the seclusion and shelter of the fig tree reading from the Law and the Prophets so that Philip's statement meant that they had found the very one of whom Nathanael's reading matter witnessed? Had Jesus so observed that reading? Had Nathanael withdrawn to pray for the coming of the Messiah? In Micah 4:4 and Zechariah 3:10 to sit under a fig tree is a reference to peace and plenty in the time of the Messiah. Whatever it was, it was sufficient for Nathanael. It called forth a confession which is almost creedal in tone. Here for Nathanael was a rabbi, a teacher, but no ordinary teacher. He was the Son of God, the King of Israel.

While the precise background is lacking for understanding both of these terms as messianic, they are definitely so. In John, Jesus is divine both in preexistence and in incarnation. Always he is the exalted Son of God, though Jesus' preferred self-designation was Son of man. Jesus did the work which his Father sent him to do. He worked as his Father worked. He did only what his Father wished. We must remember, too, that as John's account of this beginning of Jesus' public life closes with an emphasis on his sonship of God, the Synoptic account of his baptism as the beginning of his public life closes with the words of the voice from heaven, "This is my beloved Son" (Matt. 3:17).

As to the King of Israel as a messianic title, we may recall the cry of his followers at his triumphal entry into Jerusalem and into the Temple on Sunday before his death on Friday. They hailed him as Zion's King in such a tremendous demonstration that the Pharisees, regarding it as blasphemy, appealed to Jesus to stop them. His response was that on that day of all days if the people did not so acclaim him, the very stones on the path would become vocal and cry out, "Blessed is the King who comes in the name of the Lord!" (Luke 19:38).

Jesus concluded the conversation with Nathanael by indicating that he would see greater evidences of Jesus as the Messiah than Jesus' knowing his character from seeing him under the fig tree (v. 50). He would see heaven opened and the Son of man connecting heaven and earth like a Jacob's ladder with the angelic messengers of God going by means of him to and fro between God and men (v. 51). The metaphor of course is from the experience of Jacob recorded in Genesis 28:10–19. Troubled by his past and wondering about his future, Jacob slept one night on a hard pillow. He dreamed of a ladder connecting the earth where he lay to the heavens above. Angels of God were coming down to him and going back to God as messengers between the two of them. At the top of the ladder stood God to speak reassuringly to Jacob about God's purpose for him, his future, and his people through whom all the people of the earth would be blessed. By that analogy Jesus saw himself as the ultimate means of God's communication with the revelation to men. That included his incarnation among men which Nathanael had seen and had accepted. It included the "greater things" of his death and his resurrection which Nathanael would see in the future. These were included in his understanding of himself as "the Son of God . . . the King of Israel."

So ends John's introduction of the Lamb of God to the Old Israel. As the incarnate Word of God (v. 14), he has been introduced to "his own people" (v. 11). He has been introduced as the one "who takes away the sin of the world" (v. 29). John has fulfilled his mission of preparing the way for his coming and of introducing him accurately to those whom he came to redeem. At this point, John fades into the background. Jesus comes to the center of action to manifest himself to Israel as the redeeming Lamb of God.

Notes

1. Josephus, *Antiquities* XVIII 5.2.

2. This is the thrust of the Synoptic account which needs to be understood if John's abbreviated account is to be understood. See Summers, *Commentary on Luke*, pp. 45–49.

3. It should be noted here that in other places in the New Testament Jesus was identified as the Moses-like prophet. In John 6:14 some of those who ate bread-in-the-wilderness which Jesus supplied in the feeding the five thousand identified Jesus as the Moses-like prophet; Moses, too, had given bread-in-the-wilderness, the manna. John 7:40 reflects the same identification. In Peter's defense of himself and John in Acts 3:12–26, he identified Jesus as the Moses-like prophet (vv. 22–23). In Stephen's defense before the Sanhedrin, he cited God's promise of a prophet like Moses. By implication he indicated that as the Israel of the Exodus rejected Moses, so the Israel of Jesus' day was rejecting him (Acts 7:37–39), the prophet like Moses.

4. Hull, p. 222.

5. A. T. Robertson, *Word Pictures in the New Testament* (Nashville: Broadman Press, 1932), vol. 5, pp. 18–21. That is the position of *Today's English Version* of the New Testament, "The messengers had been sent by the Pharisees," p. 43–44.

6. Hendriksen, pp. 95–96.

7. Raymond E. Brown, "The Gospel According to John," 2 vol., *The Anchor Bible* (Garden City, N.Y.: Doubleday and Company, Inc., 1966), pp. 43–44.

8. Barrett, p. 145.

9. Hendriksen, p. 96.

10. Barrett, p. 145.

11. Such, with variations, is the view set out in the previously cited books by: Barrett (pp. 146–147); R. E. Brown (pp. 58–63); Hendriksen (p. 98); Smith (pp. 78–81). These are representative of many others.

12. Barrett, pp. 151–152.

13. Hendriksen, pp. 104–107.

14. We have noted previously that at the time of Jesus' calling the four fishermen, they were living in Capernaum. So the two references may represent a move from Bethsaida to Capernaum. The two towns were very close together. Both were fishing towns on the Sea of Galilee. Bethsaida was on the east side of the place where the Jordan River entered the sea, and Capernaum was on the west side. At the time of these events Bethsaida was in Gaulanitis, and Capernaum was in Galilee. At the time this Gospel was written after the Jews' dispersion by the Romans in A.D. 70, the entire territory was loosely spoken of as Galilee.

15. See discussion in Summers, *Commentary on Luke*, pp. 71–73.

II. Manifestation of the Lamb

(2:1 to 11:46)

Jesus' initial manifestation of himself to the Old Israel was through the first of his miracles (2:1–11). With it John linked the second miracle (4:47–54). It was significant to him that both took place in Cana; both took place on occasions when Jesus left Judea (Jewish territory) and entered Galilee (Gentile territory); both close with a strong emphasis on faith in Jesus. We shall, therefore, consider both of them in this initial manifestation.

In the introduction we noted the place of miracles in John's Gospel and his presenting them as signs which point beyond the miracles themselves to a more important spiritual truth. Recall his stated purpose for selecting these miracles from the many others which Jesus did (20:30–31). He selected these because they make the greatest demand on credence. He selected these for the purpose of stimulating belief that the One who did these signs was indeed the Christ, the Son of God, and that by that faith they might have the eternal life which Jesus offered. Jesus' miracles, then, were manifestations of his glory as the Redeemer whom the Father had sent.[1]

The week which began with John the Baptist's denial that he was the Christ (1:19–28) and his introduction of Jesus as the Lamb of God (1:29–36) closed with Jesus' manifesting his divine glory in turning the water to wine (2:1–11). Generally accepted, with slight reservations on the part of some, is the identification of the days of that week as follows: first day, John's dialogue with the Temple messengers (vv. 19–28); second day, he identified

Jesus to the crowd (vv. 29–34); third day, he identified Jesus to two of his disciples (vv. 35–42); fourth day, Jesus called Philip and left Judea to go to Galilee, or the reverse of these two actions (vv. 43–44); fifth and sixth days continuing the journey to Galilee with the addition of Nathanael either before leaving Judea or after arriving in Galilee (vv. 45–51); seventh day, Jesus attended the wedding feast and manifested his glory (2:1–11).[2]

Manifestation as the Giver of Signs
(2:1–11; 4:46–54)

On the third day after Jesus' calling Philip, he attended a wedding feast in Cana in Galilee. In Jewish wedding customs the initial rites between bride and groom took place in the home of the bride and then moved to the home provided by the groom for their residence. There a festival lasting up to seven days would be enjoyed by family and friends. Many questions which are posed in the commentaries, discussed at length, and then usually left unanswered because of lack of decisive evidence, need to be noted here: such as, Why was Jesus' mother there? Why was Jesus invited? Was he a relative or a friend of the bridegroom? Was the invitation related to the fact that one of his disciples, Nathanael, lived there? How many guests were present? Did Jesus arrive at the beginning or after the feast had been in progress for some time? The exegetes are right: There is no conclusive evidence because these matters are never discussed in the New Testament. They are considered important, however, because of possible bearing on: the responsible role of Jesus' mother; the diminishing of the wine before the festivities were over; the question of the need for as much wine as Jesus made.

For our purpose we may confine attention to the basic elements in the story. Jesus attended with his "disciples." Most likely this refers to those who had been with him in Judea, at least five, perhaps six people. It is strange that Barrett assumes that the probable reference is to the twelve apostles because they are mentioned in 6:67.[3] The number of disciples present may be unimportant. Their reaction to what Jesus did, however, is the most important stated result of the event (v. 11). When it became evident that the wine would not last for the remainder of the festival, it was Jesus' mother who assumed responsibility and came to him with an announcement that was really an appeal for his help, "They have no wine" (v. 3). This could be no more than the customary dependence of a Jewish mother on her oldest son, especially if her husband was not present (or not even still living as is most generally held). All interpreters understand it as an appeal for him to do something: take the news to the host since no one else had done so; go to the market and secure more wine; or work a miracle. Since Jesus had performed no miracles before this (v. 11), this last possibility seems a bit farfetched to have been in Mary's mind. Jesus' response, however, suggests that the situation was a challenge to him to do exactly that.

To our culture, Jesus' response seems to be a harsh and unfeeling thing for a man to say to his mother, "O woman, what have you to do with me? My hour has not yet come" (v. 4). Most of the interpreters find no harshness in his calling her "woman" rather than mother. They note that in 19:26, when at the cross he committed her to the care of the beloved disciple, there was only tenderness in his, "Woman, behold, your son!" followed by his words to the disciple, "Behold, your mother!" It is as if he said, "Look, he is your son now . . . . Look, she is your mother now!"

Nor do interpreters find more than slight rebuke, if any, in his words, "What have you to do with me?" It is an ancient Jewish expression in both the Old Testament and the New meaning, "What do we have in common in this matter?" Precisely the words were, "What to me and to you?" It is this which may reflect that Jesus faced a challenge to work a miracle, though Mary's appeal for help anticipated some much simpler solution to the problem. She still felt that he would do something, so she left it with him and instructed the servants to do whatever he told them.

That Jesus faced this as a challenge seems clear in his statement, "My hour has not yet come" (v. 4). For Jesus in the Gospel of John, his life moved steadily forward to one grand climactic hour when he would make the ultimate revelation of the redemptive love of God in his death on the cross. That, beyond any other thing he could say or do, would be the manifestation of God's glory. So he could pray on the night before the execution, "Father, the hour has come; glorify thy Son that the Son may glorify thee" (17:1). Frequently through this Gospel when he was faced by some tremendous challenge, it would be said of him, "his hour had not yet come" or he would say, "My hour has not yet come" (7:6,8; 7:30; 8:20; 12:23; 13:1). His words to Mary indicate that they were looking on this situation from two different viewpoints. Was it a situation for relieving an embarrassed host? Was it a situation for beginning the manifestation of himself and what he had to offer to Israel? He could respond to no voice except that of the Father.

In every action in his life, when the hour came for some partial manifestation looking forward to that ultimate one, he knew and he acted. So he did here. So he would do later when he refused the suggestion of his brothers that he go to Jerusalem for the Feast of Tabernacles and demonstrate his power. He refused saying, "My time has not yet come" (7:6). They went on without him. Later he went, too, but not until he knew that it was "time" for him to go.

John was very exact in recording the next details. He must have regarded all of them as very important. He recorded the number of the pots, six; the kind of pots, stone [4]; the size of the pots, "each holding twenty or thirty gallons" (v. 6). This Revised Standard Version reading is a round number approximation. The Greek word used indicates a measure *(metretes)* which held approximately nine gallons, and the text states that each pot held up to two or three such *metretes* (they varied in size from a content of eighteen to twenty-seven gallons each). Six such pots could hold a total of approximately 100 to 160 gallons. That much water to be used by the servants, guests, and family members in the multitude of ceremonial cleansings associated with eating and worship would not be regarded as excessive. That much wine, however, would be another matter, particularly since whatever amount of wine originally provided by the host had already been used! Interpreters cannot resist the temptation to seek allegorical overtones in this detail as well as some of the other details.

Jesus instructed the servants to fill the depleted jars with water. They did so; John notes that they were filled up to the brim—an abundance of water and a clear indication that up to this point it was water. Jesus then ordered, "Now draw some out, and take it to the steward of the feast" (v. 8). Of all the commentaries surveyed for this study, only two interpret this drawing out as drawing more water from the original source rather than from the pots.[5] This would mean that the ceremonial water in the pots remained ceremonial water but that from the same source from which it came, Jesus supplied wine. All of the others interpret the action as drawing what was unmistakably ceremonial water from the filled pots and at Jesus' instructions taking it to the steward for his tasting and approval before serving it to the guests. This is another instance in which Jesus' only action in performing a miracle was his spoken word.

When did the water become wine? While it was still in the pots, indicating that all of the ceremonial water became wine? Unless the servants noted that the water had been changed to wine, they must have wondered at Jesus' instructions. Taking water to a wine steward with the suggestion that he offer it to the guests as wine could be dangerous business for servants![6] Was only the water which they drew out to take to the steward turned to wine? There is no precise statement in the text. Most of the interpreters understand that all of the water in the pots was changed to wine, that the servants would continue to serve it until the end of the festival, and that what was left over would be the property of the bridegroom.

John's interest was not just in the ceremonial nature of the water, the fact that it was turned to wine, and the amount of it. He was also interested in the quality of the wine. Uninformed of the source of the wine, the steward tasted it and noticed that it was remarkably better than what they had been serving. He called the bridegroom to call his attention to the quality of the wine and to make what sounds like a proverbial reference to a policy of serving the best wine first and reserving inferior wine for the time when taste buds were dulled from feasting and drinking. No such custom has been identified. There may have been such a practice, or the steward may have been jesting with the bridegroom. The fact of the superiority of the wine is not challenged.

As noted above, many attempts at allegorical interpretation of this miracle have been made. Some of Jesus' miracles naturally submit to allegorical overtones. Jesus' feeding the hungry multitude in the wilderness is followed in John by his dialogue with the leaders of Israel's religion over the "bread from heaven" which Moses gave in the wilderness (the manna), the "bread from heaven" which Jesus gave in the wilderness (the loaves and fishes), and the "bread from heaven" (Jesus' body) which God gives, which men may eat and never die (John 6). In a similar way Jesus' healing of the man who was born blind led to his teaching concerning himself as the light of the world (John 9). The raising of Lazarus led to his teaching that he was the resurrection and the life (John 11). There is, however, no such clear allegorical meaning in this his first miracle.

There may be overtones of such interpretation, such as the lavishness of Jesus' love and grace, his interest in people and their needs (an anxious mother; an embarrassed host; a rejoicing wedding company). Many interpreters find allegorical overtones in comparing water with wine which in Hebrew thought was food and substance, not just enjoyment (that is, in place of the empty ceremonial religion of the Jews, Jesus gave the new wine of Christianity). There is some background for this idea in the Synoptics. While the Synoptics do not have this miracle, they do have a parabolic teaching of Jesus in which what he was offering was compared to new wine which could not be contained by the old ceremonies (wineskins) of Judaism. The teaching (Matt. 9:17; Luke 5:37–39) is associated with a wedding-bridegroom-attendants teaching (Matt. 9:14–15; Luke 5:34–35). In earlier works I have explored the relationship of miracle-story teaching in John and parable-story teaching in the Synoptics.[7] An allegorical emphasis may be supported by another method used by John. Here in the beginning of his ministry Christ offered men the best wine; in the end of his ministry, when he thirsted on the cross, men offered him the dregs of wine (John 19:29–30). This "vinegar" was the cheapest of wines which was sometimes a part of the Roman soldier's pay for his services. A like emphasis to be noted later in this study is that in the beginning of Jesus' ministry a man comes out of the "night" to Jesus and all of his life is bathed in light (Nicodemus, 3:2); in the end of his ministry a man goes out from Jesus into the "night" and for him all is dark (Judas, 13:30). This is undeniably a Johannine technique, but it is not clear that such is the case in this first miracle.

With what emphasis does the event end? There is no word about Mary's reaction to what Jesus did, or the bridegroom's, or the servants', or the guests'. John restricted his emphasis to the response of Jesus' disciples. He stated that in this "the first of his signs" Jesus "manifested his glory" and as a result "his disciples believed in him" (v. 11). Did they associate Jesus' action of changing water to wine with his presence in the world to change the devotion of Israel from meaningless ceremonial religious practice to a vital and real spiritual religious experience? Were they impressed only by his changing one liquid to another, water to wine, as Moses had changed one liquid to another, water to blood? No answer is given. Whatever they understood in it, to them it was a manifestation, a clear setting forth of his glory as John the Baptist had indicated, "We have beheld his glory, glory as of the only Son from the Father" (1:14).

They "believed in him." They had believed in him in those initial experiences with him earlier in the week. That they believed in him as a result of the miracle is not to deny the validity of that earlier belief. They were still in the come-and-see stage. Their response to Jesus' manifestation of his glory was an indication of a growing faith, a developing faith. They were convinced that they had followed the right person. Every true believer's faith should be ideally a growing faith. These disciples were devout men of the old Israel. Jesus had begun his manifestation to Israel. They committed themselves to him. Essentially the new Israel, the new people for God's redemptive witness, the church, existed in nucleus from that meaningful week.

Linked to this first miracle is the second one in John, the healing of the sick son of a king's officer (4:46–54). The word which indicates the man's position means a royal officer, the officer of the king. The king was Herod Antipas of Jewish lineage. It is correspondingly assumed that this officer was Jewish. The action of Jesus in this event is viewed as a continuation of his manifestation to Israel.

Is this another of Jesus' miracles which appears only in John, or is it to be identified with a similar event which is in the Synoptics (Matt. 8:5–13; Luke 7:2–10)? Opinion is divided. There are similarities, but the differences far outweigh the similarities. The officer in Luke was a Roman centurion; in John he was a Jewish officer of Herod. In Luke Jesus never met the centurion. The centurion first sent Jews to ask Jesus to heal his son; he had been good to the Jews and they, too, desired Jesus' help. Jesus agreed and started to the centurion's house. The centurion then sent messengers to suggest that he knew Jesus could heal the sick person, a slave, without coming into a Gentile's house. The whole event took place in Capernaum. In John the officer went from Capernaum to Cana to ask personally that Jesus come to Capernaum, seventeen miles away, and heal the sick person, his son. In Luke the emphasis is on the remarkable faith of the centurion before the healing event. In John the emphasis is upon the degree of faith which caused the officer to believe Jesus' word in a most unusual circumstance, and then the emphasis is intensified later when the sick son was healed.

Note the progress of the event and the result of Jesus' action in the Johannine account. A royal officer in Capernaum heard that Jesus had returned to Galilee and was again in Cana. He went to Cana and urged Jesus to go to Capernaum and heal his son who was at the point of death. Jesus charged the man with coming to Cana seeking "signs and wonders" to stimulate faith in him. Does this suggest that the man had heard of Jesus' previous "sign" in Cana? The probability is great that he had. The man pressed his plea that without delay Jesus go to Capernaum to heal the son. Jesus told him that a trip was not necessary. He assured the man that when he returned home he would find the son well.

The officer believed the word that Jesus spoke (v. 51) and started his return journey. Upon his arrival the next day he was greeted by the news that the boy was alive and that the fever had left him at the seventh hour on the day before. The officer reported that it was at that exact hour that Jesus had assured him that his son would live (v. 53). What was the result of this manifestation of Jesus' power to Israel? The officer believed (v. 53). Had he not already believed the day before? Yes (v. 50); so this appears to be added belief, increased belief after the pattern of the disciples who had believed before the turning of water to wine but were described again as believing after the "sign." In this second case, the man's "household" also believed; usually servants were included with family members in a household. Others in Israel shared in the faith.

It was significant to John that this was the second time Jesus had left Judea (Jewish territory), had come into Galilee (Gentile territory), and had performed a most remarkable miracle in manifestation of his glory and power. In both instances belief and acceptance had marked the manifestation. This reflects the continuing perplexity of John that Israel in vast majority could refuse Jesus—"his own people received him not" (1:11).

Manifestation as Lord of the Temple
(2:13–25)

This passage continues Jesus' manifestation of himself to Israel. Because the event took place in Jerusalem and at a Passover, it must be considered as having major importance in John's presentation. To get at the theology of the passage one needs to make a very careful review by way of intensive exegesis. A major question involved is, Did Jesus cleanse the Temple once or twice? The place of the cleansing in John is at what on the surface appears to be Jesus' first Passover after beginning his ministry. The place of the cleansing in the Synoptics is unquestionably during his last Passover, the one which resulted in his crucifixion.

There can be no question about the correct place in the Synoptics. In them, Jesus' cleansing the Temple was the thing which crystallized the Sanhedrin's determination to secure his execution that very week. The question is, therefore, Has John transposed that cleansing to this place in his Gospel for a theological purpose, or were there two cleansings? The most helpful analyses of the question which I have found are by Barrett and Brown representing the view of one cleansing and Hendriksen representing the view of two cleansings.[8] In examining the entire question, one must bear in mind that the Synoptics have only one Passover in Jesus' public ministry, but John has three definite references to Passovers attended by Jesus (2:13; 6:4; 11:55) and perhaps a fourth (5:1).[9] It is not clear, however, that these three definite ones were *separate* ones. John's placement of materials is frequently more theological than chronological.

The Temple with its sacrifices was the very center of the entire Hebrew religion. What Jesus did on this occasion struck the Jews as a threat against the Temple. Too, it appeared to them that this rabbi from Galilee was presuming to take over the operation of the Temple, or at least to determine how it was to be used, and all of that was the responsibility of the priests. Their reaction was consternation and rage. Let us review the setting, Jesus' action, and the resulting dialogue, leaving precise exegesis to the commentaries. The following is from the viewpoint that Jesus cleansed the Temple once, that the Synoptics have it where it took place, and that John introduced it early in his Gospel for a theological purpose (to show Jesus' manifestation as the Lord of the Temple which was the very center of the Hebrew religion).

Following Mark's chronology, Jesus made his triumphal entry into Jerusalem on Sunday (by our calendar) before his death on Friday (Mark 11:1–11). He entered the Temple late in the afternoon and "looked round at everything" (v. 11) before returning to Bethany with the twelve apostles. The implication is that he observed the market-like activities on that day. The next morning (vv. 12,15) he came back to the Temple, drove out the animals and the sellers of the animals, and overturned the tables of the money changers and the stations of the sellers of the doves. With only minor variations in details, this is the report of the event in all four Gospels (Mark 11:15–16; Matt. 21:12–13; Luke 19:45–46, the least in details given; John 2:13–16). He defended his action on three bases: they were defiling the Temple by turning it into a stock market (John 2:16); they were depriving the Gentiles of the only part of the Temple into which they could go for prayer to the God of Israel (Mark 11:17; Matt. 21:13; Luke 19:46); by their (implied) dishonesty and unfair business practices, they were making the Temple not a house for worshiping God but a hangout for thieves (Mark 11:17; Matt. 21:13; Luke 19:46). The latter is implied by Jesus' quotation of Jeremiah who, in a famous Temple sermon, berated the Jews for stealing and for dishonesty (among other sins) in dealing with their fellowmen (Jer. 7:8–9) and then going into the Temple, God's house, as God's forgiven people (Jer. 7:10). Jeremiah charged that their presence in the Temple in that circumstance changed it into a thieves' lair (Jer. 7:11). Jesus, who reminded some of the people of Jeremiah (Matt. 16:14), made the same charge against the Temple authorities on this occasion.

Our major interest here is in the authorities' challenge of Jesus and his response which John has *on that same day* and immediately after Jesus' dramatic and unheard-of action. An examination of that dialogue will reflect John's theological interest and purpose. We should note in passing that in the Synoptic accounts, which do not have this dialogue, the religious authorities challenged Jesus *the day following* as to what kind of authority justified his action on the day before (priestly? prophetic? messianic, remembering the messianic tribute of Jesus' followers at his triumphal entry?), and who gave him the authority (Mark 11:27–28; Matt. 21:23; Luke 20:2). That began a long, long day (Tuesday) of controversy between Jesus and the Jews—charge and countercharge, challenge and counterchallenge, dialogue, attempts to trap Jesus. The end of it was their determination to get him executed before he could leave the city when the Passover week ended. They succeeded in their determination, but they did not defeat him in his work.

In John's account the challenge was immediate and precise, "What sign have you to show us for doing this?" (v. 18). To them Jesus' action amounted to stopping the flow of animals to the altar and tax money to the treasury. It meant that he was presuming to take over the total responsibility of the Jewish priesthood. To his disciples what he had done was so drastic and dangerous that it could have led to his destruction. They remembered a line from a favorite psalm, "Zeal for thy house will consume me" (v. 17); "has consumed" is truer to the text than the Revised Standard Version's "will consume." The kind of sign which they sought was the sort of sign more often requested of Jesus' adversaries in the Synoptics (Matt. 12:38–39; 16:1–4; Luke 23:8). It was a sign which would break down resistance and cause the questioner to believe when he did not want to believe. To such a request by King Herod, by scribes, by Pharisees, and by Sadducees, Jesus had refused to show a sign.

On this occasion he gave them a sign; but in their lack of spiritual perception, it was not an answer—it was an absurdity. He said, "Destroy this temple, and in three days I will raise it up" (v. 19). The very common word translated "destroy" could be used for destroying a building or destroying a body. Jesus meant it one way; the authorities understood it another way; Jesus' disciples were completely perplexed by it until after his resurrection.

In grammatical form the verb is imperative, "Destroy this temple." Some grammarians understand it as a conditional imperative, "if you destroy." Others understand it as an ironic use; it is almost a challenge, "go on and destroy," which they could understand as his accusing them of destroying the Temple by the way they were using it. However it was understood, Jesus was putting them, the very trustees for the Temple's care and preservation, in the role of its destroyers. While the Synoptics do not have this dialogue, the subject of destroying the Temple came up at his trial and later at the trial of Stephen. It was, however, in a twisted form. In it Jesus was accused of saying that he would destroy the Temple (Matt. 26:61; Acts 6:14).

Seeing no meaning in Jesus' statement other than a literal one, they understood him to say, "The sign will be that I will raise this Temple up in three days after you have destroyed it." Pointing out the absurdity of his sign, they reminded him that the Temple had been in process of construction for forty-six years (v. 20).

What they did not say was that it was not yet finished. According to Josephus, the Temple was completed in A.D. 63, only seven years before it was destroyed by the Romans. Forty-six years beginning in 20–19 B.C. would bring the year of this dialogue to the Passover of A.D. 28. There was both incredulity and ridicule in their parting shot, "and *you* [emphatic use of the pronoun, author's italics] will raise it up in three days?" This rendering preserves the force of their statement better than "will you . . . ?"

That ended the dialogue, but John continued by adding a brief explanation of Jesus' meaning and a comment on the failure of the disciples to understand Jesus' saying. Jesus was referring to his body as the dwelling place of God in the world, his temple. That temple was going to be destroyed by the Jews, but he would raise it up in three days. Just as the verb *destroy* may mean to destroy a building or to destroy a body, the verb *raise* may mean to raise a building or raise a body; it is the verb generally used in the New Testament for the resurrection of Jesus.

Jesus was using a form of teaching found in the Old Testament and much used by the rabbis. The Hebrew word for it is *mashal*. It was a wisdom-type of teaching applying to all sorts of analogies such as proverbs, allegories, fables, example stories, riddles. This was the riddle form. The rabbi would give his students a *mashal* and dismiss them to think it through and come up with the answer. The Jewish authorities missed the point of Jesus' *mashal*. So did the disciples until Jesus was crucified and then raised on the third day. Then they remembered, "*That* was what he was talking about!"

So in the Temple riddle in John, the ultimate sign of Jesus' authority as the Son of God, and, hence, his authority over God's house, was to be his resurrection from the dead. The same is true in another riddle which is recorded in Matthew 12:38–40. The Jews asked Jesus for a sign that would compel them to believe in his authority. He responded that the only sign that would be

given was the sign of Jonah. In Luke's parallel (11:29–30) the
sign of Jonah would simply be the preaching done. The Ninevites
accepted Jonah's message and repented; the Jews were rejecting
Jesus' message and refusing to repent. His preaching was greater
than Jonah's preaching; hence, judgment would come upon the
Jews. Matthew's account extends the sign; that is, as Jonah was
three days and nights in the belly of the whale and then came
forth, so would Jesus be three days and nights in the heart of
the earth and then come forth. In John and in Matthew the ultimate sign of Jesus' authenticity was to be his resurrection.

It was important for John's purpose in writing his Gospel for
the Jews of his day that he establish early in his Gospel that Jesus,
as the Messiah, was Lord of the Temple. Indeed, in another Johannine work, which by tradition came out of the same milieu and
time as John's Gospel, Jesus as the Lamb is declared to *be* the
Temple. In Revelation 21:22 the New Jerusalem has no Temple
because the reigning God and the redeeming Lamb of Revelation
4—5 are the Temple.[10]

Following a technique in which he delighted, John used the
idea of the Temple in two senses, a lower and a higher.[11] The
Temple in Jerusalem (lower) is raised to Jesus' body as the New
Temple (higher), God's dwelling place in the world. Some interpreters extend the metaphor even beyond that to speak of the
church, the body of Christ, as the Temple that was raised up
through Jesus' resurrection. This concept is more meaningful to
Christians today than to the first Jewish readers of John's Gospel.
Unless, of course, they had read the epistle to the Ephesians!

Manifestation as the Source of the New Birth
(3:1–21)

As much at the heart of the religion of Israel as the Temple
was the proud assertion of the Jews that they were sons of Abraham. As the Temple stood materially at the heart of their religion,
their covenant relationship to God through their physical descent

from Abraham stood spiritually at that heart. Today three major religions trace their spiritual ancestry to Abraham—Judaism, Islam, and Christianity. To be a son of Abraham is an exalted privilege. One must realize, however, that to be a true son of Abraham is a spiritual matter, not a physical one. The New Testament is clear on that concept as it is clear on the fact that the concept was a stumbling block for Israel.

Their position is well represented in such statements as, "We are descendants of Abraham" (John 8:33); "Abraham is our father" (John 8:39); "We have one Father, even God" (John 8:41), which to them was the same as "Abraham is our father" of the previous reference. In succession, John the Baptist, Jesus, and Paul contended with the Jews over the inadequacy of their position. When John the Baptist detected the insincerity of many of the Jews who were coming to join his popular movement, he explained the spiritual nature of what he was proclaiming, saying to them, "Do not begin to say to yourselves, 'We have Abraham as our Father'" (Luke 3:8). He continued his rebuke of their inadequate position by saying that God could take the stones of the wilderness and turn them into better sons of Abraham than the Jews were. To be related to God spiritually required something more.

The references previously cited from John 8 are from an extended argument between Jesus and the Jews over the same matter. They equated being the sons of Abraham with being the sons of God. Jesus' insistence was that to be a son of Abraham was a physical matter, but to be a son of God required something more than that.

The same problem faced Paul in his dealing with his fellow Israelites whom he loved so much that he would have been willing to be cut off from Christ, much as that meant to him, if that would have brought them into the blessings of Christ (Rom. 9:1–5). He prayed for their salvation (10:1) and longed for the day when, through the witness of the Christians, the Jews would be brought to spiritual sonship to God (11:13–36). The entire discourse in Romans 9—11, as most of that in Galatians 3—5, is to show the Jews that to be true Israelites, true sons of Abraham, requires something more than physical relationship.

That *something more* in the insistence of John the Baptist, Jesus, and Paul is capsuled in the concept of a spiritual birth in Jesus' dialogue with Nicodemus (John 3:1–21). It was important to John that his readers understand the necessity of a new spiritual life if they were to be genuine sons of God. Early in his Gospel this dramatic encounter of Jesus and one of the most preeminent of the Jews sets out the position that as physical life comes through physical birth, so spiritual life comes through spiritual birth. And Jesus is manifest as the source of that new birth. It comes to reality out of a faith relationship to him.[12]

Out of the night, at an unidentified place in Jerusalem, a Pharisee who was a member of the Jewish Sanhedrin, came to talk about religion with the rabbi from Galilee. His name was Nicodemus. Never mentioned in the Synoptics, he has a prominent position in the Gospel of John. Besides this encounter with Jesus, he appears in 7:45–52 in defending Jesus whom the Pharisees were condemning without a legal hearing. Nicodemus appears also in 19:38–42 where he joins Joseph of Arimathea in securing permission from Pilate and in burying the body of Jesus. His initial words to Jesus indicate that he had informed himself on what Jesus was doing and he was convinced that Jesus was a God-sent teacher (3:2). He wanted to learn from such a teacher.

The pedagogical procedure known as the shock method of teaching is not new. A more shocking word could hardly be spoken to a grown man than Jesus' response to Nicodemus, "Unless one is born anew, he cannot see the kingdom of God" (v. 3). He did not make the matter particularly lucid when he continued, "Unless one is born of water and the Spirit, he cannot enter the kingdom of God" (v. 5). We do not know, of course, whether John's account includes all that was said or is a condensation. This is often the case in the New Testament.[13] We may not have the bridge between Nicodemus' opening statement and Jesus' rather abrupt response. There may have been a smooth transition, or Jesus may have simply brushed aside all preliminaries to get to the main theme, "Nicodemus, what you really need is to be born again" (author's paraphrase).

The Greek word *anothen* is ambiguous. It may mean "again" in the sense of "anew," or it may mean "from above." Nicodemus understood Jesus to mean "born anew" or "again" and asked the question which really launched the teaching, "How can a man be born when he is old? Can he enter a second time into his mother's womb and be born?" (v. 4). The question is variously interpreted as stupid,[14] gauche,[15] bewildered,[16] and wistful.[17] Stupid and gauche must be rejected; they do not fit the description of Nicodemus. Bewildered, perhaps, and wistful, definitely, fit his frame of mind. The only kind of birth he knew about was physical; that, he knew to be impossible. However impossible it seemed to be, it might be fervently desired in some circumstances—the wistful desire of starting life all over even when one is old. But how can that be? Ah! That is exactly what Jesus was talking about, but a new birth of a different kind.

Here appears again the technique of using a word in two senses, a higher and a lower. The lower is the physical birth by which comes physical life. Jesus will lift it to the higher sense of spiritual birth by which comes spiritual life. Born of the physical (flesh) produces the physical; born of the spiritual (Spirit) produces the spiritual (v. 6). That is logical and fairly clear. What he meant by "born of the flesh" is clear; what he meant by "born of the Spirit" is beginning to become clear. But what did he mean by "born of water" (v. 5)? Many theories have been presented; there are three fairly basic ones.

First, the view that "born of water" means physical birth. In this sense "born of the flesh" in Jesus' next statement would be clarification by parallel; they would mean the same and Jesus would be talking about two kinds of birth—physical and spiritual.

This idea is rather natural because it balances "born of water and the Spirit" (v. 5) with "born of the flesh" and "born of the Spirit" (v. 6). Too, it was physical birth which Nicodemus understood from Jesus' words. That is clear in his response. The grammatical form of his question anticipated a negative answer, in paraphrase, "A man cannot be born again when he is old, can he? He cannot enter into his mother's womb and be born a second time, can he?" The natural answer is no.

The objection to the theory is, in what sense can "born of water" refer to physical birth? A rather forced view which hardly deserves mention except that it is frequently suggested is that Jesus had in mind the part played by water in physical birth, the rupturing of the protective membrane in the mother, releasing water and making the passage easier for the baby.

Barrett sees as a possibility the rabbinic idea of the male semen as "water"; [18] it is so used in Pirke Aboth 3:1 and Enoch 6:2. The semen is a drop of water and hence related to physical birth. If this were the case, Jesus would be calling attention to the fact that something more than physical birth (decent from Abraham) is necessary for citizenship in God's spiritual realm.

Another view of "born of water" as reference to semen is the idea of the heavenly or spiritual seed (semen) which produces spiritual birth. The idea is developed along the lines of John 3:8–12; 1 John 3:9; 1 Peter 1:23.

In summary, it is clear that Nicodemus referred to physical birth in verse 4 and Jesus did so in verse 6. It is not clear that Jesus referred to physical birth in verse 5.

Second, the view that "born of water" means baptism. If matters of interpretation could be determined by counting the commentaries, this view would have a clear edge over all the others. Although that is true, there are objections to it. If this is the meaning, Jesus seems to have referred to three births: physical birth (v. 6); baptismal birth (v. 5); Spirit birth (vv. 5 and 6). Is there valid evidence for that? Another objection is that baptism is generally a death or burial symbol, not a birth symbol. Jesus spoke of his death as a baptism which he was to experience. He spoke of the martyrdom of some of his disciples as a baptism. Paul's classic treatment of baptism (Rom. 6) pictures it as a burial showing that in union with Christ one has died to an old life, is buried to that old life, is raised to a new resurrection life. Baptism as a death symbol is more natural than as a birth symbol.

Those who understand "born of water" as a reference to baptism are not unanimous in their views. Some understand that this water birth is a part of the saving process. Plummer, for example, writes of the "outward sign and inward grace of Christian baptism." [19] Cullmann presents the case for the necessity of baptism in line with the idea that there is no salvation outside the body of Christ (the church) and that baptism is the means by which one is incorporated into the body.[20] Beasley-Murray has a convincing rebuttal of this view.[21] Cullmann extends his view by arguing that baptism in the Christian ritual replaces circumcision in the Hebrew ritual thus opening the way for infant baptism as a saving process. He supports this by citing the fact that the indefinite pronoun (tis) of verse 5 ("one" in RSV; "a man" in KJV) really means "anybody." That would make it true of an eight-day-old baby or an eighty-year-old man!

Students in Dr. John Baillie's dogmatics class in Edinburgh in the spring of 1954 recall with amusement the day he lectured to a packed classroom on his personal views supporting infant baptism. One of his arguments was that infant baptism makes an infant a child of God, the kind of child of God that God wants it to be now; it will be a different kind of child of God later. One of his favorite students, a young minister of the Church of Scotland but in revolt against infant baptism, stood to say publicly to his beloved professor, "You are simply perpetuating the errors of Rome!"

Others understand "born of water" to refer to baptism but not as a part of the saving process. This is not as easy to delineate because of the terminology used by many. Frequently they insist that that which saves is the experience of being born of the Spirit in relationship to faith in the uplifted Christ (John 3:13–18). While thus insisting, however, they do not hesitate to speak of the "gift of grace through baptism" or the "gift of life through baptism." Such references are frequent in works previously cited: Barrett, Beasley-Murray, Dana, Dodd, Hendriksen, Plummer, Temple.

Such references are probably valid because of the close association of baptism and salvation or entrance into the kingdom. Dana treats this by indicating that in apostolic life and teaching, baptism was an inseparable part of identification with the body of Christ.[22] No controversy had arisen over the distinct relation of baptism to regeneration. The question of the ultimate essential had not been raised. This passage was never intended to settle the question of the necessity of baptism.

Beasley-Murray refutes those views which make baptism a necessity.[23] He explores convincingly the theology of John and the remainder of the New Testament showing that salvation is a matter of faith and the work of the Spirit. At the same time he rightly laments the fragmentation of the total Christian experience (repentance, confession, faith, baptism, life, sanctification) which makes it necessary for us to discuss the necessity of baptism. To those early Christians the question, Is baptism necessary? would likely have sounded very strange. Failure to recognize the place of baptism in the thinking of the early Christians may have resulted in our making it a mere symbol—so mere indeed that it hardly symbolizes anything. New Testament baptism, the dramatic picture of one's faith in and sharing in the death, burial, and resurrection of Jesus Christ, is too important for the casual air which so often surrounds it today.

Third, the view that "born of water and Spirit" represents one act, the cleansing work of the Spirit in regeneration. This view places major stress on the grammatical structure used in Jesus' statement in verse 5. Two nouns (water and Spirit) are joined by the coordinate conjunction "and" with only *one* preposition (of)—not "born of water and of Spirit" but "born of water and Spirit." This Greek construction regularly points to one act. If two acts were involved the preposition would be repeated before the second noun. If this is the meaning in this passage, two births are discussed: "natural birth" (vv. 4,6*a*) and "spiritual birth" (vv. 5,6*b*). Bultmann, who is well known for his demythologizing, is so certain that this is the true meaning that he "dehydrates" this passage by omitting "born of water" as a gloss added by a later hand![24] His removing it cannot be defended; by the science of textual criticism, the expression is a genuine part of the text. His view is that "born of water" was a churchly redaction influenced by John 6:51–58, a doctrine of baptism to go with the doctrine of the Eucharist.[25]

Calvin is certain that water and Spirit mean the same thing in the passage.[26] He understands "water" as referring to the inward cleansing and quickening which the Spirit works in the believer. He points to a similar construction in John the Baptist's witness that when the Messiah came he would baptize in the Holy Spirit and fire—one preposition meaning one act. The Revised Standard Version's repetition of the preposition is not true to the Greek text (Matt. 3:11).

Titus 3:5 has been cited as another parallel of this construction, "He saved us . . . by the washing of regeneration and renewal in the Holy Spirit." He saved us, that is, by the cleansing renewal which the Holy Spirit works in regeneration. By this construction John 3:5 means, "born of the Holy Spirit's cleansing."

Whatever Jesus meant by "born of water," all interpreters agree that the most important idea involved in this passage is the necessity of being "born of the Spirit." Nicodemus thought in terms of physical birth. He knew the absurdity of becoming again a babe-in-womb to be born "again." He knew the wistful dream of starting life all over, born "anew." He was bewildered at Jesus' affirmation that one must be born again or anew or from above.

Jesus made it clear that like begets like (v. 6). Human nature
(flesh) can produce only human nature (flesh). Man's physical birth
gives him physical life; it cannot give him spiritual life. In his
natural birth, man inherits a natural body with passions according
to its nature. The longer he lives the more involved he becomes
in the things of the flesh. He is frustrated in his desire and attempt
to break away from undesirable involvements. Yet it is just that
which Jesus was offering Nicodemus, to be born again, born from
above, born of the Spirit. Even Nicodemus, old (likely), set in
his Pharisaic, legal bondage, could be born again, could be made
a new person.

To Nicodemus' plaintive, "How?" Jesus responded with an illustration from the wind. Here again is the lower-higher method.
In Greek the word *pneuma* means either "wind" or "spirit." In
Hebrew the same is true of *ruach*. One cannot know the origin
of the wind (its whence) nor can he know its destination (its
whither), but he can experience the reality of its presence. No
more can one understand the initiatory activity of the Spirit in
regeneration nor the ultimate reach of the Spirit's purpose in
regeneration, but he may experience the reality of it.

Jesus: Nicodemus, do you hear that wind *(pneuma)?*
Nicodemus: Yes.
Jesus: Where does it come from?
Nicodemus: I don't know.
Jesus: Where is it going?
Nicodemus: I don't know that either.
Jesus: Then how do you know it is there?
Nicodemus: I hear it; I feel it; I experience the reality of it.
Jesus: Ah! That's the way it is with one who is born of the Spirit *(pneuma)*.
He experiences the present reality of it, the mysterious, sovereign work-
ing of God. Believe that, Nicodemus. Give yourself up to the sovereign
will of the Spirit of God. Be born again!

To a second "How?" from Nicodemus (v. 9), Jesus explained
that it was a matter of faith, faith in him, the Son of man who
had descended from heaven as the manifestation of God and

God's way for men. He illustrated from the history of Israel in the wilderness (v. 14). Sick people, who in faith that God would heal them, looked up to the serpent which God had commanded Moses to lift up and were healed of their physical ills (Num. 21:4–9). By the same analogy, people, who in faith that God will heal them spiritually, may look up to the lifted-up Son of man and be spiritually healed, saved. In John 8:28 and 12:32–36 the "lifting up" of Christ is a reference to the cross. To believe in him is to have new life here and eternally.

The paragraph which follows Jesus' illustration is one of the best known and most loved in this Gospel and in all of the Bible, 3:16–21. It rests the entire quest of man for salvation, for new life on faith in God's Son. God so loved that he would not see man in sin and do nothing about it. In the Son of his love, he moved redemptively into man's experience even when it required the sacrifice of that Son. So could he save man from the total fragmentation of sin. So could he save him to the total integration of the life that comes by being born of the Spirit. Jesus offered that new birth with its new life to Nicodemus. Subsequent actions of Nicodemus in this Gospel indicate that he accepted it. When he went out from that encounter with Jesus, it was no longer "night."

Manifestation as the Source of the
Water of Life
(4:1–45)

In the more expansive literary structure of John's Gospel, there is a similarity of pattern in Jesus' leaving Judea and arriving in Galilee in 1:43–2:11 and in 4:1–45. In the former he left the Jewish territory of Judea; he arrived in the Gentile territory of Galilee; he performed a miracle; the faith of his disciples was increased. In the latter he left Judea; he arrived in Galilee; he performed a miracle; the faith of the king's officer increased, and his household believed with him. There is, however, one striking difference in the two journeys; on the latter he went through Samaria. His encounter with the Samaritan woman enriches our understanding of Jesus' theology, his method of working with those who need salvation, and his training of his messengers of salvation.

In the more restricted literary structure of the Gospel, there are some striking differences between Jesus' encounter with one who was seeking salvation (Nicodemus) and one who seemed in every way to resist the salvation offered (the Samaritan woman). One was a man; one was a woman. One was from the viewpoints of religion, morals, and social standing an ideal man—a Jew, a Pharisee, a member of the supreme court of Israel. The other was from all of these viewpoints the farthest possible removed from the ideal—a Samaritan, with an abortive form and concept of religion, five times married, and now living in adultery with a sixth man. That which makes the entire matter of supreme importance to Jesus and to us is that *both of them needed salvation,* and in Jesus both of them found it.

John began his account of Jesus' encounter with this woman by stating that in going from Judea to Galilee, Jesus "had to pass through Samaria" (v. 4), or "must needs" go through Samaria (KJV and ASV). The construction involves some kind of necessity, but what kind was it? It does not mean that there was no other road from Judea to Galilee except the one through Samaria. There were two other major roads, one to the west up the coast line and one to the east through Perea. Some interpreters find only a geographical necessity in John's statement. If one wanted the shortest and most convenient route, he would take the one through Samaria. Barrett says that the route was desirable and that John's verb "conveys no more theological significance than Josephus's." [27] His reference is to Josephus' statement that when going to and from Jerusalem for festivals, the Galileans' custom was to go through Samaria. Bultmann states that John's verb has the same "harmless meaning" of the Josephus reference.[28] Plummer indicates that Jesus went that way because he felt no need for avoiding Samaritan hostility by crossing the Jordan and going through Perea as Jews sometimes did.[29]

Other interpreters, however, understood a divine necessity in John's account.[30] The verb which John used always involves a necessity if a desired end is to be realized. In this use it is most often translated "must"; one must do something if a desired end is to be realized. Understood in this way, John's use carries the sense of a theological necessity. The necessity may have been that Jesus might follow the direction of the Father's will for his life. Or it may be that a manifestation of himself as Redeemer must be made even to the hybrid Samaritans with their incomplete form of the Hebrew religion. Indeed, in this instance the two were the same. It was under the guidance of the Father's will that Jesus went to offer the "living water" to the Samaritans.

The Samaritans were a mixed race resulting from centuries of intermarriage of Jews with Gentiles from the time of the Babylonian captivity. Their offer to help the returning exiles in the rebuilding of the Temple was refused. The Jews would not permit them to help in the rebuilding of God's house when they had been unfaithul to God's laws. Subsequently they built their own temple on Mount Gerizim. Even after it was burned by John Hyrcanus the high priest of the Jerusalem Temple in 128 B.C., they continued to worship there.[31] That history supplies the background for Jesus' dialogue with the Samaritan woman.

While John's use of time (Jewish or Roman) is not always clear, the entire circumstance of this event indicates that Jewish time is involved in the "sixth hour" here (about noon). On the outskirts of the town of Sychar they stopped at a famous well. Jesus stayed to rest while the disciples went into the town to find food. As he sat by the well, his entire appearance expressed extreme weariness and thirst. A woman of the town came to the well and filled her water pot. Each would know the other's background; no greeting would be expected. The natural sequence appears to be that when she had filled her water pot and was ready to leave, Jesus broke the silence with his request, "Give me a drink" (v. 7). Her response was one of surprise, a twofold one likely. She may well have been surprised that he would speak to a woman. She probably knew that in Jewish custom men did not speak to women in public, not even to their wives. She was certainly surprised that a Jew would ask a Samaritan for a drink. The next sentence could be her ironic reminder but it is almost universally regarded as John's explanation for any readers who would not be familiar with Jewish-Samaritan relationship and customs, "For Jews have no dealings with Samaritans" (v. 9).[32] This translation, as well as that of the American Standard Version and King James Version, is really an overstatement. Even the Pharisees permitted the use of eggs, fruits, and vegetables from Gentiles. Jesus' disciples had gone into a Samaritan town in quest of food. *Today's English Version* has the accurate meaning of the word in rendering the sentence, "Jews will not use the same cups and bowls that Samaritans use." It was a matter of religious, ceremonial food laws. The Samaritans cherished the Pentateuch, rejecting the remainder of the Hebrew Scriptures, but they did not practice the laws of ceremonial purity and were regarded by careful Jews as unclean. By offering to drink from her water pot, Jesus was exposing himself to ceremonial uncleanness; that surprised her.

Jesus' response to her statement was even more surprising. He told her that if she had known "the gift of God" and the true identity of the one who had asked of her a drink, she would have asked him for a drink and he would have given her "living water." In her response and in his, the pronouns are emphatic: "*You* are asking *me* for a drink?" He was a Jew; she was a Samaritan; he needed something which she had; he was asking for it— water for his physical need. In Jesus' view and response the situation is reversed. He had something which she needed, so he responded, "If you really understood the situation, *you* would have asked."

Here we note the first of several instances in this event in which John's lower-higher use appears. They will be developed in sequence: water, worship, food, sowing, harvesting. She had water (material) which he needed and for which he asked. He had living water (spiritual) which she needed but for which she was not asking. He was ready to give it when she came to understand and to accept.

Some interpreters understand "the gift of God" in verse 10 to refer to Jesus as it does in 3:16; he is God's gift. In the immediate context, however, it seems better to understand it as God's gift of salvation as represented in the "living water" which Jesus had to give her. The Son whom God gave (3:16) and the salvation which he gives are, of course, inseparably united. As the Jewish religious authorities puzzled over Jesus' new Temple *mashal*, as Nicodemus puzzled over his new birth *mashal*, so the woman puzzled over his living water *mashal*. All asked the same question, How? In Jewish thought and Scriptures, "living water" meant running water in contrast to still water. A favorite sermon text of my high school preaching days was Jeremiah 2:13 which registers God's complaint against Israel,

> For my people have committed two evils:
>   they have forsaken me,
> the fountain of living waters,
>   and hewed out cisterns for themselves,
> broken cisterns,
>   that can hold no water.

In Zechariah 14:8 and Ezekiel 47:9 are other references to the virtue of living water. The woman may have had in mind the flowing spring which fed the water standing in the one-hundred-foot shaft of Jacob's well. That misunderstanding may indicate the scoffing nature of her rejoinder. Since Jesus did not even have a rope bucket for getting down to the water in the shaft, how was he going to get to the flowing water which fed the well (v. 11)? He must think he is greater than Jacob who got the well by digging down to the spring.[33]

Frequently a person in John's Gospel uses words which, unknown to the speaker, carry a double meaning. Here is a case. Jesus *was* greater than Jacob the ancestral head from whom the Samaritans traced their lineage through Joseph. He also had living water to offer, greater than any water Jacob ever gave. Pointing up the nature of that superiority, Jesus assured her that the water from Jacob's well, the water which he had asked of her, had the power to satisfy thirst temporarily, but that one who drank of the living water which he was offering her would never thirst again; it would be within that one a living fountain for eternal living (vv. 13–14). Compare John 7:37–38 which contains Jesus' promise that the thirsty one who drinks of him by faith will have rivers of living water flowing out of his heart. John identified those "rivers of living water" as the Holy Spirit.

Was the woman still speaking in half-humorous, half-scoffing banter when she asked Jesus for a drink of that marvelous water (v. 15)? Never thirst again? Never have to come to the well every day or twice a day? How convenient. Was she still thinking only of a sort of magic water which this man can bestow as "the gift of God" (v. 10)? Or was there some dim beginning of a realization that he was talking of something more than material water? Was there in her question some of that wistfulness of Nicodemus in his question about starting life all over again (3:4,9)?

Whatever her thoughts, Jesus knew that before she was a proper recipient for that living water she had to know what was involved in a genuine relationship to God. He startled her to a consciousness of her sin, always a barrier to a geniune relationship to God, by his order, "Go, call your husband, and come here" (v. 16). Startled and perhaps also perplexed by so abrupt a change of subject in their dialogue, she answered curtly, "I have no husband." That did not settle the matter. Jesus agreed on the accuracy of her statement but pointed out that he knew she had lived with five husbands and was now living in adultery with a man who was not her husband (vv. 17–18). Plummer suggests that the emphatic position of the pronoun, "not *your* husband," may imply that he was some other woman's husband.[34] There is no indication of how the five marriages had ended. Had she outlived five husbands? Had she been cast off by all or some of them? Interpreters agree that the implication is that her record of five husbands was not a wholesome one. Jewish practice regarded three marriages as maximum even when Hillel's lax interpretation of Deuteronomy 24:1 was followed. It is not likely that Samaritan laws were any more generous. Whatever her blotched marriage record, she was then living in adultery, perhaps with another woman's husband.

That was a subject of conversation less desirable than bantering about drinking water. She made an abrupt change. Unless her reputation for immorality had traveled as far as Judea or Galilee, this man must have the kind of knowledge which is possessed only by God's prophets. Perhaps he could settle for her a controversy which had raged for centuries between his ancestors and hers over the proper high place for worship—Mount Zion in Jerusalem or Mount Gerizim in Samaria. Once the Samaritans had had a temple on Mount Gerizim, but it had been destroyed 150 years before. The Jews still had their Temple in Jerusalem, and three times a year she saw pilgrim caravans going there to worship.[35] Where "ought" one to go to worship? Can one get nearer to God on Mount Gerizim or Mount Zion? That is the essence of her question (vv. 19-20).

The higher-lower technique appears again. She spoke to him of a geographically oriented worship on a specific mountain, Zion or Gerizim—either/or, not both. Jesus spoke to her of a spiritually oriented worship which can no more be localized than God can be localized. If one worships a deity which can be localized, limited to a particular mountain or shrine, he must go to that place to worship. If, however, one's deity cannot be so localized, neither can his worship be localized. So it was with the God whom both Jews and Samaritans sought to worship, but they seemed so often

short of the realization that he could be worshiped at *either* Mount
Zion or Mount Gerizim or at *neither* Mount Zion nor Mount
Gerizim (vv. 21–24).

His first words were a promise, "The hour is coming when
neither on this mountain nor in Jerusalem will you worship the
Father" (v. 21). Now, her concept of worship was wrong. The
time was coming when she would realize that genuine worship
relates to the God who is worshiped, not to the place of worship.
"You worship what you do not know" (v. 22) refers to the partial
revelation of God which the Samaritans had because they accepted only the Pentateuch and rejected the remainder of the
Hebrew Scriptures. That limited them in their approach to worship. "We worship what we know, for salvation is from the Jews"
(v. 22) refers to the complete revelation of God through the Scriptures all of which the Jews (except the Sadducees) accepted. The
Pentateuch (the Law) revealed sin; the Prophets revealed the
sin-bearer. The Law revealed the need of salvation; the Prophets
revealed the provision of salvation. From this viewpoint the Jews
were clearer in their knowledge of God than were the Samaritans.
The Jews' religion included the glorious hope of salvation through
God's Redeemer. The Samaritans' religion had but a dim reflec-
tion of that.

Jesus continued, "But the hour is coming, and now is" (v. 23).
This is a language pattern of Jesus in John's Gospel. See a similar
use in 5:25–29. In both of these passages, there is the tension of
the now and the not yet of eschatology which is so much a part
of the Synoptic Gospels. "The hour is coming" looks to the future.
"The hour is coming and now is" looks to the present as a time
of fulfillment. "The hour is coming and now is" (4:23) sees the
time of true worship as the time of Jesus' presence and revelation
that "God is spirit" (v. 24) and that true worship is spiritual after
the nature of the God who is worshiped. God seeks worshipers
who worship with that understanding. That is not to discount
the importance of a place where those who worship may go for

private or community worship. It does, however, eliminate once and for all the idea that worship is limited to such a place. "God is spirit" (4:24), "God is light" (1 John 1:5), "God is love" (1 John 4:8—these Johannine expressions are not definitions of God. They are descriptive of God's dealings with men, and they are elements of a true concept of worship.

With an air of being out of her depth in such consideration of God and a proper relationship to God, the woman said, "I know that Messiah is coming (he who is called Christ); when he comes, he will show us all things" (v. 25). These appear to be strange words for a Samaritan. They did not look for a messiah in the sense in which the Jews did. They looked for "the one who returns," (a prophet like Moses according to Deut. 18:15–19, a part of their Pentateuch). They expected him to be a specialist in interpreting the Law. They did not use the word *messiah* for "the one who returns." John used it because it would be more meaningful to his readers than the Samaritans'.

Jesus' surprising confession to her was, "I who speak to you am he" (v. 26). Any response she might have made was prevented by the return of the disciples. When she saw them, she left her water pot and hurried to town. Interpreters divide on whether she left it so Jesus could get the drink he had requested or whether she was in such a hurry that she forgot it. Probably she cared not if he and all the others (twelve?) drank from her water pot; she had news which was too good to keep.

Surprised to find Jesus talking to the woman, the disciples withheld their questions and offered him the food which they had brought from the town. He responded with another *mashal*, "I have food to eat of which you do not know" (v. 32). He moved from the lower, material food to the higher, spiritual food. His disciples no more understood his meaning about food than the woman had understood his meaning about water. They spoke among themselves of the unlikelihood that anyone (especially in Samaritan territory) had given him food. There was no evidence that the woman had given him food. What did he mean about his having food unknown to them?

His explanation did not mean that he had no need for physical food. The incarnation was real. Jesus got tired, sleepy, thirsty, and hungry as other people do. Here he spoke of a higher food which sustained him in that higher life of his commitment to the will of the Father; hence, his words, "My food is to do the will of him who sent me, and to accomplish his work" (v. 34). The pronoun is emphatic, "*My* food." That which sustained him was his aim and purpose to carry out the Father's will. That complete conformity of Jesus to the will and work of the Father is a recurring note in John (5:30; 6:38; 11:4; 12:49–50; 14:31; 15:10; 17:4). Did he consider their offer of physical food a temptation to divert his attention from the need of the Samaritans, the fragmented woman who had just left and the spiritually deprived people ("men" KJV) to whom she had gone to witness? His words from the wilderness temptation of the Synoptic Gospels come to mind, "Man shall not live by bread alone" (Luke 4:4). Bread was necessary, but his commitment to the will and work of the Father was more necessary. No physical need could turn his attention from the opportunity at hand to manifest to the Samaritans the redemptive love of God.

He continued by moving to another lower-higher instruction. "You say, don't you, that it is still four months before the harvest comes?" (author's translation). The form of the question indicates that the answer will be yes. It may have been a proverb which Jesus applied ("Four months between sowing and harvesting"). It may have reflected some discussion of the group along their journey, such as, "The farmers are sowing; in four months they will be harvesting." Jesus wanted them to see an *unexpected* harvest of a different kind, an immediate gathering of people, even Samaritans, for God. "I tell you, lift up your eyes, and see how the fields are already white for harvest" (v. 35). Couple that with the statement in verse 30 that when the woman invited the men

of the town to go out to the well and see a man who had supernatural knowledge by which he had told her the story of life,
"They went out of the city and were coming to him" (v. 30).
You can just see them strung out along the path, hurrying, shoving
for position in their eagerness to see such a man. Here, Jesus
indicated, was a harvest opportunity for which they did not need
to wait four months. As a picture of plenty in Amos 9:13, this
year's sower caught up with the reapers who were still harvesting
last year's crop, so in Jesus' words the reapers in this instance
have caught up with the sower.

He spoke of two kinds of sowing, two kinds of reaping, and
two kinds of wages. Farmers sow wheat; they reap wheat; they
receive wages. Jesus has sown the word; his disciples have an
immediate opportunity to reap sheaves for God; their wages can
be told in terms of eternal life for those whom they harvest for
God.

Back to verses 28–29. The woman sought out the people of
the town. "Men" is likely a general reference to people. Although
the definite article is used, "the men," it does not necessarily
justify the idea that she sought out the six men whom she knew
best from her relation to them. Her report was the sort of overstatement which excited people make. Jesus had not told her
everything which she had done, though her life with five husbands
and a paramour covers a great deal of territory! Her question is
fascinating, "Can this be the Christ?" She would likely have used
their word for "the one who returns."

The Greek people had an effective precision in asking questions
by using negative particles which indicated the kind of answer
anticipated. In verse 33 the Greek particle *(mē)* which introduces
the question, anticipates the answer no—"No one has brought
him anything to eat, has he?" No. In verse 35 the Greek particle
(ouk) anticipates the answer yes—"You say that it is yet four
months before harvest comes, don't you?" Yes. The Greek particle
(mēti) in verse 29 reflects an uncertain frame of mind about what

the answer will be, "You don't suppose, do you, that this might be the Christ?" It is as if she thinks the answer is yes, but she thinks they will answer no.

They were, nevertheless, stimulated to go to see for themselves, half believing and yet doubtful. At their request, Jesus and the disciples spent two days in witnessing to them. There was a harvest. Many believed because of the testimony of the Samaritan woman (v. 39). Many others, unconvinced by her testimony, were convinced by Jesus' teachings (vv. 41–42). Their testimony was "We know that this is indeed the Savior of the world" (v. 42). They had drunk the water of life, God's gift of salvation, from its very Source.

Manifestation as Lord of the Sabbath
(5:1–47)

"Lord of the Sabbath" as a title for Jesus is borrowed from the Synoptic Gospels. As they walked one sabbath along a path through the grainfields, Jesus' disciples had taken ripened heads of grain, rubbed them in their hands to separate grain from chaff, and had eaten the grain. Deuteronomy 23:25 reflects approval of one's plucking another man's grain by hand and eating it but to thrust in one's sickle was forbidden! The fact that the disciples were doing this on the sabbath caused the Pharisees to object that they were breaking the law which prohibited labor on the sabbath. Jesus used examples from Israel's history to justify "law-breaking" as the Pharisees were defining it; such as 1 Samuel 21:1–6 and Numbers 28:9–10. He then quoted Hosea 6:6 to show that in God's view a merciful attitude to others is more important than religious rituals. He concluded with the very revolutionary statement, "For the Son of man is lord of the sabbath" (Mark 2:28; Matt. 12:8; Luke 6:5). While that language is not used in this event in John, the principle is embedded in Jesus' statement, "My Father is working still, and I am working" (5:17). It was his response to the Jews' challenge that he was breaking the law of sabbath observance which was one of the two reasons that caused their determination to put him to death (v. 18). On another occasion he had assumed lordship of the Temple (2:13–22). Now he was compounding the crime by assuming lordship of the sabbath.

The occasion was his presence in Jerusalem for a feast. We have noted earlier that textual variants on the grammatical construction ("the feast" or "a feast"?) make it impossible to tell whether this was a Passover feast or a Tabernacles feast. The question is unimportant as far as this event is concerned. It is important in the question as to the number of Passover festivals attended by Jesus according to the Gospel of John.

From the viewpoint of the text of the New Testament, the location of this event was for centuries a problem. Three different names appear in different manuscripts—Bethsaida (which has the strongest manuscript support), Bethzatha, and Bethesda. The most certain we can be from the textual readings is that it was near the pool where the sheep were washed before being sacrificed, just northeast of the Temple. Brown's [36] treatment of the problem is very helpful. The indispensable work for understanding this entire problem and for ascertaining the unquestionable location and description of the place is by Jeremias.[37] The rediscovery of the pool may be dated from 1888. After a series of limited but important excavations, the pool has been excavated on a massive scale since 1949. It had been lost to the eyes of man so long that many critics rejected the authenticity of this miracle because there was no visible evidence for such a pool. No wonder, excavations have revealed that the floor of the two pools enclosed within the five porches was forty-five feet beneath the present surface level! So much was the accumulated debris of the centuries since the destruction of the city in A.D. 70.

The entire structure was large.[38] The implication of verse 3 is that this was a regular gathering place for people with various physical handicaps—blindness, paralysis, crippled conditions.

Other than verse 7, the original text of the Gospel contained no explanation as to why they were there. The last clause in verse 3 and all of verse 4 of the King James Version appears to be a late addition to explain the lame man's statement in verse 7. Tatian's arrangement of the four Gospels about A.D. 190 included the explanation, but it does not appear in the Greek manuscripts until the fifth century. It is clear from verse 7 that occasionally there was some sort of turbulence in the water and that the people believed that the first person who got into the water after the disturbance would be healed. At least the lame man of this event believed that. That is why he was there and likely why many of the others were there.

Was there an angel stirring up the water as the interpolated verse 4 indicates? Noting the very prominent ministry of angels in the events of the New Testament, Hendriksen states that we cannot rule out such a source for the agitation of the water.[39] The agitation, however, could have been from some natural cause. Several interpreters suggest agitation from the springs which fed the pool or from some process of drainage and filling. Hendriksen calls on us to stress the fact that Jesus' healing of the man was not ascribed to any angelic action or any medicinal value of the water. Jesus did not even use the water, though on other occasions he used a variety of physical actions: touching the tongue of a man with a speech impediment; thrusting his fingers into the ears of one whose hearing was to be restored; making a poultice of clay and spittle to anoint the eyes of a blind man.

Had other people been healed here? The lame man thought so. Except for the interpolated verse 4, there is no statement that there had been other healings. Again, we cannot rule out the possibility. There are evidences in the New Testament of God's honoring a very simple, naive faith that needed something material for an anchor: the woman who touched the hem of Jesus' robe (Luke 8:44); those on whom the shadow of Simon Peter fell (Acts 5:15–16); the aprons and handkerchiefs that were carried from Paul to sick people (Acts 19:11). God does sometimes work in mysterious ways his wonders to perform.

While it may be necessary for us to a consider all of these matters in trying to get at the significance of this the third of John's signs, our main focus must not be on a series of questions and suppositions about other miracles. It must be on this miracle and its place in the experience and teaching of Jesus and subsequently in John's presentation of Jesus. There was one particularly pathetic man whose situation arrested the attention of Jesus. He had been an invalid for thirty-eight years (v. 5). The thirty-eight years indicates the gravity of his case. It has no more symbolic meaning than the eighteen years of the woman whom Jesus healed of curvature of the spine (Luke 13:16).

Jesus approached the man at the point of the one thing he wanted above everything else, 'Do you want to be healed?" (v. 6). Knowing that that was the very reason that he was there, feeling absolutely helpless to do anything for himself, and having not a single person to help him, the man may have felt that Jesus' question was foolish or even cruel. Here, however, was one person at least who had noticed him enough to show some interest in him. Did his heart beat a bit faster with the thought, Perhaps he will help me get into the pool the next time the water is troubled? Feeling that his wish to be healed was too obvious for response, he simply pointed out to Jesus why he could not be healed (v. 7). Was there a note of request in his statement? "If I just had *someone* to help me, . . ." Did he know Jesus from some other miracle which he had done? There are prior references in John to miracles which Jesus performed in Jerusalem (2:23; 3:2). Did Jesus interpret his reply as a call for help? We do not know. We know that he did have someone, but that someone did not need troubled water as a tool, whatever the source of the troubling. Jesus spoke and his words were command and

challenge, "Rise, take up your pallet, and walk" (v. 8). Healing
was instant; obedience was instant. He took up his pallet and
started walking.

Enter the watchdogs of orthodoxy. "The Jews" of verse 10 must
have been Pharisees. They stopped him to charge him with being
a lawbreaker, "It is not lawful for you to carry your pallet." Doubtless they had in mind Exodus 20:10, "You shall not do any work"
on the sabbath. How much work is there in carrying a *krabbatos*
(poor-man's pallet) across town? Not much, and it was not the
kind of labor prohibited by the Exodus law anyway. But the Pharisees would not even lift saliva from their mouth to rub on their
sore eyes on the sabbath because it meant carrying a burden.
The man defended his action by referring them to one who at
that moment was probably greater in his eyes than their ceremonial laws. He was carrying his pallet because the man who had
healed him told him to. He had been healed without the help
of the pool; he did not have to stay at the pool; the man had
told him to take up his pallet and walk, probably to go home.

Healed you? On the sabbath? Ah ha! Another man had broken
the law. Their ceremonial laws also prohibited any form of healing
on the sabbath. "Who is the man . . . ?" They would charge
him too. The healed man could not point Jesus out because, as
he often did, Jesus had withdrawn from the scene of excitement
over one of his miracles. That stopped the discussion temporarily.
John did not stop at that point. The sign had been accomplished.
But that to which the sign pointed was John's major concern:
Jesus' manifestation of himself even to the leaders of the religion
of Israel as the Lord of the sabbath.

Continuing his account, John reported that at some later time
Jesus found the man in the Temple and said to him, "See, you
are well! Sin no more, that nothing worse befall you" (v. 14).
"See" is another example of John's dramatic "behold" or "look"—
consider the wonderful change in your condition. "Sin no more"
indicates Jesus' awareness of some kind of sin in the man's life.

There is no indication that Jesus was relating the sin to the man's crippled condition in a cause-and-effect sort of way. That was a standard thought in Jesus' day, but on other occasions he absolutely rejected sin as a solution to the problem of the source of physical calamity.[40] It is entirely possible that the lame man had been blaming his crippled condition for those thirty-eight years on God and that his sin was his bitterness, hostility toward God. The sins of the spirit are as vicious and as destructive of character as the sins of the flesh. Witness Galatians 5:19 wherein the two are equally linked as evil. The "nothing worse" of Jesus' warning is generally regarded as God's judgment—get your heart right with God; there are worse things than physical ills.

The man went to the Jews and identified Jesus as the one who had healed him (v. 15). His motive is not indicated. Did he fear their threat because he had been breaking their law? Did he trust Jesus to make a better defense of his carrying his pallet on the sabbath than he had made? The Jews began their persecution of Jesus as a lawbreaker (v. 16). He could have been charged on two accounts: breaking the law by healing on the sabbath; breaking the law by encouraging the healed man to carry his pallet on the sabbath.

Jesus justified his action in a way that infuriated the Jews. He said, "My Father is working still, and I am working" (v. 17). To what extent they would have understood that statement alone to be Jesus' claim that he was the Son of God may be open to question. By the time his discussion in verses 19–46 was over, however, it was unmistakably clear that he was claiming precisely that. So John's explanation in verse 18 may reflect the Jews' attitude at the end of the long defense more than at the beginning. John wanted his readers to understand that the Jews were so crystallized in their opposition to Jesus that they were determined from that time forward to kill him. What were their reasons? He was in their eyes a lawbreaker, a serious charge within itself; he claimed to be the Son of God which to them meant that he

was claiming equality with God, the sin of blasphemy which in
the days of Moses would have resulted in the guilty one's being
stoned to death.

In his defense, Jesus went back to the Genesis account of creation which was behind the sabbath law of Exodus 20:10. After
six days of creative activity, God rested on the seventh day and
hallowed it as a memorial to his creative work (Gen. 2:1–3). Jesus'
point in his statement "My Father is working still" is that the
Genesis passage does not imply that God never worked after
completing the initial creation. He went right on working in and
with his creation. The word translated "still" is extensive in force
(right up to now). Link the Genesis passage with this statement
of Jesus and then link them with Revelation 21:5 in which the
eternal, Creator God of the throne scene in chapter 4, worshiped
for his creative work (Rev. 4:11), says, "Behold, I make all things
new." At the end of the Bible as at the beginning, God works
in his creation.

The Jews knew that God did not stop working when the first
star appeared on Friday night and the sabbath began! Of course
he worked—in sustaining his creation, in creating life, in granting
redemption, in judgment on evil. Their God was a continually
working God. That was what Jesus meant, and it was the reason
which he gave for his own working on the sabbath. As the Son
of God, he did as his Father did; he worked that which was good
for man, as the sabbath was good for man. In a similar controversy
with the Pharisees on another occasion, he stated that the sabbath
was made to serve man, not to be served by man (Mark 2:27–
28).

In an extended discourse on his work as the Son of God (vv.
19–46), Jesus set out basic ideas and reasons for his work. (1) As
the Son he did not work independently, "of his own accord";
he did only what the Father did, the same kind of work (v. 19).
(2) Because the Father loves his Son, he reveals to him all that
he is doing in order that the Son may do the same (v. 20). Moreover

Jesus indicated that they were destined to see the Son do "greater works" than healing the lame (v. 20). These "greater works" are identified in verses 21–22 and 25–29 as exercising the power of judgment and the giving of life. (3) For anyone to fail to honor the Son by acknowledging him as the Son is to fail to honor the Father. In John, one cannot have the fatherhood of God unless he confesses the sonship of Christ. (4) To hear the Son's word (the very word he was speaking to them in this encounter) and to believe in him is to escape judgment and to possess eternal life (v. 24). The one who identifies with the Son, by faith in him, has already started living that eternal life.

In verse 25 Jesus took up again the statement of verse 21 that the Father had given to the Son the responsibility of giving life. In Jewish religious thought, the exercise of judgment and the giving of life were regarded as the prerogatives of God alone. It was Jesus' claim that the Father had given these two prerogatives to him which convinced "the Jews" that he should die for blaspheming God. In this passage, verses 25–29, Jesus put two kinds of "giving life" in contrast. It is the higher-lower method again, but one may argue as to which is higher and which is lower. The two kinds of life which he gives are the life of regeneration (vv. 25–26) and the life of resurrection (vv. 28–29). In developing them, Jesus used his "the hour is coming and now is" and his "the hour is coming" formula, but he reversed the order observed in his use of them with the Samaritan woman (4:21,23).

"The hour is coming, and now is" introduces the raising of life of those who are spiritually dead (vv. 25–27), Those who are spiritually dead hear the voice of the Son of God and respond to it in faith. They come to experience life, the eternal life of verse 24. Eternal life is a distinctive Johannine concept. While the sense of duration usually understood in the word *eternal* is a part of the concept, it is not all of the concept. The emphasis is on the quality of that transcendent life upon which one enters to live now and forever. The Father has entrusted to the Son the prerogative of giving such life. And the hour "is"; it is presently working. One who believes receives even now this life which is like that of the Father and of the Son (v. 26). He does not have to wait for the future to be thus raised up to a new kind of life.

"The hour is coming" (v. 28) looks to another kind of raising to a new kind of life the giving of which the Father has granted to the Son. This is the resurrection from the dead. If Jesus' listeners wondered at the idea of his giving spiritual life, let them wonder even more at his giving resurrection life. If "the Jews" of this controversy were indeed Pharisees, this would be all the more striking to them. Whereas the Sadducees denied the resurrection of the body, as well as any other kind of life after death, the Pharisees held firmly to the doctrine of resurrection. Now their antagonist, this lawbreaker, was claiming that God has turned over to him the power and authority of the resurrection.

"The hour is coming" looks to a future time; in John 6:39,40,44, and 54, that future time is designated "the last day." So Jesus could not add "and now is," because the resurrection was (and is) future. "All who are in the tombs" refers to those who are physically dead (v. 28). They, too, are destined to hear the voice of the Son, to respond to its authority, and to come forth in resurrection (v. 29). For some it will be a life-kind of resurrection (the redeemed); for others it will be a judgment-kind of resurrection (the unredeemed).[41] Those who claim that in verses 25–26 John has demythologized the Synoptic teaching on the resurrection of the dead by equating resurrection with regeneration, do well to observe that if such is true, the demythologizing is reversed in verses 28–29, and *the last word is an affirmation of the doctrine of the resurrection.* The Son exercises both the life giving of regeneration and the life giving of resurrection.

In the closing part of his discourse, Jesus pointed out to the Jews the very strong witness to his sonship to God. It is a fourfold witness. (1) John the Baptist as a burning and shining lamp wit-

nessed to it (vv. 33–36). (2) The Father himself witnessed to it
(vv. 37–38). (3) The very works which Jesus was doing in obedience
to the Father witnessed to it (v. 36). (4) Moses in the Scriptures
witnessed to it (vv. 39,45–47). His reference is likely to Deuteronomy 18:15–19. The construction in verse 39 may be a simple
statement of fact as it appears in the Revised Standard Version,
"You search the scriptures." If so, it is a comment that they search
their Scriptures for evidence of the coming of the Messiah, but
they are missing the fact that he is the Messiah of whom the
Scriptures witness. Or the construction may be an imperative
as it appears in the King James Version, "Search the scriptures."
In this case it would be a challenge to the Jews to go to their
Scriptures and search them for evidence that their witness points
to him as the Messiah. He did not, however, show optimism that
they would so interpret that witness (v. 47).

The discourse made it very clear to the Jews that Jesus did
understand himself to be the Son of God whom the Father had
sent into the world to do his work, even when that work involved
action which the authorities regarded as lawbreaking. John's summation of verse 18 was accurate. They sought to kill him because
he assumed the role of lordship over the sabbath, and he assumed
the role of sonship to God making himself equal to God. It is a
bit surprising that John did not conclude the encounter with his
favorite reason for their not killing Jesus right then, "his hour
had not yet come."

Manifestation as the Bread of Life
(6:1–71)

The four Gospels contain at least thirty-five specific miracles
which Jesus performed.[42] In addition to these there are several
references to occasions on which Jesus performed multiple healing miracles of different kinds. Of all of his miracles only one
appears in all four Gospels—the feeding of the five thousand (Mark
6:30–46; Matt. 14:13–23; Luke 9:10–17; John 6:1–14). It must have

been very widely used by the early Christians.

In developing their particular emphases, the writers used the miracle in different ways. In Luke the only real emphasis is on Jesus' compassion for the hungry people. That element is in the other Gospels, too, but there are other emphases which overshadow it. In Matthew to some extent and especially in Mark, there are strong overtones of an attempt of the people to get a revolution started with Jesus as their leader—a political, military messiah. For examples: (1) They were out in a desert place (where traditionally revolutions started in Israel). (2) There were many who "were coming and going" (Mark 6:33) suggesting an air of secrecy. (3) When Jesus saw the crowds they reminded him of "sheep without a shepherd" (Mark 6:34), an expression for an army without a leader or a nation without a leader in the Exodus experience of Israel (Num. 27:16–23). On that occasion it was another "Jesus" who became that leader; Jesus is the Greek form of Joshua. (4) It was a crowd of men almost if not completely to the exclusion of women and children; Matthew's "besides women and children" (14:21) may be rendered "apart from" ("to the exclusion of"). (5) The twelve apostles may have shared in the wishes of the people. Jesus had to compel them to get into a boat and leave before he could dispel the crowd. (6) Mark's closing comment on the entire event is that, "they did not understand about the loaves, but their hearts were hardened" (6:52). Hardened because he would not be that kind of messiah?

John noted that emphasis too. Jesus perceived that the people were going to seize him forcibly and make him their king (v. 15). It was near the time for Passover (v. 4); they may have been thinking of carrying out their plans in Jerusalem. There is no evidence that Jesus attended that Passover. Ironically it was at the Passover one year afterward that he was executed on the charge that he was a revolutionist. John, however, did not develop that emphasis. He focused on what happened on the next day when, in the synagogue at Capernaum, Jesus discussed with the people who had participated in the miracle (v. 25) and with their leaders ("the Jews," vv. 41,52) the ultimate significance of the miracle—the meaning to which the sign pointed. That dialogue, preserved only by John, provides one of the most dramatic of his manifestations to Israel—his manifestation as the Bread from heaven, or the living Bread. Four major ideas from that dialogue must be examined.

First, **God provides physical bread for physical man** (vv. 1–15). This is the miracle itself. The occasion was Jesus' withdrawal with the twelve for some quiet time of rest after they had returned from a preaching mission through Galilee and had made their report to him (Mark 6:30–31). Matthew includes as a part of Jesus' motive for withdrawal the news of the beheading of John the Baptist (14:13). The crowd of people from whom they were trying to withdraw thwarted that attempt. When they learned where Jesus was going, they took off on foot around the north shore of the Sea of Galilee as Jesus and the twelve were going by boat from the west side to the east side. Luke 9:10 indicates that they stopped near Bethsaida. There the crowd found them; Jesus would not send them away. He spent the day in teaching them about the kingdom of God and in healing the sick (v. 11).

Having finished his teaching and being reluctant to start the crowd to their homes hungry, knowing that he was going to feed them (a typical Johannine notation, 6:5–6), he tested the faith of Philip whose home was nearby in Bethsaida. "How are we to buy bread, so that these people may eat?" Philip did not even suggest that they ask Judas Iscariot their treasurer (John 12:4–6) how much was in the money bag. He made a rapid estimate that at regular wages a man could work two hundred days and not have enough for each of the people "to get a little" (v. 7). Had Philip forgotten how Jesus supplied enough wine for a wedding party some time before this?

Andrew did a bit better. He was aware of the presence of food in the company. He reported the presence of a boy who had five barley cakes and two fish, a boy's lunch.[43] Andrew's question was, "But what are they among so many?" (v. 9). Was he remembering that Jesus had turned a large amount of water into an equal amount of wine and wondering if Jesus could do something with the boy's lunch? That is rather doubtful. The total Gospel account points up the total lack of resources available to the apostles to relieve the crisis. They had not enough money (v. 7), not enough food (v. 7), and not enough shops if they had the money (Luke 9:12). The Luke reference contains their suggestion that Jesus dismiss the five thousand plus people to go to the villages in the territory to buy food; that would have required a lot of villages. They had one resource, however, which they were overlooking; Jesus was there and he was in control (v. 6).

The next action was simple and direct. At Jesus' instructions, the twelve organized the company into convenient groups to sit (recline, as in banqueting) on the grass. He took the boy's lunch, gave thanks for it, and broke it into serving pieces which were passed to the people until all had "as much as they wanted" (v. 11) and had "eaten their fill" (v. 12). Jesus then instructed the twelve apostles to gather up the broken pieces which had not been used. Each one returned with a basket filled with the surplus food. This plus the fact that more than five thousand people had been fed emphasized the *quantity* of Jesus' provision as in the miracle at the marriage feast the best wine emphasized the *quality* of Jesus' provision.

What was the reaction of the people who experienced this bounty? Luke contains no reaction whatever. His account closes with the gathering of the fragments. He omits the next materials which are contained in the other Gospels. His next event is the confession at Caesarea Philippi which probably occurred near the Feast of Tabernacles about six months later.

Mark and Matthew state that immediately after the gathering of the fragments Jesus compelled the apostles to get into a boat and cross over to the other side of the sea while he dismissed the crowds (Mark 6:45; Matt. 14:22).[44] By another miracle of Jesus they were rescued from a vicious storm and arrived on the west side of the sea at Gennesaret (Mark 6:53; Matt. 6:34) about three miles from Capernaum where John reports their arrival (6:16,21).

John's report of the reaction of the people to the miracle (vv. 14–15) may throw some light on Matthew and Mark's report of Jesus' immediate dismissal of the twelve and then the dismissal of the people. Relating Jesus' giving them bread in the wilderness to Moses' giving Israel the manna in the wilderness, the people concluded that Jesus was the expected prophet-like-unto-Moses Messiah of Deuteronomy 18:15–19. The nearness of Passover with the Exodus setting may have contributed to their conclusion (v. 4). In their enthusiasm they were ready to take him by force (a word for capturing someone), take him to the Passover, and make him their king (v. 15). If the apostles were about to be swept along by the movement, Jesus would have to get them away before he could dispel the crowd. They wanted a military messiah who could lead them in their revolt. In time of war it would be of inestimable value to have such a leader and provider as Jesus. He, however, knew that he was not that kind of messiah, He broke up their efforts effectively. The "king" idea does not appear in John again until it becomes a major part of Jesus' trial before Pontius Pilate.

Second, **God provides spiritual bread for spiritual man** (vv. 16–59). Verses 16–24 link the miracle with Jesus' interpretation of its spiritual significance on the next day. Having dismissed both the apostles and the crowd, Jesus went up on the mountain overlooking the place of the miracle to pray. John gives only the fact of his going up on the mountain. For the other details we are indebted to the Synoptics. Jesus' practice of withdrawing to pray in times of great popularity is a theme of the Synoptics, particularly of Luke. While he was there, a storm swept down upon the sea, endangering the lives of the apostles. Jesus went to their rescue, walking upon the water, the fifth of John's signs.

He quieted their fears and apparently quieted the storm (John 6:21; Matt. 14:32, "the wind ceased") though this is not given with the detail of the Synoptic miracle of his quieting a storm on another occasion (Matt. 8:23–27; Mark 4:38–41; Luke 8:22–25).

Some of the people delayed their departure, perhaps waiting for Jesus to return. When he had not returned on the next morning, they took boats which had come from Tiberias during the night and crossed back to the west side to seek Jesus. They found him at Capernaum (vv. 22–24). They asked, "Rabbi, when did you come here?" (v. 25). The interrogative particle may mean "when" or it may mean "how." In this instance it seems almost to imply both. ("When did you arrive and how did you travel?"). Note in verse 22 their careful observation that there had been only one boat at the scene the day before; the apostles had left in it; Jesus had not been with them. Were they suspecting another miracle? Had they heard from the apostles about how he had come, and were they asking him to confirm it?

Jesus' response sounds as if he so interpreted their question, "You seek me, not because you saw signs [plural], but because you ate your fill of the loaves" (v. 26). He charged them with not being so interested in his power or its source as in his provision for their physical need. He counseled them to be more concerned about spiritual food which endures to eternal life than material food which is perishable and at best can sustain only temporal life (v. 27). Only he, the Son of man on whom God the Father has set his seal of approval, could supply that food. He *gave* them the physical food; they must *work* for the spiritual food which he can supply. Physical food was important for them, but it was just an illustration of the spiritual food which God was offering them in him. They asked, "What must we do, to be doing the works of God?" (v. 28). He answered that the only work which God would accept was that they believe in him whom God had sent (v. 29). In this sense, believing in him is working and working is believing in him.

Their next question was a call for a sign that he was really sent of God, a sign that would make seeing and believing one and the same (v. 30). They gave him an example as if asking a question. They cited a parallel between Moses' giving food to their fathers in the wilderness and Jesus' giving food to them in the wilderness. Both the manna and the multiplied loaves were miracles. The manna convinced their fathers that God had sent Moses. Did Jesus mean for the multiplied loaves to convince them that God had sent him? Beneath the surface was the question, "Are you the prophet-like-unto-Moses?"

They called the manna "bread from heaven" (v. 31). Jesus granted that the manna could be properly called "bread from heaven," but he emphasized that the real giver of the bread was not Moses but God. He added that God is also the giver of "the true bread from heaven" of which the manna was only parabolic. The true Bread from heaven which God gives is the One who comes down from heaven and gives life to the world (v. 33). The expression here translated "the one who comes down from heaven" may also be translated "that which comes down from heaven" (RSV) with the sense that "the true bread" is the bread that comes down from heaven as God's gift, Christ. The personal translation seems more accurate in this chapter in which the one coming down from heaven is Christ himself and by his coming he gives life to the world (note this use in vv. 35,38, and 58). As he offered the woman of Samaria the Water of life and she replied, "give me this water" (4:15), so he offered these people the Bread of life and they replied, "give us this bread" (6:34). In each instance, however, the request reflects incomplete, if not erroneous, understanding of what Jesus was offering.

In response to their request, Jesus followed the same theme, but he spoke more plainly because they did not see that he was not just *offering* them the life-giving bread from heaven; he *was* that life-giving bread. So he spoke, "I am the bread of life" (v. 35). To come to him and to believe in him are to be equated. So also to come to him and to believe in him is to eat the Bread

of life and nevermore hunger or to drink the Water of life and
nevermore thirst (v. 35). He recognized that they had seen him,
and they had seen him multiply the bread and fish, but they
did not yet believe in him. They had not come to him in the
sense of commitment to him. Observe the concept of coming
to him in verses 35,37,44,45, and 65. To come to him is to believe
in him. Those who believe in him are the Father's gift to him,
and he rejects none of those whom the Father gives him (v. 37).
It is for the very purpose of doing the Father's will that he has
come into the world. It is the Father's accomplished will that
negatively he should lose not one of those who come to him
and positively he should give eternal life (regeneration) to them
here and now and that he should raise them up (resurrection)
at the last day (vv. 38–40).

Enter "the Jews" (v. 41). They murmured their displeasure at
his claim to be the Bread from heaven. Whatever density of understanding lingered on the part of "the people" who experienced
the miracle and initiated this theological discussion with Jesus
(vv. 22,24,25), the Jews understood him and were offended at
his claim. Usually "the Jews" in John refers to the religious authorities in Jerusalem. Were some of them present at the miracle and
in the synagogue for this dialogue? It is possible. These, however,
may have been the Jewish authorities in Galilee. Note their acquaintance with Jesus' family background (v. 42). Essentially they
were saying that Jesus did not come down from heaven; he came
from Nazareth. Another case of a prophet without honor in his
own country.

Jesus addressed himself pointedly to their complaint (vv. 43–
51). In order for one to come to him, that one must first be drawn
by the Father (v. 44) and taught by God (v. 45). In the Synoptics,
in John, and throughout the New Testament, the matter of salvation is always God's first move. Apart from God's initial action
in offering salvation, no one can be saved. God draws men by
love, by acts of mercy, by the giving of his Son for their redemp-

tion. That comes first, but there must be the response of receptivity through faith on the part of the one who is drawn. The Jews were not interested in that; they were interested only in winning a theological argument. Jesus made the case very plain for them; the decision was theirs. They had been drawn by God, taught by God, though they had never seen God as Jesus had seen God (v. 46). He had seen God; he knew the will of God; he told them "truly, truly" that the only way to eternal life was for them to believe in him, the Bread of life, whom God had sent (vv. 46–48).

He reminded them that their forefathers ate the material bread from heaven (the manna), and they perished; it was only for physical life. He offered himself to them as the true Bread from heaven which they might eat and live forever. He offered his own flesh (a death reference) for the life of the world (v. 51).

Jesus spoke verses 35–40 to clear up the misunderstanding registered in verse 34. He spoke verses 43–51 to clear up deeper misunderstanding registered in verses 41–42. Seeming even further darkened in their misunderstanding, the Jews argued violently among themselves asking the perplexed "how" of Nicodemus (3:9) and the Samaritan woman (4:9). "How can this man give us his flesh to eat?" (v. 52). Literally, the question is one of *ability*, "How is this man able to give to us his flesh to eat?"

For them to eat his flesh, he would first have to die. He was claiming that God was his Father. Apart from the blasphemy of that claim, how could the Son of God die? He was claiming that he was able to do what Moses could not do, give them eternal life. How? He was claiming that he was giving his physical death for their spiritual life. How? Their messianic anticipation did not include his death; it embraced only glory and triumph for him. Their word which is translated "this man" and literally means "this person" may have been used in contempt that he, a lawbreaker, could be God's agent for giving them eternal life by his physical death.

Jesus' closing words anticipate in John his eucharistic words in instituting the Lord's Supper (Mark 14:22–25; Matt. 26:26–29; Luke 22:19–20). On that occasion Jesus took from the Passover table bread to represent his body and wine to represent his blood. He gave to them these symbolic elements to eat and to drink in memorializing his death for man's life. Note in Luke 22:20 that Jesus identified his blood symbolized in the wine with the new covenant which God had promised through Jeremiah (31:31). John's Gospel does not have the institution of the Lord's Supper, but he has an almost identical teaching of Jesus in this dialogue with the Jews over eating his body and drinking his blood.

To have spiritual life one must "eat the flesh of the Son of man and drink his blood" (v. 53). His flesh is genuine food and his blood is genuine drink (v. 55). The one who eats his flesh and drinks his blood abides in him and he abides in that one (v. 56). As "the living Father" sent the living Son into the world, whoever eats the flesh and drinks the blood of the Son will have eternal life; he will live forever as the Father and the Son live forever (v. 57). That is what eating the living Bread means (v. 58).

Third, **many refused the Bread of life** (vv. 60–66). A consistent pattern in John is that wherever Jesus taught and worked, a division among the people resulted; some rejected him; some accepted him. On this occasion, many of those who rejected his teaching were called "disciples" (v. 60). The word means "learners." They had attached themselves to him and the apostles; they followed him to listen and to learn. They may have possessed a genuine hunger to know more about God, and they were looking to Jesus for guidance. This teaching, however, was more than they could take. "This is a hard saying" (v. 60) does not mean hard to understand. It means hard to accept. Their problem was that they *did* understand. Jesus was teaching that as the Messiah he would die. They could not accept that. Their words "who can listen to it?" may mean just that; who can listen to that kind of teaching? On the other hand the pronoun may refer to Jesus, "who can listen to him?"; who can learn from such a teacher?

Jesus sensed their frame of mind and their disillusionment over his teaching. He proposed an even greater demand on credence. He asked them if they were offended over the idea of the Messiah's death, how would they respond if they saw him ascend to heaven from whence he had been telling them that he had descended? (vv. 61–62). John's Gospel does not contain the account of Jesus' ascension. Likely at this point Jesus was making reference to the total experience of his death, resurrection, ascension to the Father who had sent him, and perhaps the sending of the Holy Spirit (vv. 62–63). Would they believe then? They must get past their crude thinking about actually eating his physical flesh and drinking his physical blood. They must understand that life is a gift of the Spirit. It is the Spirit of God who gives spiritual life to men of faith but not to those who cannot really believe because they cannot get beyond the barrier of the physical to experience the reality of the spiritual (v. 64). Jesus knew that with all his potential, Judas, one of the twelve, was of the same frame of mind as these "disciples" who went back and no longer followed him with the hope of learning from him (vv. 64–66). Rejection by many in Galilee thus followed the pattern of rejection by many in Judea (5:16–18).

Fourth, **the apostles had confidence in the Bread of life** (vv. 67–71). Some reject; some accept. On this occasion the acceptance of his teaching is an act of the apostles. Jesus challenged their loyalty with a question which breathes the tone of appeal to loyalty, "Will you also go away?" (v. 67). The negative participle which introduces the question indicates Jesus' anticipation of their answer "You do not wish to go away, too, do you?" Simon Peter spoke for the group in answering no. Another of the dramatic experiences of Jesus included by the Synoptic writers but not by John is the confession at Caesarea Philippi. When Jesus questioned the twelve about expressed opinion of the people about

him and then about their conclusion about him, it was Simon
Peter who voiced the opinion of the group in confessing Jesus
to be the Christ (Matt. 16:16). As close as John comes to a Petrine
confession is this passage (vv. 68–69).

There are three elements in Peter's confessional response to
Jesus' question. (1) "Lord, to whom shall we go?" (v. 68). This
reflects a recognition of their need. There was a compulsion upon
them for life commitment to someone. They were conscious of
no one else to whom they might go. Some of them had once
followed John the Baptist. He had introduced them to Jesus and
had since been executed by Herod Antipas. They had no one
else to trust and to follow. If not Jesus, then back to the fishing
nets and the tax tables. (2) "You have the words of eternal life"
(v. 68). The construction is not an emphatic one. The statement
is the simple but moving reason for their staying with him. They
had found the one whose very words (the term means "spoken
words") conveyed the message of eternal life, the transcendent
life here and forever. (3) "We have believed, and have come to
know, that you are the Holy One of God" (v. 69). They had a
felt need; they had found that need adequately met in him; now
through the words of Simon they make their confession of faith.
It would be difficult to frame a more emphatic and dramatic
confession. Let us read it precisely from the grammatical construction. "We have believed and continue to believe and have come
to know and still know that you are the Holy One of God." What
more needs to be said?

Jesus' final word is a sad one of caution to Simon Peter about
the inclusiveness of his "we." There were twelve of them. Jesus
had chosen them from all of his learners (disciples) to follow him,
to learn from him, to share in his work. One of the twelve, however, had already set himself on a course that could mean only
tragedy and ruin. The eleven did not know that but Jesus did.
That one would ultimately slander him (the meaning of the word
devil) by betraying him to his death on the charge of treason
against Rome. How far Judas had already gone in his deviation

from loyalty, we do not know. We do know that the climax came in the last week of Jesus' life with the twelve. Be careful, Peter, how you say, "we."

Manifestation as the Teacher of Israel
(7:1 to 10:42)

In the structure of John, this long central section is a theological unit. It is broken, however, into multiple literary segments. The unit is built around two visits of Jesus to Jerusalem: the Feast of Tabernacles (October) and the Feast of Dedication (December). The line of division between the two is not clear. Some interpreters think that the Feast of Dedication does not begin until 10:22 where it is first introduced. Others think that it begins at 10:1 with the good shepherd allegory. The following exposition is presented from the viewpoint that 7:1 to 10:21 took place at Tabernacles and 10:22–42 took place when Jesus returned to Jerusalem for Dedication.

The materials of the Feast of Tabernacles are divided into a general background followed by at least two, perhaps three, teaching sessions. The organization which is followed in this exposition is a simplified one, built around the two specific days in which Jesus taught (7:14,37). Much more complex organizations appear in different commentaries. On a day designated only "About the middle of the feast" (v. 14), Jesus taught on (1) The source of his teaching and (2) Lawbreaking or Law Keeping. On "the last day of the feast," (v. 37) he taught on (1) The living water and (2) The light of the world. This may have been one extended session, or it may have been two shorter ones related to two of the major Temple services of the festival: the water service (7:37) and the light service (8:12). Jesus' giving sight to the man who was born blind (ch. 9) carries forward the light of the world theme (9:5), and it merges into the good shepherd allegory (10:1–21). Theologically they both belong to the light of the world section (8:12–59).

Both that day and the entire festival week ended with the

Jews hopelessly divided in their appraisal of Jesus. Many of them said that he was demon possessed. Others, even while rejecting his teachings, pointed to his miracles and said that a demon-driven person would not do such works: healing a man who had been an invalid thirty-eight years (ch. 5); giving sight to a man who had been born blind (ch. 9). When Jesus returned in December for the Feast of Dedication they had had two months to consider the issue. Immediately they confronted him with the demand for a straight, clear answer to their question "Are you or are you not the messiah?" (10:24, author's translation). When he had responded to that question, they attempted to stone him to death for blasphemy in calling himself the Son of God. He left the Temple, Jerusalem, and Judea, crossed over into Perea, and carried on his ministry there (10:40–42).

Jesus and his disciples went to Jerusalem for the Feast of Tabernacles (7:1 to 10:21). The theme of conflict appears even in the setting of the journey to Jerusalem for the feast conflict between Jesus and his brothers. Assuming that he would go, his brothers urged him to take the opportunity to manifest himself openly "to the world" (v. 4). Their argument was that being the Messiah was a very public matter. It could not be "in secret." He should let his followers in Jerusalem "see the works" which he was doing in Galilee. Their suggestion has a ring of sympathy for his messiahship. John, however, makes it clear that his brothers did not believe that he was the Messiah (v. 5). They may have been thinking that to show himself as the Messiah in Jerusalem would lead to his being rejected by the authorities and to his giving up the Messiah business. A sixth-century manuscript has the word "then" at the end of verse 5: "For even his brothers did not believe in him then." It cannot be regarded as an accurate reading. Doubtless it was added by some scribe because after Jesus' resurrection his brothers apparently did believe that he was the Messiah (Acts 1:14; 1 Cor. 9:5; Gal. 1:19). By early church tradition the "James" of Acts 15:13–29 was a brother of Jesus and the author of the epistle of James. Too, by early church tradition another of Jesus' brothers wrote the epistle of Jude.

Jesus rejected their suggestion. He said that they did not require any special time to go to the feast. They could go any time they wished. He could go, however, only when his "time" had fully come (v. 8), and it had not yet come (vv. 6,8). He would know when the time came for him to make any move related to manifesting himself. Ultimately Jesus' time or hour in John was the time of his glorifying the Father through his death and resurrection. Note 13:1, "Jesus knew that his hour had come" and 17:1, "Father, the hour has come." Until then, every move he made was related to that hour and to the will of the Father for him. So he said, "I am not going up to this feast" (v. 8). Some manuscripts have, "I am not yet going up to this feast."

He did go. His brothers went on apparently to be there for the beginning of the feast. Likely they traveled in a caravan of friends and relatives according to the custom. Jesus left later and in far less public way, "in private" (v. 10). Alone? Accompanied by his apostles? By a different road? No indication is given. The Jews expected him to attend the feast as any other Jewish man would. As time passed and he did not arrive, they became impatient, "Where is that man?" (v. 11, author's literal translation). Before he arrived they were already divided into those who said, "He is a good man" and those who said, "No, he is leading the people astray" (v. 12). They were probably thinking of his previous visit and the authorities' charge that he was a lawbreaker who also encouraged others to break the law. All of their talk was rather secretive, however. They would not speak openly until the authorities had come to an official position on what should be done with him (v. 13). Such was the atmosphere for his teaching!

The first teaching session is reported in 7:14–36. When the week was half over Jesus arrived, entered the Temple, and started teaching. Rabbinical teaching was carried on in the porticoes

which surrounded the open court which in turn surrounded the
main Temple buildings. In a normal situation the place would
be crowded with pilgrims as well as local people. Tabernacles
was the most joyous and most popular of all of their festivals.

The subject matter of Jesus' opening teaching is not stated.
The peoples' reaction to his teaching is stated. They were amazed
at his teaching because he had no official rabbinical training. Matthew 7:28–29 has a similar response of the people who heard
Jesus' Sermon on the Mount. On that occasion they remarked
that his teaching had a ring of authority which was absent from
the rabbinical teaching which consisted of stringing together quotations from the rabbis who had preceded them. The part of
Jesus' teaching, which John reports, grew out of their question
which was essentially, "Where did he get his learning when he
has never had any teachers?"

He addressed himself first to the source of his teaching (vv.
16–18). His teaching did not originate with him; it originated
with God who had sent him to teach. No, he did not get his
learning from the official sources at the human level. He got it
from the official source at the divine level. There was a way by
which anyone could test his teaching to see if he got it from
God. "If any man's will is to do his will," God would reveal to
that one whether the teaching had its source in God or whether
Jesus was acting independently (v. 17). This is a tremendous statement on the subject of knowing God's will. A constant cry of
God's people, old or young, is, "How can I know God's will?"
There is no better starting place than in Jesus' statement, "If
any man's will is to do his [God's] will . . . ." The starting place
is not the desire to *know* God's will; it is the desire to *do* God's
will. Do you want to know it? Then seek for a willingness to *do*
it, and he will reveal it.

Jesus' position was that if the Jews were really open to do what
God wanted done, they would know that what God wanted done
was what Jesus was doing. He was not seeking his own glory by

acting on his own authority. He was seeking God's glory by acting on God's authority. And "in him there is no falsehood" (v. 18), or more literally "no unrighteousness."

That statement was Jesus' transition to the second point of his address, "Lawbreaking or Law Keeping?" (vv. 14–36). He went back to the controversy over his action and teaching on his prior visit when he had healed the lame man on the sabbath and had been charged by the authorities with breaking the law (5:1–47). On that occasion they had determined to kill him (5:18). Now Jesus asked them why they wanted to kill him as a lawbreaker when they were all lawbreakers. They broke in to charge him with madness and to deny his charge that they wanted to kill him (v. 20). If his listeners were pilgrims from outside of Jerusalem, they may not have known of the authorities' determination to kill him.

Ignoring their interruption, Jesus went on to admit that he had healed a man on the sabbath. In doing so he had broken their law; it was a part of their oral law but not a part of Moses' written law. He charged the Jews, however, with breaking their own law and, by their own interpretation, Moses' law in their practice of circumcision. Although circumcision had been their practice from the time of Abraham (Gen. 17:12), it became a matter of law in the Mosaic code (Lev. 12:3). Every male child was to be circumcised on the eighth day. If he was born on the sabbath, the eighth day would be the sabbath. This posed a dilemma. Should they break the sabbath law in order to obey the circumcision law or should they break the circumcision law, postponing circumcision one day, in order to obey the sabbath law? The rabbinical decision had been to break the sabbath law in order to maintain the circumcision law. Rabbi Hosea had said, "Great is circumcision since it overrides the stringent Sabbath." [45] Jesus concluded by calling upon his hearers to make a judgment in the matter. If the rabbis and all Jewish parents who had a male child broke the sabbath by performing surgery on one organ of an eight-day-old child, why did they condemn him as a law-breaker when he healed the whole body of a thirty-eight-year-old man? Judge by what is right, not by what appears to be right (vv. 23–24).

The immediate result of this teaching session was more indecision and confusion. The people of Jerusalem had two problems: (1) Since the authorities had determined to kill Jesus (5:18) and since he was continuing to teach right there in the Temple and they were doing nothing about it, could it be that they had decided that Jesus really was the Christ (vv. 25–26)? [46] (2) If that was true, what were they going to do with their tradition that no one would know where the Messiah would come from? And even they knew where Jesus came from, Nazareth. Jesus' response was that they did not really know where he came from, why he had come, or who had sent him (v. 28). They knew his name; they knew his family background; they did not know the most important thing about him—his mission in the world. He was the Son of God, but they knew neither him nor God who had sent him (vv. 28–29).

In anger, some sought to make a citizen's arrest on the spot. They were unable to do so because "his hour had not yet come" (v. 30). Many others believed in him because of the miracles which he was performing; they could not anticipate a messiah who would do more than he was doing (v. 31). The Pharisees joined the Sadducees (chief priests) in sending members of the Temple guard to make an official arrest. They did not return until the last day of the festival, and even then they returned with no prisoner (vv. 45–46). John gives no reason for the delay; he may have understood it in the usual way, "his hour was not yet come."

Jesus' second teaching session is reported in 7:37–52 and 8:12 to 10:21. The first part took place in the Temple (7:37 to 8:59). The second part took place outside the Temple but apparently nearby (9:1 to 10:21). The setting is very briefly given. It was "in the treasury" (8:20, see above note) and it was "on the last

day of the feast, the great day" (7:37). Interpreters are divided
as to whether this means the seventh day or the eighth day.[47]
The Feast of Tabernacles began on the sabbath and closed on
the sabbath. The first seven days consisted of sacrifices, procession-
als, and praise services memorializing the forty years of their
fathers' living in tents with their needs provided by God as they
moved from slavery in Egypt to national status in the land of
God's promise. To the Old Testament prophets those were the
greatest days in Israel's history, days when God dwelt with his
people. The eighth day was a day of rest as any other sabbath
but with special sacrifices because it was the closing sabbath of
this very special week as well as the closing sabbath for all of
the festivals for that year.

The living water teaching (37b–52) was related to the water sacrifices of the week. On each of the first seven days, a priest filled
a gold pitcher with water from the pool of Siloam and carried
it to the Temple. Joined there by the worshipers, some of whom
may have accompanied him to and from the pool, he led a processional of praise around the Temple area to the altar of burnt
offerings where he emptied the water into a silver basin. The
people sang Isaiah 12:3, "With joy you will draw water from the
wells of salvation." This memorialized God's giving water to Israel
during their desert wanderings of the Exodus (Ex. 17:2–7). In
the New Testament days, the service had added the element of
prayer to God for winter rains looking to the next year's crops.
On the seventh day, the procession went around the altar seven
times.

If Jesus' teaching in 7:37–38 came on the seventh day, it was
likely timed dramatically at the end of this symbolic outpouring
of water. As the water gushed from the rock at Meribah to satisfy
the physical thirst of the Israelites of Moses' day, so Jesus, like
the rock in a dry land, offered spiritual water for the spiritual
thirst of the Israel of his day. Plummer's view is that on the eighth
day the teaching would have been all the more dramatic.[48] They

would have had their seven days of ritual water sacrifice and their singing of drawing water from the wells of salvation. Now that it was all over, their spiritual thirst would not have been assuaged. They would still be in need of water that would satisfy that thirst. Jesus offered them that kind of water.

As to the woman at the well in Samaria, Jesus offered to the people at the Temple in Jerusalem "living water" (vv. 37–38). He stood as a prophet of old would have stood, openly and authoritatively. He cried aloud in tones of strong emotion; the Revised Standard Version's "proclaimed" is inadequate for this setting. "If any one thirst," the modal construction is one of strong probability. Jesus knew the hearts of men and their deep spiritual drives. He knew the strong probability of the spiritual thirst of the worshipers. "Let him come to me and drink"; Jesus was the real source for their satisfying their thirst. Not the rock at Meribah, not the pool of Siloam or the Gihon springs which fed it, *Jesus* was the source for their real need. "Let him drink"—as simple as that. The water is available, but each one must drink of his own will and for his own salvation.

How does one "drink" of the water which Jesus offered? By believing in him. In John the ultimate act of sin is always unbelief in Jesus, and the ultimate act of obedience is belief in him. Furthermore, the one who believes, who drinks of the water which he offers, will not become a self-enclosed, stagnant pool. Out of his innermost being will flow "rivers of living water" for the blessing of others. The one who receives the water becomes a supplier of water for others. The symbol cannot be pressed too far. Christ is always the real supplier of the water.

Jesus related this promise to their Scriptures (v. 38). No specific passage is cited. There is a strong flavor of Isaiah in this entire teaching. "If anyone thirst, let him come to me" sounds very much like Isaiah 55:1, "Ho, every one who thirsts,/come to the waters."

"Out of his heart shall flow rivers of living water" sounds very much like Isaiah 58:11, "And you shall be like a watered garden,/ like a spring of water,/whose waters fail not." John explained that by the rivers of living water flowing out of the believer, Jesus was referring to the Holy Spirit. That sounds very much like Isaiah 44:3, "For I will pour water on the thirsty land,/and streams on the dry ground;/I will pour my Spirit upon your descendants. The explanation anticipates the John 14 and 16 teachings of Jesus about the coming of the Holy Spirit after his glorification through death, resurrection, and ascension.

The immediate result of this teaching is seen in the divided opinion of the people (vv. 40–52). Some said, "This is really the prophet," probably meaning the prophet like Moses. Others said, "This is the Christ [Messiah]." Some responded to that by indicating the unlikelihood that the Messiah would come out of Galilee and the fact of the Scriptures that the Messiah would come out of Bethlehem (Mic. 5:2). Some wanted to seize him (compare v. 30), but no one actually laid hands on him.

At this point John recorded the return of the Temple guard to report to the Sanhedrin members who had dispatched them to arrest Jesus several days before, the day of Jesus' teaching "about the middle of the feast" (vv. 14,32). They had not arrested Jesus. When the Sanhedrin members asked why, their response was, "No man ever spoke like this man!" (v. 46). They were impressed doubtless by what he said, what he claimed that he could do, and his manner of authority in it all. The Pharisees accused them of having been duped by Jesus as they felt the common people had been (v. 49). Their contemptuous "this crowd" probably indicates a large company of the uncultured *am haares,* "people of the earth," who made no attempt at knowing and keeping the rabbinic laws. In contrast, the Pharisees pointed out what they thought was true that no Pharisee and no Sanhedrin member had believed in Jesus. Nicodemus, who was both a Pharisee and a Sanhedrin member (3:1), spoke up to point out that the Pharisees who were so zealous to keep the law were breaking it by condemning a man without a trial (vv. 50–51). They turned their scorn from the crowd to Nicodemus and insulted him by suggesting that he must be a Galilean too if he would defend a Galilean. They counseled him to search the Scriptures and "see that out of Galilee ariseth no prophet" (ASV). Their specialty was law, not history! Several Old Testament prophets had come from Galilee. Ever hear of Nahum and Jonah?

The light of the world teaching begins at chapter 8:12 and is doubtless related to a second of the major services of the week.[49] On the first day of the week the four huge gold lamps in the court of the women were lighted. By their traditions, the glare of the lights could be seen in every courtyard in Jerusalem. One line of tradition held that during the week women on the outskirts of the city could thread a needle by the light! The light symbolized the pillar of fire which led Israel during the Exodus wanderings (Ex. 13:21). It spoke of God's presence and guidance of his people. Evidence is not clear as to whether the lamps were lighted every day or only once for the week. Some Jewish authorities hold that they were lighted only once. Maimonides was positive that the lighting was repeated daily.

Whatever the case, Jesus would have chosen the most strategic moment for his opening statement, "I am the light of the world" (v. 12). The pronoun is emphatic—"I alone," "I and no other." The psalmist of ancient Israel sang with confidence, "The Lord is my light and my salvation" (27:1). In rabbinic Judaism, one of the names of Messiah was Light. In 1 John 1:5 the message which God's Son, Jesus Christ, left for his followers to proclaim was that "God is light and in him is no darkness." To his disciples Jesus once said, "You are the light of the world" (Matt. 5:14). In all of these references, light is not a phenomenon of the natural universe. It is a soteriological function. It is active in the world of men, leading them toward the ultimate good which the benevolent Creator offers. So when Jesus stood in the Temple, in the very place where the phenomenal lamps of gold were lighted to remind the people of God's saving presence, he was saying that God's salvation was resident in him and functional through him. He was indeed this world's light.

"He who follows me will not walk in darkness." The pillar of fire which led the Israelites in the Exodus did not stand still. It moved; if they were to have its benefits, they had to follow. So Jesus is to be followed. The Father's blessing for the one who follows the Son is deliverance from darkness (evil) and the gift of "the light of life," the living light. The light gives life as the water of 4:10,14 gives life and as the bread of 6:35,51 gives life. Interrupted by the Pharisees, Jesus had to drop the teaching on light.[50]

The Pharisees interrupted Jesus' teaching because they thought they had caught a way of defeating him by his own words. That was their sole interest, not to learn from him but to discredit him in the minds of those who did want to learn from him. In verses 14–29 Jesus addressed himself to the Pharisees in responding to their charge. He had said, "I am the light of the world." They said that his statement constituted bearing witness for himself and by their rabbinical laws one could not bear testimony in his own behalf. By the Mosaic code one witness was not adequate in capital cases, and that was what the Pharisees wanted, his death. In capital cases at least two, and in some cases three, witnesses were required (Num. 35:30; Deut. 17:6; 19:15). Jesus called upon this law in his own case (vv. 17–18). He had a two-fold witness. His Father bore valid witness for him, and he bore for himself witness that was valid even though it was in his own behalf (vv. 14–16).

They caught at his word "Father" again. Prior to this they had determined to kill him for calling God his Father. Now he was repeating the blasphemy. Pushing the matter they asked, "Where is your Father?" (v. 19). His response was in the rabbinical *mashal* type of answer: If they really knew who he was, they would know who his Father was. They wanted to arrest him but could not "because his hour had not yet come" (v. 20).

Jesus spoke to the Pharisees as he had spoken to their officers earlier (7:33). He was going away soon. They would seek him but not find him because they could not go where he was going. He was speaking of his death. Inevitably they would succeed in bringing him to his death. He would go to the Father. They could not go to the Father because they were rejecting the Son. To refuse to believe in him was to die in their sins (8:24). His words would be vindicated in his death. Then they would know of his oneness with the Father. "I always do what is pleasing to him" (8:29). Who else could ever make that claim?

There were many who "believed in him" because of those sayings (v. 30). The primary reference was to his sayings in verses 14–29, but probably his teachings of the entire day were included. How genuine was this belief? Was it a belief unto salvation? Was it a superficial act of the moment which would wither in the shallow soil of their lives? Tragically it seems to have been the latter. When his dialogue with them was over, they too were ready to stone him to death (v. 59).

First, Jesus indicated that the test of genuineness was to *continue* in his work, not just to make a quick momentary response. Such continuing would bring them to full realization of the truth and that truth would make them free. They retreated to their sonship-to-Abraham argument. They were Abraham's children through the son (Isaac) of the freewoman (Sarah), not the son (Ishmael) of the slave woman (Hagar). They had never been in bondage.

Jesus explained that he was talking about enslavement to sin and being set free from such slavery. As evidence of their spiritual bondage to sin, they had been trying to kill him even though they were physically descended from Abraham. He hinted here that Abraham was not really their father (v. 38); he repeated that hint in verse 41 after they had insisted again that Abraham was their father. This was the problem which we have previously discussed regarding their view that to be descended from Abraham who was in covenant relationship with God was all they needed to be rightly related to God.

They became angry; they pressed their sonship back beyond Abraham to say that God was their Father and they were his legitimate sons (v. 41). Jesus then went beyond the hints of verses 38 and 41 to charge that their father was not God but the devil (v. 44). The word *father* is used in three different ways in this dialogue. God is the Father of Jesus Christ (v. 38). Abraham is the physical father of the Jews (v. 39). The devil is the spiritual father of the Jews (vv. 41,44). From the beginning of man's knowledge of the devil, he has been known as a murderer, perhaps an indication that the devil was involved in Cain's murdering Abel (Gen. 4:8). If they were sons of God rather than of the devil, they would hear his words which were from God (v. 47). In their hostility they countercharged that Jesus was a demon-driven Samaritan. Likely this is an indication of their knowledge of his two-day ministry to the Samaritans (4:4–54). It could mean that his understanding of God was as inadequate as that of the Samaritans. Jesus rejected that charge with the statement that everything he did was to honor God, and if anyone would keep his word, he would never die.

That confirmed them in their view that he was demon driven right out of his mind! Never die? The prophets died. Abraham died. "Are you greater than our father Abraham?" (v. 53). "Who do you claim to be?" Jesus answered that he was one who kept the word of the God whom they claimed as their Father, that the Father glorified him because of that obedience, and that Abraham saw his day and rejoiced (v. 56). They scoffed that Abraham had seen his day; that implied that he had also seen Abraham's day but he was not yet fifty and Abraham had died hundreds of years before (v. 57). Jesus' answer to that kind of thinking was, "Before Abraham was, I am" (v. 58). Two verbs express the true situation—"Before Abraham came to be" expresses being

with reference to origin. "I am" expresses being without reference
to origin. Abraham was of the temporal order. Christ was of the
eternal order.

His teachings overwhelmed and frustrated them: God was his
father; he was from above as they were from below; God had
sent him into the world, and he always did those things that
were pleasing to God; he could give life and deathlessness to
anyone who really believed in him and kept his word; he existed
before Abraham came into being. They could not comprehend
it, but they regarded his teaching as blasphemy. They took up
stones intending to stone him to death, which would have been
an act of mob violence. While they were choosing the stones,
he concealed himself from them and left the Temple. Their attempt to stone him may be additional evidence that this teaching
was on the seventh day of the festival rather than the eighth, a
sabbath. It is doubtful that they would have taken up stones on
the sabbath thus breaking the sabbath law in order to kill him.
He had come to the feast secretly (7:10); he left secretly (8:59).
His brothers were right: he went to Jerusalem and manifested
himself openly; he was rejected. They were wrong at one point;
the rejection did not cause him to give up his ministry as the
one whom God had sent.

Jesus' light of the world teaching is carried on beyond his leaving the Temple. "As he passed by" (9:1) seems naturally to relate
to his going "out of the temple" (8:59). If "the last day of the
feast" (7:37) was the seventh and, hence, not a sabbath, the Jews
would have had no sabbath problem to deter them in trying to
stone him, but the healing of the blind man could not have taken
place then because it took place on the sabbath (9:14). On the
other hand, if "the last day of the feast" meant the eighth day,
this healing could have taken place on that day only *if* the Jews
were so angry that they were willing to break their sabbath law
in order to stone him. With the apparent impossibility of being
absolutely certain about these matters, all we can state for sure

is that soon after the attempted stoning (either on the same day or the next day or the next sabbath), Jesus healed the blind man on the sabbath and related it to his light of the world teaching (9:5) of the festival week (8:12–59).

The place appears to have been the Temple area. The man was a beggar; the Temple area was a popular place for beggars (see a similar event in Acts 3:1–10); the man seems to have been well known (v. 8) by people who were concerned about sabbath laws (v. 14); the people had no problem in reaching the religious authorities to report the matter (v. 13). From some unidentified source Jesus and his disciples knew that the man's blindness was congenital. The Pharisees knew that the man's parents reported that his blindness was congenital, but that knowledge could have come after the event. The fact that his blindness was congenital is an important part of the miracle and all of the discourses which followed it.

The disciples of Jesus shared a general, Jewish, religious thought of the day—that all suffering in the world was related in some way to sin. As to the source of the sin which resulted in the evil, they thought in terms of three categories: (1) the sin of Adam, (2) the sin of the parents, (3) the sin of the individual. The sin of Adam as the general foundation for all sin might be understood from Genesis 3:17–19. The sin of one's parents as the cause for congenital affliction could be understood from many Scripture passages (Ex. 20:5; 34:7; Num. 14:18; Deut. 5:9; 28:22). One's own sin as the cause for affliction could be understood from many passages (such as Deut. 28:15–68; Jer. 31:30, denying the people's crutch reflected in 31:29, "my parents are responsible for my sin"). To think, however, of one's being born blind because of his personal sin is not so easy to explain. What were the disciples thinking?

Two explanations have been proposed. One, God in his omniscience knew that when the person came to maturity he would commit some great sin. Accordingly he punished the person for the sin long before it was committed by having him to be born blind. Two, even when he was in his mother's womb the person had committed some sin which resulted in his being born blind.[51] The Jewish people accepted the idea of conscious emotional response and action of souls in the prenatal state. An example of a good action may be seen in Luke 1:41. When Mary greeted Elizabeth who was in the sixth month of her pregnancy, the unborn babe made so strong a movement that Elizabeth interpreted it as leaping "for joy" (v. 44). An example of evil action may be seen in rabbinic interpretation of Genesis 25:26.[52] As the twin sons of Isaac and Rebekah were being born, Esau emerged first with Jacob grasping his heel as he was born second. This was interpreted as attempted murder, Jacob trying to prevent the birth of Esau. Or attempted stealing, Jacob wanting the right of the firstborn and trying to prevent Esau from being born first.

For the disciples, then, their question was a no-nonsense one, "Who sinned, this man or his parents, that he was born blind?" (v. 2). The grammatical construction indicates a specific act of sin which caused the specific condition of affliction, literally, "Who committed a sin with the result that this man was born blind." [53] They were looking back for a cause of the blindness. In his response, Jesus challenged them to look forward for a purpose in the condition, "It was not that this man sinned [again, a specific act of sin], or his parents, but that the works of God might be made manifest in him" (v. 3). Here, as in other cases, Jesus did not involve himself in speculative questions as to the cause for some tragedy. Compare Luke 13:1–5. He rather directed attention to the need of action by way of personal responsibility on the part of the questioners.

They were interested in how the man came to be in that condition; Jesus was interested in what they could do to get the man out of the condition. In being healed of his unexplainable blindness, he would become an example of God's great mercy rather than of his wrath. Jesus joined the disciples with himself in saying,

"We must work the works of him who sent me" (v. 4). Actually the disciples took no active part in the performance of the miracle. Jesus, however, joined them to himself in the social outreach of the "works" for which the Father sent him into the world. They shared in what he was doing in the preaching missions on which he sent them as recorded in the Synoptics. They would continue to share in the Father's "works" even after Jesus returned to the Father (chs. 14—17).

"While it is day" (v. 4) pointed first to doing the Father's work during the earthly life and ministry of Jesus. His "day" was while he was here in the days of his flesh. Their "day" was also during that time, but it would stretch on beyond that to include their entire lifetime. Opportunity has its limitations; "night comes" is a reminder of the end of opportunity. As long as Jesus was in the world, he was commissioned by the Father to be "the light of the world" (v. 5) and to bring that light to mankind. His immediate opportunity was to bring physical light to an unfortunate man who knew only physical darkness. The miracle would accomplish that. But the miracle was a sign pointing to his giving spiritual light in place of the man's spiritual darkness. That comes later in verses 35–38.

Jesus mixed spittle with clay, smeared it on the eyes of the blind man, and told him to go to the pool of Siloam and wash it off. Many elements combine in this miracle. Both clay and spittle were used in medicinal ways in that day.[54] Jesus used them apparently to focus the man's attention on the fact that he was going to do something to help his eyes. On some other occasions he acted in a similar way: touching eyes; putting his fingers in ears; touching a tongue. On still other occasions he simply spoke the healing word. In this case he may have been calling attention to the necessity of a believing response on the blind man's part. There is a strong Johannine mystique involved in this action. Over and over during this festival week Jesus had spoken of his having been "sent" by God. Now as the "Sent One" he sends the man to the pool of Siloam which meant "sent" to wash from his eyes elements commonly used in healing. There was no Naaman-the-Syrian hesitancy (2 Kings 5:10–14) on the man's part! He went immediately, and when he had washed off the clay poultice, the darkness no longer held his eyes.

John's account moves in a straight line to the theological complexities and significance growing out of the miracle. First, when the man returned to his home, his neighbors and acquaintances were completely perplexed. Some were certain that he was the blind beggar whom they had known. His demeanor was so changed, however, that others said that he only looked like that beggar. He said, "I am the man" (v. 9). In response to their request for an explanation of his sight, he made a very factual report, but the facts had important implications. "The man called Jesus" (v. 11) had healed him. He healed him by smearing his eyes with a mud mixture and sending him to Siloam to wash the mud away. He went; he washed; he looked up (literally), the Greek word for receiving the ability to see. He did not say it because at the moment he did not know it, but his life would never be the same again. He knew the one who had healed him only by name and by action, but he was destined to know him much better.

Recognizing this as a case of lawbreaking by one who had been guilty of such before and had been arguing the matter with the authorities during the feast, the perplexed people took the man to the Pharisees and reported it. By their laws Jesus could have been charged as a breaker of the sabbath law simply by kneading the clay and spittle into mud. He was also guilty for practicing healing on the sabbath. At the Pharisees' request the man repeated the healing process which Jesus had used. The report divided the Pharisees into two groups. One group stressed Jesus' breaking the law as evidence that he was not from God. Another group stressed Jesus' healing the blind man as evidence that he was not a sinner. They asked the healed man what he thought about Jesus, and he answered, "He is a prophet" (v. 17). This meant that he viewed Jesus as one who was sent as God's messenger.

In their dilemma (v. 16), the Pharisees decided that no miracle had taken place. They referred the matter to the man's parents. In simplified form their questions with the parent's answers were three: (1) "Is this your son?" "Yes." "Was he born blind?" "Yes." "How is that now he can see?" "Ask him; he is old enough to speak for himself." John explained that their third answer grew out of fear of reprisal from the Pharisees if they admitted that Jesus had healed their son. The authorities had already agreed that if anyone confessed that Jesus was the Messiah, he would be put out of the synagogue, literally, "desynagogued." To be banned from the synagogue could be for thirty days or for longer, even for life. It also included prohibition of approaching within six feet of anyone who was not under such a ban.

The Jews pressed their case by confronting the healed man again. They could no longer deny the miracle; now they tried to discredit Jesus as the one who had done it. They would discredit him by putting their superior knowledge up against the man's opinion. "We know that this man is a sinner" (v. 24) is a very clear statement. Their pronoun is emphatic, *"We* know . . . ." The man had said, "He is a prophet." Their words "Give God the praise" are not so clear. Actually their word was "glory" rather than the Revised Standard Version "praise." They may have meant for him to give credit for the miracle to God rather than to Jesus. They may have meant for him to glorify God by denying his confession that Jesus was a prophet, one of God's messengers.

The healed man's response was to fall back on personal witness. He did not know enough to judge whether the man was a sinner; they were the ones who had that kind of knowledge. There was one kind of experiential knowledge which he had and they did not have, "I was blind, now I see" (v. 25). That is the hardest kind of evidence to refute! They asked him to tell them again what Jesus had done in giving him his sight. Perhaps they hoped to pick up some detail by which they could show him from his own testimony that what Jesus had done constituted lawbreaking.

Impatient with their quibbling in the face of clear facts, he responded by making fun of them. He had told them just minutes before, and they would not listen. Why did they want to hear it again? His pronoun is emphatic and his question anticipates a negative answer, *"You* are not wishing to become his disciples, too, are you?"* (author's literal translation). He knew the answer to that question! The word which is translated "too" ("also" in KJV and ASV) is ambiguous. Some interpreters understand it as an indication that the man considered himself a disciple of Jesus or of being on the verge of becoming one. Others understand it to relate to the known disciples (apostles in the Synoptics) who were there in Jerusalem with Jesus. The latter seems more likely. Either would be a satirical reference. These Jews become Jesus' disciples? Not likely!

Their response was to ridicule him. In what they regarded to be an extreme expression of contempt, they charged him with being a disciple of that one, unwilling even to pronounce Jesus' name. Their pronouns "you" and "we" are emphatic: *"You* are that one's disciple; *we* are Moses' disciples" (author's translation). They were certain that God had spoken to Moses. They had in their Scriptures the life of Moses from birth to death. They had no evidence that God had spoken to Jesus; they had no record of where he had come from (v. 29). They rejected his own insistence that he had come from God. The man once blind responded to that in strong sarcasm. To him it was something at which to marvel that Jesus had healed him, a man born blind, and they would deny that Jesus had come from God. God does not help sinners to heal blind men; he helps sincere worshipers to do so, those who do his will (vv. 30–32). This one of whom they were speaking with such contempt could do nothing if he had not come from God (v. 33). To these authorities that was the proverbial last straw. They were the professionals in all questions of

religion. He, in their opinion, was a total sinner. Yet he was trying
to teach them (v. 34). "They cast him out" does not likely mean
that they pronounced sentence of excommunication upon him.
The word for "desynagogue" (v. 22) is not used here. Such sentence of excommunication would have to come from the entire
Sanhedrin. Likely it means that in sheer exasperation over what
had come to be a harangue, they terminated the matter by expell-
ing him from whatever place they were meeting (v. 34).

That did not end the sequence of events. Jesus heard of their
action. He sought the man and asked him, "Do you believe in
the Son of man?" (v. 35). This is regarded as the correct reading
though some good manuscripts have "Son of God." The man's
response reflects respect for Jesus. Remember that he had not
seen Jesus; he had only heard his voice. Did Jesus identify himself
to the man? Did someone tell him that this was Jesus? His answer
indicated an openness of faith, so he must also have had some
understanding of the meaning of "Son of man." He was willing
to put his faith in the Son of man if Jesus would identify him
(v. 36). For Jesus it was a matter of self-identification. He made
it in a very forceful way for one whom he had healed of congenital
blindness: "You have *seen* him" (author's italics); the very sight
you have received has introduced you to him. "It is he who speaks
to you" (v. 37). You have seen him; you have heard him; you
already know him. Jesus' identification of himself to this man is
very much like his self-identification to the Samaritan woman
(4:26). Such self-identification Jesus reserved for very special cases.
The man's confession was complete, "Lord, I believe"—the ultimate act of obedience in John (v. 38). "And he worshiped him."
Basically the word meant to prostrate one's self before the object
of worship. While bowing or kneeling would satisfy the act, prostration before Jesus would have been very much in order when
the magnitude of the blessing he had bestowed in the healing
was considered.

The man received his physical sight, the dispelling of his physical darkness, in one dramatic event. His receiving spiritual sight, the dispelling of his spiritual darkness, came in a series of steps. Verse 11, "The man called Jesus . . . ." Verse 17, "He is a prophet." Verse 25, "One thing I know, that though I was blind, now I see." Verse 31, "If any one is a worshiper of God and does his will." Verse 33, "If this man were not from God, he could do nothing." Verse 38, "Lord, I believe." He had found the Light of the world.

Jesus looked at the man who had come into the light of God. He looked at the watching Jewish religious authorities who were remaining in their self-imposed darkness and planning to kill him. Then he uttered a sentence that reaches from the mountaintop of joy to the slough of despair, from the weal of the redeemed to the woe of the unredeemed (v. 39). His coming into the world was primarily for redemption, but it inevitably meant judgment also; it was judgment in relation to man's response to God's offer of love. "That those who do not see may see" speaks of those who, like the man who was born in darkness, come into the full light of God's redemption in Christ. "That those who see may become blind" speaks of those who, like the privileged religious authorities, thought they had everything, but they lacked the one thing that was essential—a faith acceptance of Jesus Christ as the one sent from God. The light only made them blinder. The same glaring light which illumines the road for one traveler blinds another so he cannot see the road. It depends on the direction one chooses to travel.

There were Pharisees standing near enough to hear Jesus' conversation with the new believer and to hear Jesus' summary sentence. They asked Jesus if what he had said meant that they were the blind ones (v. 40). In that case, of course, the formerly blind man would be the seeing one. In a *mashal* type of answer he indicated that their very insistence that they could "see," that they were capable of spiritual perception, was a part of their blindness and, hence, a part of their sin in rejecting him (v. 41).

If they were really incapable of spiritual perception, they would not be guilty in rejecting him. The sentence structure is a contrary to fact condition. The true condition was that they were capable of spiritual perception and, therefore, they were guilty for not exercising it.

He used an illustration (10:1–5) to make understanding easier for them, but John states that they did not understand it. It is a situation similar to Jesus' use of parable stories in the Synoptics. Those who really wanted to learn understood them; those who were crystallized in their opposition to him did not understand them. His illustration was one of shepherds and sheep stealers and sheep folds. The true shepherd enters the door to feed and protect the sheep. The sheep stealer avoids the door and climbs over the wall to steal and destroy the sheep. The sheep know the difference between the protector and the destroyer.

When the Jews failed to understand his allegory, he approached it from a different viewpoint and further elaboration (vv. 7–18). He identified himself as the door by which the sheep enter the fold. By a double metaphor **he is also the Good Shepherd who provides for the sheep,** protects the sheep even to the point of laying down his life for the sheep.[55] The religious authorities of Israel are the thieves who refuse to go in by Christ, the door, and their relation to the sheep is one of destruction. Rather than dying for the sheep, they flee when danger comes and leave the sheep to the wolves. The Good Shepherd's supreme motive is to provide for the sheep the abundant life. There are other sheep which he has to bring from another fold. When he has brought them, there will be one shepherd, the good one, and one flock. This is generally understood as a reference to the Gentiles who are to be brought into the one flock of God. Robinson interprets it as a reference to the Jews of the dispersion.[56] The Father loves the Son because as the Good Shepherd he lays down his life for the sheep. From the Father he has the authority to lay down his life and to take it up again—death and resurrection.

Thus Jesus closed his teachings on the light of the world. The man who received his sight, both physical and spiritual, was illumined by the light; he saw to enter the door for life with the Good Shepherd and God's sheep. The Jews remained in their spiritual blindness, shunning the light, missing the door and life with the Good Shepherd and God's sheep. Rather than that, they were the enemies of both the Good Shepherd and God's flock.

John concluded that long section with the characteristic indication of the division of opinion among the Jews (v. 19). One part of the schism believed that Jesus was demon driven and that to listen to him was a waste of time (v. 20). The other part, though unwilling to believe in Jesus, were convinced that one who taught in such way and opened the eyes of the blind could not be demon driven.

Two months later Jesus returned to Jerusalem for the Feast of Dedication and started teaching again (10:22–42). The Jews who had opposed him to the point of wanting to kill him on his last visit gathered around him with a pointed challenge. They asked for a clear unambiguous answer to their question (no allegory this time, please). They wanted a yes or no to their question which essentially was, Are you or are you not the Messiah? Jesus responded that he had already told them plainly, but they would not believe it. Beyond his words, his works bore clear witness to him. These were works which they had seen, the healing of the lame man at the pool and the healing of the man born blind. He had done them in his Father's name, which meant as his Father's representative, doing what the Father would do if he were present as Jesus was (v. 25). He went back to his Good Shepherd analogy of his last teaching in Jerusalem. They did not believe him because they were not his sheep. His sheep knew him and were eternally secure in his keeping (vv. 27–29). He and the Father were one (v. 30), one in purpose, one in plans, one in work to realize that purpose and those plans.

To the Jews he was blaspheming again in making himself equal
with God. They took up stones again with the intention of killing
him. He challenged them by indicating that he had done many
good works for the Father and asking them to name the specific
one for which they desired to stone him (v. 32). Was it for healing
the lame man? Was it for giving sight to the blind man? Should
one be put to death for such works as these? They answered
that they were intending to stone him not because of the miracles
but for his teaching. He was a man but he was teaching that he
was God (v. 33). On an earlier occasion they had said that he
was making himself equal to God (5:18). Such teaching they regarded as blasphemy. In the days of Moses that sin was punishable
by death. Under Rome the Jews did not have the power of capital
punishment (John 18:31). What they were planning was mob violence, lynching in modern terms.

Jesus turned their own language, interpretative slogans, and
Scriptures against them. He cited Psalm 82 which pictures God
assembled in council with his human judges, rulers, princes. In
verse 1 these judges are called "gods." The word is the one used
for God *(elohim)*. God chides these "gods" for their lack of justice
in judging (vv. 2–5). Then in verse 6 God says, "I say, 'You are
gods, sons of the Most High, all of you; nevertheless, you shall
die like men, and fall like any prince.' " There, Jesus reminded
them, was a place where God himself called men "gods." Then
he cited one of their favorite principles for interpreting Scripture—"Scripture cannot be broken" (v. 35). Whether Jesus en-
dorsed the principle or did not endorse it is not indicated. He
was assuming their endorsing it and he was using it to this effect:
If in your own Scriptures, men are called "gods," and if the Scriptures cannot be broken (proved wrong), why is it blasphemous
for me to say, "I am the Son of God"? (vv. 35–36). From their
interpretive stance, it was an unanswerable argument.

He concluded by asking them for fair dealing. He asked that

they consider the kind of works he was doing. Were they the kind of works that would be characteristic of God—mercy to the lame; mercy to the blind? If not, do not believe me. If so, believe the works even if you do not believe me. His works should convince them of the oneness which existed between Father and Son (vv. 37–38). Their response was one so often repeated in the history of men. When they could not win by logic, they resorted to violence. They tried to seize him intending probably to drag him from the Temple and stone him. He escaped and left Judea (v. 39). He went across the Jordan into Perea where John the Baptist had preached in the days when Jesus began his ministry. The people who had followed John welcomed him. They noted that, "Everything that John said about this man was true" (v. 41). Many believed on him.

There is no indication of the length of his ministry in Perea. Nor is there any indication as to whether he ever went back to Galilee. When compared to the Synoptics, there is in John a large gap in Jesus' ministry. The next event in John is the raising of Lazarus which seems to have been shortly before the Passover at which Jesus was executed. That meant a span of about four months between his leaving Jerusalem at the end of the Feast of Dedication and his return for Passover. The Synoptics, which have none of the materials of John 7—11, record an extensive ministry of Jesus in Galilee right up to his leaving to go to the Passover.

The only reason we can suggest for John's gap is the sometimes elusive "theological purpose." John presents Jesus' conflict with the Jerusalem authorities in what appear to be three successive festivals: Tabernacles (October), Dedication (December), Passover (April). Everything moves in a straight line to one dramatic event: his rejection by Israel, his death, his resurrection. Whatever materials he may have had which did not contribute to that theme he omitted.

Manifestation as the Lord of Life
(11:1–46)

Theologically this is one of the most important chapters in the Gospel of John. It marks the climax of Jesus' manifestation of himself to Israel in the most stupendous of his miracles. It marks the official decision of the Sanhedrin to seek Jesus' death. *Chronologically,* if one seeks to establish a sequence of Jesus' movements in the closing events of the Gospels, it is one of the most baffling chapters in all four Gospels.

John's sequence is, on the surface, a rather simple one. Jesus left Jerusalem after the Feast of Dedication in December. He went to southern Perea and carried on a ministry there (10:40–42). After an unspecified time he returned to Judea (Bethany) for the raising of Lazarus (11:1–53). He left Jerusalem and went to Ephraim in the hill country a few miles north of Jerusalem (11:54). He returned to Jerusalem for the Passover in April (12:1). That is a three and one-half months span including only one specific event.

Mark's sequence (10:1) has Jesus leaving Galilee and going to "the region of Judea and beyond the Jordan" (Perea). Jesus' ministry there was a brief one as he traveled with the apostles arriving in Jerusalem (Mark 11:1). The only place-name mentioned is Jericho as they approached Jerusalem. There is no indication of when he left Galilee for the Passover.

Matthew's sequence is identical with Mark's, but he has more teaching of Jesus along the way—two chapters to Mark's one. Jesus left Galilee (Matt. 19:1), was in Jericho (Matt. 20:29–33), and arrived in Jerusalem (Matt. 21:1). Such a journey would anticipate no more than three or four days.

Luke's sequence is the most complex of all. Jesus and the apostles left Galilee to go to Jerusalem for the Passover "when the days drew near for him to be received up" (9:51). "He set his face to go to Jerusalem" (v. 51), but the journey does not appear to have been a direct one. In 9:52–56, he is in Samaria. In 10:13–16, he is denouncing Chorazin and Bethsaida, towns in Galilee. In 10:38–42, he is in the village of Mary and Martha which we know from John 11:1 to have been Bethany in Judea. In 13:22,31–35, Pharisees are warning him to get out of the territory of Herod Antipas which could have been either Perea or Galilee. In 17:11–19, he is on the border between Galilee and Samaria. In 18:35 to 19:28, he is in Jericho. In 19:29, he arrives in Jerusalem. Most of the events and teachings in these ten chapters are in Luke only.

Did he do all of that back and forth travel between setting his face to go to Jerusalem (Luke 9:51) and arriving in Jerusalem (19:29)? Not likely. It appears more likely that the "Journey to Jerusalem and Death" is a theological theme in Luke. From that viewpoint, Jesus "set his face to go to Jerusalem" (9:51) soon after the confession and transfiguration experiences which focused on his death (9:22,31). So as "he went on his way through towns and villages, teaching, and journeying toward Jerusalem" (13:22), everything he did was embraced within that theme. In carrying out the theme, Luke used materials from numerous ministries of Jesus to show the nature of his ministry as he journeyed beneath the shadow of the cross. He fitted the materials into that theme. The period of time covered was likely six or seven months.[57]

The thrust of this review is that we can establish no more than a very tentative sequence of Jesus' activities in those closing months of his ministry. It seems wise to look at the events from the viewpoint of their relationship to the climax in his death and resurrection. That appears to be what John has done. There are touch points here between John and the Synoptics, but their importance in his purpose and presentation is minor.[58] A major question from a Synoptic studies viewpoint relates to their omission of the raising of Lazarus, but that is not for this Johannine study.

We know Lazarus of Bethany only from this event. Highly conjectural efforts to identify him with the Lazarus of Jesus' example story in Luke 16:19–31 are just that; they are too fragile to be called evidence. We know his sisters Mary and Martha and something of their respective temperaments from the Luke 10:38–42 event. Mary is further identified here and in John 12:3 as the woman who anointed Jesus at the banquet on Saturday. The sisters sent word to Jesus that Lazarus was ill; later developments indicate that he was at that time near to death. Jesus responded that the end result of this experience would not be death but glory for both God and the Son of God (11:4).

At this point, questions begin to arise. Where was Jesus when the messenger (or messengers) reached him? Was his statement in verse 4 his response to the sisters? Did the messenger return with it? Did he arrive before Lazarus died? If so, did Lazarus hear the message? These and multiple others are found in the commentaries. For these and most of the others, answers are conjectural only. Some of the answers might help us in our understanding; others might satisfy our interest but add nothing of substance to our understanding.

It does appear likely that Jesus' response was his message to the sisters. It may be reflected in verses 7–13 that the apostles heard it, too, and that it encouraged them in their trying to discourage Jesus from going to Bethany (vv. 8,12). If Lazarus was not going to die (v. 4), why should Jesus risk death in Jerusalem (v. 8)? Close examination indicates that Jesus did not mean that Lazarus was not going to die. The grammatical construction permits the meaning "this illness will not end in death," rather it would end in the glory of God and the glorification of the Son of God. If that was Jesus' meaning, it indicates that he knew that Lazarus would die, and he knew that he would raise him from the dead. The apostles did not so understand it; whether the sisters did is open to question.

What precisely did Jesus mean that this illness would eventuate in the glory of God and the Son of God? Did he mean that the nature of the raising of Lazarus would cause people to glorify God and the Son of God? That happened when he restored life to the widow's son at Nain (Luke 7:15–17). Or is this an example of double meaning in John? In Jesus' prayer on the night of his arrest, he carried the glorification of God and of the Son of God even to his death on the cross (17:1). It was the raising of Lazarus which brought about the official Sanhedrin decision which ultimately led to his death (v. 53). Was that what he meant? The emphasis is a distinctive of John; in the Synoptics the emphasis on the Sanhedrin's determination to execute Jesus is his cleansing of the Temple. Always in John, events move ultimately to the glorification of God through the death and resurrection of the Son. That would be clear to Jesus in this instance. It was not likely clear to his hearers on this occasion. They were not yet ready to grant that he would die, much less, then, that death could be glorification.

On the surface, the connection between verses 5 and 6 seems very strange. The "so" of verse 6 indicates that Jesus stayed where he was two days after hearing of Lazarus' illness because he loved Lazarus and his sisters. From the human viewpoint it would appear that love for them would have prompted his leaving to join them immediately. Jesus, however, was not moving from the human viewpoint; he was moving from the divine viewpoint. His reason for waiting is embedded in his statements in verses 4 and 15: Verse 4, the end result of Lazarus' illness was not death; it was life for him and glory for God and his Son; verse 15, the end result for the apostles would be an additional increase in their still-growing faith in him and in God's purpose for him.

When Jesus proposed that they return to Judea (v. 7), the apostles resisted it, reminding him that the last time he was there the Jews had attempted to stone him to death (10:31,39). In fact, the Jews had tried to kill him the last three times he had been there: 5:18; 8:59; 10:31. Jesus' first response was again by way of riddle. In 9:4 he had said, "We must work the works of him who sent me while it is day; night comes, when no one can work." His "day" for working was the time that he was living; death would bring his "night," no more opportunity to work. That same viewpoint is expressed in his response here in verse 9. "Twelve hours in the day" represented his "day" (of 9:4) for working. All work then was done in the daytime. "The night" (v. 10) represented the same thing which it represented in 9:4—the end of an opportunity to work. So here in the case of Lazarus, there was an opportunity for him to work; he could not pass it up.

His second response to the resistance of the apostles focused on Lazarus' situation; Lazarus had fallen asleep and Jesus was going to awake him (v. 11). He was still speaking in riddle; sleep was a metaphor for death (see Luke 8:52). Still resisting, the apostles seized upon that as a good sign (v. 12). Sleep during illness was good. The sick one would awake with fever reduced and body rested. Jesus then "told them plainly" (v. 14), not in a *mashal* (riddle), not in a figure of speech (metaphor) but openly, "Lazarus is dead." Two days before that, the word of Lazarus' sickness had come by messenger from the sisters. Now Jesus had learned that Lazarus had died. How had he learned it? Apparently by that divine knowledge so often stressed in John. He knew it by revelation from the Father. Precisely when Lazarus had died is not clear. It depends on how long it took Jesus and the disciples to travel to Bethany. When they arrived, they learned that Lazarus had been dead four days. It simply is not clear as to how that fact links: (1) the time of his death, (2) the time of Jesus' awareness of his death, and (3) the time of their journey from wherever they were to Bethany.

We have noted above that Jesus told the disciples that for their sake he was glad that Lazarus had died. Out of it all, their faith in him was to be strengthened. How often seeming tragedy for one person results in spiritual growth in others. When they knew that he was determined to go even at the risk of his life, they resigned themselves to it with Thomas perhaps voicing the viewpoint of all of them in his words, "Let us also go, that we may die with him" (v. 16). It was a bold resolution which they lacked the courage to carry out. When the crisis hour came, one of them betrayed him; one of them swore that he was not even acquainted with him; nine of them ran to hide; only one went all the way to the cross, John the beloved.

Jesus arrived at Bethany four days after Lazarus died (v. 17). The customary mourning of relatives and friends lasted normally at least seven days. Family friends were present to share the grief of the sisters. Included were "many of the Jews" (v. 19) who had come out from Jerusalem. They were family friends; Jesus was a family friend; not all of these Jews, however, appear later to be Jesus' friends (vv. 37,46). Learning that Jesus was finally approaching, Martha went to meet him, away from the crowds whether friends or enemies. Her greeting, which would be repeated later by Mary, likely reflects their conversation in the days of Lazarus' illness, "Lord, if you had been here, my brother would not have died" (v. 32). They were surely aware of his having healed the lame man at the pool and the man who had been born blind. Likely they knew of his other healing ministries. They believed that he could heal Lazarus, but he did not come in time (v. 21,32).

The sisters may have known of his having raised others from the dead: the daughter of Jairus (Luke 8:40–56) and the son of the widow at Nain (Luke 7:11–17). The news of the latter had reached from Galilee to "the whole of Judea" (v. 17). Martha's next words indicate her belief that God would grant to Jesus anything which he asked "even now" (v. 22). Although Lazarus was dead, he was not beyond the power of God working through his Son. It appears that at this point she was bold enough to think of such a miracle. As if responding to her suggesting the possibility of such a miracle, Jesus said, "Your brother will rise again" (v. 23). Martha took his verb "will rise again" to be a reference to the resurrection of the dead, a doctrine accepted by the Pharisees. It appears to have diverted her thought from her tentative suggestion about his ability to restore Lazarus to life. She responded with her confession, "I know that he will rise again in the resurrection at the last day" (v. 24). She used his verb "will rise again" and the noun derived from it "resurrection." That, however, was not what Jesus meant.

Jesus' answer was one of the most dramatic and stupendous of all of his many I-am claims, "I am the resurrection and the life" (v. 25). As in other such cases, the construction is emphatic, "I alone," "I and no other." This proclamation recalls his claim in 5:25–29 that the Father had committed to him the authority to give life by both regeneration and resurrection. Continuing, he made proclamations which are basic to the entire subject of life, death, and beyond death.

"He who believes in me, though he die, yet shall he live." In this statement, "die" refers to physical death and "live" refers to spiritual life. One may experience physical death, but because of his faith indentification with Jesus Christ, he has entered upon a spiritual life which transcends death's dissolution of physical life. Lazarus presumably had believed in Jesus; he had experienced physical death; nevertheless, he still lived spiritually. An added dimension of that life is to be the ultimate resurrection from physical death, a life-kind of resurrection (5:29). Not even physical death can make any essential break between the believer and his Lord (1 Thess. 4:13–18).

"Whoever lives and believes in me shall never die" (author's translation). In this statement, "lives" refers to physical life and "die" refers to spiritual death. The one who lives physically and believes in Jesus Christ has already entered upon a spiritual life which guarantees that he will never experience spiritual death. The grammatical construction is the Greek double negative which is the strongest way of expressing the negative idea (bad English but perfect Greek) "he shall not never die," and Jesus added "forever."

Martha was overwhelmed by the depth and comprehensiveness

of Jesus' claim. When he asked her, "Do you believe this?" she could respond only in a broad general confession of her faith in him which assumed her faith in anything which he said, "Yes, Lord; I believe that you are the Christ, the Son of God" (v. 27). To accept that truth and all that was involved in it meant that whether she understood or did not understand it, she believed his word.

Martha left Jesus there and went to bring Mary to him. At the news that Jesus had arrived and wanted to see her, Mary arose and without a word left the room and the mourners. Assuming that she was going to the tomb to wail, they followed. When she reached Jesus she fell before him and uttered the same words which Martha had used earlier, "Lord, if you had been here, my brother would not have died" (v. 32). She believed that he could have spared their grief and could have prevented Lazarus' death if he had responded immediately to their message. With those words Mary began weeping anew. The Jews who had come out from Jerusalem (v. 19) joined her in weeping. In their mind, he had come too late.

Jesus was not immune to human grief and affliction; "he was deeply moved in spirit and troubled" as he looked on the weeping sisters and their friends (v. 33). John used two verbs to describe Jesus' reaction to the scene. "Deeply moved" translates a word of strong emotion which is used in other places to describe Jesus' feelings in confronting the sick and afflicted (Mark 1:43; Matt. 9:30). "Troubled" is a verb to describe agitation. John used it with the reflexive pronoun, "he shook himself with agitation" or "he was deeply agitated." As the group moved on toward the tomb, Jesus wept with them. While he did not regard Lazarus' death as tragedy, he shared their grief in their sense of loss in that death. Some of the Jerusalem Jews noted his weeping as an indication of his love for Lazarus (v. 36). Others, not so generous in their feelings toward Jesus but feeling their loss in Lazarus' death, commented caustically that if he really cared he could have come to prevent Lazarus' death; they remembered his healing the man born blind (v. 37).

They came to the cave where Lazarus was entombed. Again Jesus was shaken by agitation (v. 38). Why? Was he not about to end all of this grief and wailing by bringing Lazarus back to life? Yes; that had been his clear intention for several days (vv. 6,11,14–15). Was his agitation a matter of impatience with the mourners? In view of his sharing their sense of distress (v. 35), that does not appear to be the case. Can his being deeply moved in spirit and agitated reflect his genuine emotion as he faced the challenge of death and moved to overome it? Shortly he would face that challenge in his own experience. He knew that he would be executed at the approaching Passover. For the preceding six or seven months, he had tried frequently to get his disciples to believe that. Even though he accepted it as a part of the Father's will for him, it was still a challenge, that club which the devil uses to keep men enslaved to the fear of the ending this life (Heb. 2:14). He stood before the tomb that had held his friend for four days; death's challenge was real and agitating.

He ordered the opening of the tomb, and men were ready to obey him. Martha who had ventured faith in a possible miracle a bit ago (vv. 21–22) found her faith not so strong. She reminded Jesus that Lazarus had been dead for four days. By this time, according to their views, the spirit would have ceased to hover about the body with the hope of returning to it; decay would have set in. If Jesus had arrived before Lazarus' death, he could have healed him. Even if he had arrived during the first three days, he could have raised him to life. But now Martha's "he has been dead for four days" meant "it is too late." Jesus' answer, "Did I not tell you that if you would believe you would see the glory of God?" meant correspondingly, "Martha, where I, the resurrection and the life, am present, it is *never* too late!" Where the Lord of life is present, the powers of life over death are already at work.

Alas for him who never sees
The stars shine through his cypress-trees!
Who, hopeless, lays his dead away,
Nor looks to see the breaking day
Across the mournful marbles play!
Who hath not learned, in hours of faith,
The truth to flesh and sense unknown,
That Life is ever lord of Death,
And Love can never lose its own! [59]

"Take away the stone" (v. 39). They did so. Jesus stood before
the open tomb and prayed. He thanked his Father for always
hearing him when he prayed. He told the Father that he never
doubted that he heard him when he prayed. He prayed aloud,
however, because he wanted the people to hear him talking to
the Father in order that they might know that the Father had
sent him (vv. 41–42). Continuing in a loud voice so the crowd
could hear, he cried, "Lazarus, come out" (v. 43). This sentence
is not really a translation. The text has three words: a noun and
two adverbs, literally, "Lazarus, here, outside!" What words to
probe, to examine, to explore for depth of implication! Lazarus
emerged from the cave wrapped in the cloth strips appropriate
for burial in Jewish customs, with the turban-like cloth about
his head. Jesus ordered the people to free Lazarus of those tokens
of death (as he had freed him from the reality of death?). More
words to probe, examine, and wonder at, "Unbind him, and let
him go" (v. 44).

Thus ended the seventh, the most dramatic, of John's signs.
We do not speak of difficulty when divine powers are involved.
From the human viewpoint, however, it is the one which makes
the biggest demand on credence. How did those present react
to it? Is it strange that there is no word of Lazarus' reaction or
Martha's or Mary's (not at least until later, 12:1–7) or Jesus' disciples? The reaction which was necessary for carrying forward
John's account as Jesus moved toward the cross is given. "Many
of the Jews," friends of Mary and present to share her grief, "be-

lieved in him" (v. 45). They were the ones who were open to belief in Jesus and acceptance of him as the one whom God had sent. Others, however, were not open to that belief and acceptance. They went back to Jerusalem and reported to the Pharisees what Jesus had done. Doubtless these were the Pharisees who for months had been determined to bring Jesus to his death. Now they had to act. They had to bring death even to the one who had manifested himself as the Lord of life.

Notes

1. Organization of the Gospel of John around the miracles or consideration from the viewpoint of their centrality has been a popular approach. Representative of many are: T. C. Smith, "The Book of Signs," *Review and Expositor,* Fall 1965, pp. 441–458; Robert T. Fortna, *The Gospel of Signs* (Cambridge: Cambridge University Press, 1970); Hull, who presents John, chapters 2—12 under the theme, "The Book of Signs," pp. 227–324.

2. Recommended commentaries on this miracle and representing a variety of viewpoints are: Barrett; R. E. Brown; Bultmann; Hendriksen; Lenski; R. V. G. Tasker, "The Gospel According to St. John," *The Tyndale New Testament Commentaries* (Grand Rapids: Wm. B. Eerdmans Publishing Company, 1960); A. Plummer, "The Gospel According to St. John," *Cambridge Greek Testament for Schools and Colleges* (Cambridge: University Press, 1905).

3. Barrett, p. 159.

4. They were ceremonial pots. If a stone pot became defiled ceremonially, it could be used again after cleansing. If an earthen pot became defiled, it could not be cleansed; it had to be broken (Lev. 11:33).

5. Westcott, pp. 37–38; Hull, p. 231.

6. The RSV translation "steward" is one of several options which translators use. The Greek word means "master of the couches," that is, the reclining couches used by the guests at the table. The man may have been appointed by the bridegroom, or he may have been elected by the guests.

7. Summers, *Commentary on Luke,* pp. 68–70; Ray Summers, *The Secret Sayings of the Living Jesus* (Waco: Word Books, Publisher, 1968) pp. 38–41.

8. Barrett, pp. 162–169; R. E. Brown, pp. 114–127; Hendriksen, 121–128.

9. This reference is to Jesus' going to Jerusalem for "a feast" (clearly the best manuscript reading) or "the feast" (some manuscript support but not the best). Usually "the feast" in Jewish use meant Passover, but sometimes "the feast" referred to Tabernacles. We cannot, therefore, be certain of the identification of this one.

10. See Summers, *Worth Is the Lamb,* pp. 211–214.

11. We will see this method used very extensively in subsequent sections such as the Nicodemus encounter, the Samaritan woman encounter, and the Bread of heaven discussion.

12. Much of the following study of John 3:1–21 has been published in another form: Ray Summers, "Born of Water and Spirit," *The Teacher's Yoke: Studies in Memory of Henry Trantham,* ed. E. Jerry Vardaman and James Leo Garrett, Jr. (Waco: Baylor University Press, 1964), pp. 118–128. In that form the material is longer, more detailed, and more technical.

13. See Alan Richardson, "The Gospel According to Saint John," *Torch Bible Commentaries* (London: SCM Press, Ltd., 1959), p. 68.

14. E. C. Colwell and E. L. Titus, *The Gospel of the Spirit* (New York: Harper and Brothers Publishers, 1953), p. 43.

15. Richardson, p. 71.

16. H. E. Dana, *The Heavenly Guest* (Nashville: Broadman Press, 1943), p. 46 and Plummer, p. 94.

17. William Temple, *Readings in St. John's Gospel* (London: Macmillan and Co., Ltd., 1961), p. 44.

18. Barrett, pp. 174–175. G. R. Beasley-Murray, *Baptism in the New Testament* (New York: St. Martin's Press, 1962), p. 228 rejects this and all other references to physical birth.

19. Plummer, p. 95.

20. Oscar Cullmann, *Baptism in the New Testament* (Chicago: Henry Regnery Company, 1950), pp. 23–53.

21. Beasley-Murray, pp. 216–226.

22. Dana, *The Heavenly Guest,* pp. 45–46.

23. Beasley-Murray, pp. 296–305.

24. Bultmann, pp. 138–139.

25. The commentary cited in the previous reference is the 1971 English translation of the German edition published in 1950. In his *Theology of the New Testament* (New York: Charles Scribner's Sons, 1951), I, pp. 139–142, he did not press this idea but indicated that in the form in which John 3:5 has come down to us it teaches new birth through baptism.

26. J. Calvin, *The Gospel According to St. John,* 2 vols., trans. T. H. L. Parker (Grand Rapids: Wm. B. Eerdmans Publishing Company, 1959), I, p. 65.

27. Barrett, p. 193.

28. Bultmann, *Commentary,* p. 176.

29. Plummer, p. 114.

30. See varying and penetrating statements from this viewpoint in R. E. Brown, p. 169, "God's will or plan is involved"; Hendriksen, p. 155, "to do the will of the One who had sent him and accomplish his work"; Hull, p. 250, "not as a geographical necessity but as a divine constraint."

31. Even today the small remnant of the Samaritans carries on some worship on the site of that temple. The Feast of the Passover is their most cherished festival.

32. It may not be a bad pun to note that the verb used transliterates as "synchronize." The Jews and Samaritans did not mesh.

33. There is no Old Testament reference to Jacob digging the well, but from antiquity, it has been known by that name. It was near the field Jacob had given his son Joseph.

34. Plummer, p. 119.

35. Jews were expected to go to Jerusalem each year for Passover, Pentecost, and Tabernacles.

36. R. E. Brown, pp. 206–207.

37. Joachim Jeremias, *The Rediscovery of Bethesda,* "New Testament Archaeology Monograph No. 1," ed. Jerry Vardaman (Louisville, Ky: Southern Baptist Theological Seminary, 1966). This book is presently available only from Editor Vardaman, professor of biblical archaeology, Cobb Institute of Biblical Archaeology, Mississippi State University, University, Mississippi.

38. Excavations reveal that it was a trapezoid measuring 164 feet on the north, 215 on the south, 309 on the west, and 314 on the east. The four sides were pillared porticoes making four of the five porches. The fifth ran from the east side to the west side near the middle making two pools completely surrounded by porticoes.

39. Hendriksen, p. 191.

40. For examples see John 9:3 to be considered later and Luke 13:1–5.

41. For more extensive treatment of this passage and the entire New Testament doctrine of the resurrection, see Summers, *The Life Beyond,* pp. 30–94. For this passage see particularly pp. 53–55.

42. Some interpreters find thirty-seven by counting two summary statements as separate miracles embedded in other miracles: 6:21, "and immediately the boat was at the land to which they were going," embedded in Jesus' walking on the water; 11:44, "The dead man came out, his hands and feet bound with bandages,"embedded in Jesus' raising of Lazarus.

43. TEV translates "boy." RSV retains "lad" as in KJV and ASV. The word is used only here in the New Testament. In the Septuagint it is used of Joseph at the age of seventeen (Gen. 37:2,30). We cannot be certain about the age of this boy.

44. Mark has a troublesome statement that Jesus instructed them to "go before him to the other side, to Bethsaida" (v. 45). Bethsaida, however, was on the east side where Luke and John place the feeding of the crowd. To harmonize the records, some interpreters have tried unconvincingly to create another "Bethsaida" in the vicinity of Capernaum where the apostles landed after the storm, according to John, or Gennesaret, according to Mark and Matthew. Other solutions have been suggested. The truth remains that if one must have a clear solution to the problem, he must wait. Such a solution simply is not available now.

45. See Barrett, p. 264 for numerous rabbinical quotations on overriding the sabbath law by keeping the circumcision law.

46. The precise location of his teaching this day is not indicated. The teaching on the last day was "in the treasury" (8:20). That was so close to the priests' chambers that they were practically within hearing distance.

47. Some interpreters state no position as to the seventh or eighth days (Calvin, Hovey, Hull). Plummer interprets Jesus' teaching from the view that it was the eighth day. Barrett, Brown, and Lenski understand the seventh day to be the one designated and interpret from that stance. Barrett and Lenski, however, think that which day it was is of minor importance.

48. Plummer, p. 177.

49. This omits 7:53 to 8:11 which by manuscript evidence cannot be defended as taking place at this point. It is omitted by all of the best manuscripts. In other manuscripts it appears in several different forms and at several different places. Some manuscripts have it after John 7:36; others have it after John 21:24. Some have it after Luke 21:38. It is widely accepted as an authentic event, but there is no widely accepted agreement in locating it. For me, it bears many similarities to events of Jesus' controversy with the religious authorities during his last week in Jerusalem when they tried to trap him in so many ways related to law interpretation. It is omitted from this discussion because it is not significantly related to the activities and teachings of that day, and it breaks the flow of Jesus' teaching in using "water" and "light" services of the festival.

50. He picks it up again in 9:5, "As long as I am in the world, I am the light of the world." He proceeds then to give man physical light (9:6–8) and then leads him into spiritual light (9:35–38).

51. Some writers suggest the possibility of their having included transmigration of souls or preexistence of souls. That is extremely doubtful. It could not be based on their canonical Scriptures, and it is doubtful if they would have been acquainted with the idea which was reflected later in some of the Hebrew wisdom writings.

52. H. L. Strack and P. Billerbeck, *Kommentar zum Neuen Testament aus Talmud und Midrash*, 6 vols. (Munich: Beck, 1963), II, pp. 250–251, 527–529, and 544.

53. So Barrett, Brown, Hendriksen, Lenski, and others.

54. I have found no reference to their having been used together as Jesus used them here.

55. By a similar double metaphor the redeeming Lamb of Revelation 5 comes to be the providing Shepherd of Revelation 7, supplying food and shelter for God's flock. See Summers, *Worthy Is the Lamb*, pp. 135, 152.

56. Robinson, "The Destination and Purpose of St. John's Gospel," p. 128.

57. For an extended presentation of this theme and method in Luke, see my *Commentary on Luke*, pp. 122–231.

58. Such as the Luke account of Jesus' visiting in the home of Mary and Martha (10:38–42) and as Mark's indication of Jesus' making Bethany his stopping place at a later visit to Jerusalem during the Passover (11:11; 14:3).

59. John Greenleaf Whittier, "Snow-Bound," *The Complete Poetical Works of Whittier* (Boston: Houghton Mifflin Company, 1894), p. 401.

III. Rejection of the Lamb

(11:47 to 12:50)

John's account of Israel's final and irrevocable rejection of Jesus begins with a decision of the Sanhedrin very soon after the raising of Lazarus. When the Pharisees heard the report of the miracle and its results, they were greatly alarmed. Some of their own number were going over to Jesus' side and believing in him (v. 45). In an unofficial capacity, they joined the chief priests in assembling the Sanhedrin to consider the matter (v. 47). That was a strange combination of forces, Sadducees and Pharisees, but they saw Jesus as a common enemy and a dangerous one.

"They were saying" (v. 47) better translates John's verb than "[they] said" (RSV). It is the continuous repetition of the same question by different voices suggestive of disorder, something like, "They kept on saying, 'What are we doing?' " The implied answer is, nothing. There had been determinations to kill him (5:18) and threats to stone him (8:59; 10:31), but actually they were doing nothing. On the other hand, Jesus was doing greater things everytime he came to Jerusalem: healing a lame man; giving sight to a blind man; raising a dead man. They had ceased to deny his miracles. They granted the validity of what he was doing (v. 47), but they were so crystallized in their opposition to him that they would not grant the validity of his sonship of God. They saw him as a potential military messiah who could arouse such a following that the Romans would take from them what limited freedom they possessed (v. 48). Their "holy place" was the Temple and their "nation" was their identity as a political unit, though under severe restriction by the Roman armies quartered there to maintain Rome's interests. When the kind of uprising which they feared finally came about (A.D. 66–70), it resulted in those very tragedies. The Temple was destroyed and the nation of Israel was ended, but it was not at the instigation of a man like Jesus or people like his followers.

Finally, the high priest Caiaphas took charge. He was high priest from A.D. 18 to 36 and was noted for his displays of contempt for friend and foe alike and for his ruthlessness in the exercise of his authority. His words to the Sanhedrin were scathing, literally, *"You* don't know nothing" (v. 49). The pronoun is contemptuously emphatic, and his double negative charges absolute ignorance and ineptitude. *He* had the answer: "It is expedient for you that one man should die for the people, and that the whole nation should not perish" (v. 50). He bowed before the bad politician's favorite household god, expediency. Perhaps it was the only god he knew. The Romans had a word for it: "Not what is best, but what is necessary." His meaning was clear; it was necessary for Jesus to die rather than for the nation to die. They could not let Jesus go on until his movement reached the revolutionary proportions which would bring the Romans who would destroy the Jews. *The man must die!*

John, however, understood Caiaphas' words in an entirely different way. His fateful words in that fateful year were the words of one who as high priest unconsciously prophesied Jesus' sacrificial death not only for the nation of Israel but also for the children of God scattered throughout the world (vv. 51–52). But Caiaphas' words had deeper meaning: (1) it was necessary for Jesus to die; (2) it would be one man dying for the nation; (3) his death would not be just for the Jews; it would be for those who through Jesus' death would become "the children of God . . . scattered abroad," the Gentiles. *The Lamb must die!*

The Sanhedrin accepted Caiaphas' recommendation with, of course, his meaning. From that moment they started planning how they could bring Jesus to his death (v. 53). It was an official decision; the official sentence would be pronounced at his trial. It would not be easy to bring about his death, but it was inescapably necessary. They would find a way.

The "therefore" of verse 54 links Jesus' action to the Sanhedrin's decision. Because of that decision he withdrew from the public scene. He "no longer went about openly among the Jews" (v. 54). His "hour" had not yet come, but it was not far off. With the apostles, he withdrew to the wilderness country near Ephraim. The town is generally identified with the Old Testament town of Ephron and thought to have been about twenty miles north of Jerusalem. There he would remain until his return to Jerusalem for the Passover and the "hour" toward which he moved.

When the time for the Passover drew near, "many went up from the country to Jerusalem before the Passover" (v. 55). Many efforts have been made to determine the probable attendance at a Passover in Jesus' day. By tradition, Passover day had become joined to the Week of Unleavened Bread which followed it and which was one of the three festivals which male Jews were required to attend. It had all come to be regarded as one festival and was sometimes referred to as Passover and at other times as Unleavened Bread. Estimating the number of male Jews by fairly reliable knowledge of the population, the Passover attendance has been fairly well determined at about 100,000 including other family members who would go with the men. No one takes seriously Josephus' 2,500,000! The many who went before the week started did so in order to secure ceremonial purification in order that they might participate in the week's services. This practice was based both on Old Testament regulations and developing traditions.

For this particular week there was unusual excitement in the air. Many had never seen Jesus. They had heard of him and of what he had done. They were especially excited about seeing

Lazarus (12:9). They had heard, too, about the Sanhedrin's official decision. They were speculating about Jesus' action; would he or would he not come to this Passover (v. 56)? From the human viewpoint, why should he? Why should one go deliberately to the place where he faced certain death? From the divine viewpoint, he should and he did. Sensing the growing excitement of such an emotional crowd, the Sanhedrin gave an order making it legally mandatory that if anyone knew where Jesus was, he should report it in order that they might arrest him (v. 57).

In the opening discussion of John 11, we observed the extreme difficulty in trying to determine the sequence of Jesus' movements in the closing months and days of his ministry. The four Gospel writers differ greatly in the material which they include from his words and works as well as the order in which they use it. They follow their distinct theological emphases with three basic but differing approaches: (1) Matthew-Mark; (2) Luke; (3) John.

At John 12, Mark 11, Matthew 21, and Luke 19:28, they come together for the events of Jesus' last week in Jerusalem, his death, and his resurrection. At some points they are very close together. At others they are apart in materials used (John 14—17 for example is not in the Synoptics) as well as in their methods of presentation. As long ago as 1882, Plummer (whose commentary is so freely used by all contemporary ones) gave sound appraisal and reminder: "We have not sufficient data for harmonizing this latter portion of S. John with the Synoptists. In the large gaps left by each there is plenty of room for all that is peculiar to the others." [1]

For an understanding of the events, teaching, and theology of the entire week, one needs to study the four Gospels together. This volume, however, must concentrate on John's account, his theological purpose, and his method of carrying out that purpose. Cross reference to the other Gospels will be limited to those elements which seem to be very essential.

According to John's account, Jesus and the apostles in returning from Ephraim (11:54) arrived in Bethany, "six days before the

Passover" (12:1). Although that is a very exact statement of time, it is ambiguous because of the problem of John's view of Passover Day of that week in comparison with the Synoptic view of the two. Was Passover Day a Friday in the Synoptics and a Saturday in John? That problem will be considered in the exposition of John 13—18. At this point we need to note only that Jesus arrived in Bethany in time for a dinner on Saturday night before the triumphal entry on Sunday. John used the supper in several ways. It was likely an expression of gratitude to Jesus for his having raised Lazarus from the dead. It was an occasion which brought out the true character of Judas Iscariot as this climactic week started. It contributed to the decision of the Sanhedrin to kill Lazarus as well as Jesus. It contributed to the growth of the crowds who welcomed him at his entry into Jerusalem to begin the week which would end in the tragedy of death and the triumph of resurrection.

John gives no location for the supper. Mark and Matthew identify the place as the home of Simon the leper. Nothing more is known about him; he may have been healed of his leprosy through the ministry of Jesus. It may well have been an occasion in which four devoted friends expressed their gratitude for Jesus' ministry of mercy. Lazarus was a noted guest. Martha helped to serve. Mary sought a way to express the magnitude of her gratitude and devotion to Jesus. Note the similar conduct of the two sisters in Luke 10:38–42. It was a brave thing for the friends to do. The religious authorities had ordered that anyone who knew where Jesus was should report it in order that they might arrest him to kill him. These friends welcomed him with a banquet, the news of which spread quickly to Jerusalem (vv. 9–11).

According to the custom at formal meals, the diners reclined at the table. Mary found her way of expressing her devotion by anointing Jesus' head (Mark and Matt.) and feet (John) with a twelve-ounce bottle of very expensive perfumed oil. Beyond the lavishness of her gift, she ignored social custom by loosing her hair publicly and using it to wipe his feet. It was admittedly an extravagant and rare display of devotion. Mark and Matthew report that the disciples complained indignantly at the waste when there were so many poor people who could have been helped by her selling the oil and giving them the money. John reports that it was Judas Iscariot who led the complaint. Their estimate was that on the market the perfume would have sold for "three hundred denarii" (v. 5). That was the equivalent of three-hundred-days' wages for a working man.

John also gives the reason for Judas' complaint. He was the treasurer of the group; he carried the money box for the group's supplies; he was a thief who stole from the group funds to supply his personal needs (v. 6). That was retroactive insight. As the group looked back later on Judas' subsequent betrayal of Jesus for money, they could understand many things which they did not even observe when these things were taking place. The same sort of retrospective understanding is reflected in verse 4. John also indicated in an aside comment that Judas had no concern for the poor (v. 6*a*). He made no comment regarding the concern, or lack of it, of the rest of the apostles who had also suggested such an offering for the poor (Mark 14:5; Matt. 26:9).

Jesus looked upon Mary's action and the apostles' reaction in an entirely different way. His response to them was, "Let her alone" (v. 7). Their criticism may have been a case of the poor carping at the wealthy. There are evidences that the family was wealthy. They had a private burial cave (11:38); only the wealthy had that. Mary had a bottle of perfume that would have cost a working man a year's wages. So, in their minds, if she had that kind of money, why wasn't she helping the poor rather than wasting money in such display of sentiment? They had no evidence, of course, that she was not helping the poor or that she had not already made the traditional Passover gift to the poor!

Jesus gave them another way of looking at the situation. First, he said, "Let her keep it for the day of my burial" (v. 7). That is the Revised Standard Version translation, one of many which struggle with the grammatical construction in variant manuscript readings. A more precise, albeit rough, translation is, "Leave her alone in order that she may keep it for the preparation for my burial" (author's translation). This sounds as if she had been interrupted in her anointing him, and Jesus was suggesting that she neither sell it nor anoint him now, but that she keep it to anoint his body at his death at the end of the week. Mark (14:3) and Matthew (26:7), however, have a very graphic picture of her breaking the fragile container and "pouring" its contents over Jesus' head (and body, Matt. 26:12?). That suggests that she had none left to keep for any kind of future use.

Indeed, in the Mark (v. 8) and Matthew (v. 12) accounts, Jesus stated that Mary had done this as a preanointing of his body looking to his burial at the end of the week. Interpreters differ in their views. Some think that Mary did this consciously; that is, she believed that he would be put to death; she doubted if in the circumstances she would be permitted to honor his body by anointment; she saw this as a good and perhaps last opportunity to do so. Others think that she did it unconsciously; that is, she did not do it for that reason, but essentially, Jesus said, that was what it amounted to. It was something like the case of Caiaphas who spoke words with one intent, but in a very exact way, they had meaning of which he was not aware (11:51). Jesus' interpretation of what she had done was true. That was the only such anointing of his body which any of his inner circle of friends would do. On Friday evening after he was buried, some women who had followed him in Galilee bought anointing ointments for that purpose (Luke 23:55-56). But when the sabbath had passed and they went on Sunday to anoint his body, it was no longer in the tomb; he had arisen from the dead (Luke 24:1-10).

Jesus' second statement to the apostles was a reminder that they were never without an opportunity to aid the poor, "The poor you always have with you," a quotation of Deuteronomy

15:11. There was still opportunity for them to fulfill the Passover custom of giving to the poor (John 13:29), even at that Passover. Jesus was not insensitive to the poor and needy. His record was very clear on that. That the poor were always about them was not only scripturally true, it was situationally true. Because of underproduction and overproduction, the land was crowded by the poor and the beggars. It has been estimated that when Jesus fed the five thousand, three-fifths of them had never before had a fully satisfying meal.

In dramatic contrast to the ever-present opportunity to do something for the poor, Jesus reminded them "but you do not always have me" (v. 8). Soon he would be with them no more. Let anyone who had anything he wished to do for Jesus act with haste. How sad that on the night of his betrayal he would say almost the same thing to Judas (13:27). In both parts of his rejoinder, Jesus put great stress on his death: Mary had preanointed his body for burial (v. 7); he would not be with them much longer (v. 8). Still they would not believe that he was to die. They would resist that part of his teaching to the very end.

Hearing that Jesus was in Bethany with Lazarus, a great crowd came out from Jerusalem (v. 9). They wanted to see Jesus. For many it would be their first time to see the teacher from Galilee, the one whose followers looked upon as the Messiah. They wanted to see a man who could raise the dead. They also wanted to see the man whom he had raised from the dead. Here was their opportunity to see the two together! It was an excited crowd that made its way from the city to the village. The chief priests responded with another decision. The situation was growing more and more critical. Lazarus was a living example of Jesus' power. They could not refute that. Where logic could not prevail, perhaps force could. They decided to kill Lazarus, too, because on account of him, many of the Jews were turning in faith to Jesus (v. 11). There is no record that they succeeded in killing Lazarus. They did succeed in prevailing upon the Romans to kill Jesus, but that did not stop his work. Soon after his death, even "a great many of the priests" were converted to the Christian faith (Acts 6:7). Could any of these priests have been among those priests?

On the next day, Jesus made his triumphal entry into Jerusalem. It further incited the determination of the Jewish authorities to kill him. All four Gospels contain this important event. They make the same basic presentation. Major differences consist of blocks of material contained by one Gospel but not by one or more of the others. John's account does not have the long, carefully made preparation for the entry which the Synoptics have (Mark 11:1–8; Matt. 21:1–6; Luke 19:29–36). On the other hand, the Synoptics do not have John's lengthy section following the entry in which the request of Greeks to see Jesus launched a major teaching of Jesus (12:20–50). This event fits most naturally right after the entry.[2] Robertson, for no indicated reason, puts it on the day following.[3]

A great crowd of the festival pilgrims heard that Jesus was on his way into Jerusalem. They went out to meet him (v. 12). The Synoptics appear to have a crowd gathering along Jesus' way and going with him. The picture is that of two crowds meeting, gathering about Jesus and the apostles, and accompanying him into Jerusalem and the Temple in a tremendous praise processional.

They understood from his riding a donkey that he was coming as the Messiah, according to the prophecy of Isaiah (62:11) and Zechariah (9:9). "Fear not, daughter of Zion;/ behold, your king is coming,/ sitting on an ass's colt!" (author's translation). They gave him a royal welcome, lining his path with their robes, waving palm branches of joy as if it were Tabernacles rather than Passover, and shouting their acclaim. Different people doubtless cried out different tributes: "Hosanna!" "Blessed is he who comes in the name of the Lord." "The King of Israel!" "Hosanna in the highest." "Blessed is the King who comes in the name of the Lord!" "Hosanna to the son of David." [4]

John reports that the disciples, apparently the twelve, did not understand this while it was taking place. After Jesus' death and resurrection ("when Jesus was glorified"), they remembered the scene, the tributes, and the application of the words of prophecy to his entering Jerusalem in this manner. His implication is that in looking back from the perspective of Jesus' death and resurrection, they understood what the entry was all about. Jesus was offering himself to Israel as the Son-of-David Messiah. Israel understood that and cried out their welcome.

The crowd that went out to meet him (v. 12) went in part because of the testimony of the people who had witnessed the raising of Lazarus (v. 17). They had heard of the miracle; they had not seen Jesus; still they gave him a messianic welcome. By the Synoptic accounts, they accompanied him right into the Temple, praising him to the extent of infuriating the Pharisees who regarded it as blasphemy. John reports the frustration of the Pharisees (v. 19). They felt that the whole mass of Israel was going to follow Jesus. But that was on Sunday. By Thursday the tides had all turned against him. By Friday, Israel was crying, "Crucify, crucify!" He would not be the kind of messiah they wanted.

The Pharisees' lament "the world has gone after him" (v. 19) was the logical place for John to report the coming of the Greeks who wanted to see Jesus. It also appears to be the most natural place for it to have occurred. These Greeks were Gentiles who had become proselytes to the Hebrew religion and were attending the Passover for worship.[5]

For some reason, concerning which we can only speculate, the Greeks made their request to Philip, "Sir, we wish to see Jesus" (v. 21). Philip reported their request to Andrew who is noted in John for bringing people to Jesus (1:40–41; 6:9). The two of them took the report to Jesus. In the Good Shepherd teaching, Jesus had said to the Jews, "I have other sheep, that are not of this fold; I must bring them also" (10:16). In this request of Gentiles to see him in this situation in which the Jews could not bear the sight of him, he recognized that the climax of his ministry had come. When he was lifted up, he would draw all men to himself (v. 32). These Greeks were a token of Gentiles who would come to his light.

Now he could say, "The hour has come for the Son of man to be glorified" (v. 23). He continued to speak of his death, using the analogy of a seed, a grain of wheat which can produce no other wheat unless it dies (v. 24). It falls into the earth like a body which is buried. It gives itself up to a dissolution which is like death. It comes to life again producing much wheat (v. 24). Not just one grain of wheat results from the death and burial, but many. That is like his parable of the sower, the seed, and the soil (Matt. 13:23). In that parable, however, the seed was "the word of the kingdom" (v. 19). In the present analogy of his death the seed is the sower. Jesus is that sower who, like a seed, will be planted at Passover, but what a harvest will come at Pentecost! [6]

He continued by saying that to love life is to lose it in a self-interest which rules out any concern for others. To hate the life of destructive self-interest, however, is to keep the genuine life eternally. Those who follow Jesus must go where he goes; even if that means death, his servant must go with him. The one who serves him, even if it means death, will be honored by the Father (v. 26). To die to self in service to Christ is not loss; it is gain. His disciples needed to be reminded of that fact during that week. Later they would need its encouragement even more. One must bury himself somewhere if he is to bear fruit for God. In what corner of the field one is buried matters only in relation to the Father's will. The field is still the world (Matt. 13:38).

At that emotion-packed moment Jesus prayed. John does not have Jesus' agony prayer in the garden of Gethsemane. His emotions on that occasion and his prayer as he faced death on the morrow are very much like this situation. In John, "Now is my soul troubled" (v. 27) is very much like, "My soul is very sorrowful, even to death" (Mark 14:34; Matt. 26:38). In John, "What shall I say? 'Father, save my from this hour?' " is very much like, "My Father, if it be possible, let this cup pass from me" in Matthew (26:39). In John, "No, for this purpose I have come to this hour. Father, glorify thy name" (vv. 27–28) is very much like, "Nevertheless, not as I will but as thou wilt" in Matthew (v. 39). In both cases, Jesus felt that death was very near.

Even while committed to the Father's will, he struggled with the prospect of the shameful and agonizing death of a Roman cross, with the sin of the world focused upon him as if he were the greatest of all sinners. In the first clause of verse 27, the word "troubled" is the one used for his agitation at the tomb of Lazarus (11:33). There he faced the challenge of death in the experience of a friend; here he faced the challenge of death in his own case, just as he would again in Gethsemane. It was a time for prayer, but what kind of prayer? Should he pray for the Father to save him from that hour? He felt that he could not pray that prayer because it was for that very hour that he had come into the world. His ultimate manifestation of the Father's love for sinful humanity would be through his sacrifice on the cross. Compare Paul's affirmation in Romans 5:8, "God shows his love for us in that while we were yet sinners Christ died for us." In Gethsemane he would pray in effect, "Father, if there is any other way, let this cup pass from me." There was no other way.

Victory came for him as he prayed the only prayer which he felt that he could pray, "Father, glorify thy name" (v. 28). A voice came from heaven saying, "I have glorified it, and I will glorify it again" (v. 28). On two other occasions this phenomenon had come to him. All three times, his death was at the center of what the voice said. At his baptism the voice had said, "Thou art my beloved Son; with thee I am well pleased" (Mark 1:11). That identified the nature of his messianic role after the pattern of the suffering Servant (Isa. 42:1; Ps. 2:7). At his transfiguration

the voice had said, "This is my beloved Son, with whom I am
well pleased; listen to him" (Matt. 17:5). On that occasion, the
words were addressed to the apostles instructing them to listen
to what Jesus had been saying to them about his death which
would come soon in Jerusalem (Luke 9:22,31). In this third instance, the voice assured him that God would glorify his name
through the death which he faced that very week (v. 28).

Jesus heard and understood. The people heard but did not understand. Some thought an angel had spoken to him, but others
thought they had heard thunder (v. 29). That was tragic because
they needed the assurance of God's glorifying his name through
Jesus and his death more than Jesus did (v. 30). Jesus' next words
were words of judgment and of salvation. His coming death meant
judgment upon this world of sin. It meant the ultimate overthrow
of Satan (v. 31). It also meant salvation as an accomplished fact
for all who would receive it. When he was lifted up on the cross,
suspended between heaven and earth as if neither would have
him, he would draw all men to himself (v. 32). That drawing of
all men would include the Greeks as well as the Jews.

The people responded to his statement that both judgment
and salvation would result from his death. They were more interested in his saying that he would die than in his speaking of
crucifixion (v. 33) as the manner of his death. He had said that
the Son of man was to be glorified (v. 23). The Son of man was
a messianic figure, and they thought rightly that he was applying
it to himself. But now he was saying that the glorification would
come through his death (v. 33) and in their views, the Messiah
was to live forever (v. 34). They were perplexed. So they asked
him pointedly, "Who is this Son of man?" (v. 34). In other words,
"Are you the Son of man (Messiah), and if so, how can you say
that you are going to die?"

Jesus went back to his claim (chs. 8, 9) that he was the Light
of the world. Some of his listeners would have heard him on
that occasion; others would have heard about it. For others it

was a new teaching. He gave it to all of them in the form of metaphor. The Light (Jesus) was still present and available to them (v. 35). They should seize the opportunity to take advantage of that Light, to walk in it rather than in the blinding darkness of this world. They should believe in that Light and become sons of light (v. 36). It was their decision and time was short.

In John's account, Jesus withdrew himself from the public scene at this point (v. 36*b*). Few of those present would see him again until they saw him lifted up on the cross. John appraised the situation clearly. Jesus had done many signs in their presence (v. 37). His ministry there in Jerusalem had included the greatest of his miracles: the healing of a man who had been born blind; the raising to life of a man who had been dead for four days. They could not deny the miracles. Still they refused to accept him as the Son of God who was to die for their sins and the sins of the world. It was a case of seeing but not seeing. They saw physically, but they did not see spiritually. They saw the signs, but they did not see that to which the signs pointed, Jesus as the long-anticipated Messiah.

John related their situation to the lament of Isaiah, "Lord, who has believed our report?" (Isa. 53:1). There is a plaintiveness about the cry which borders on the force of an optative, "Oh, that someone would believe our report." When God had commissioned Isaiah to preach (Isa. 6:10), he had told him how hard the people were and how hard his task would be. The more he preached, the harder they would become. The more they looked, the less they would see. Eyes are blinded and hearts are hardened when men refuse God's offer of mercy.

The last part of John's quotation from Israel has troubled interpreters. It seems to mean that God blinded the eyes and hardened the hearts of the people so they would not see and understand and turn, in which case he would have to heal them (v. 40*b*). It is instructive to note that in all rabbinical use of the Isaiah passage, the meaning is understood as conditional rather than purposive.

That is, *if* they should see and understand and turn, God would forgive them. That view may be supported by the fact that Isaiah's vision closed on the remnant note so prominent in Jewish theology (and Pauline theology), that hopeless as the task seemed, there would be a believing remnant who would experience forgiveness (Isa. 6:13).

In the case of Jesus and his manifestation of himself to Israel, there was both acceptance and rejection. There were some of the Jews, even some of the authorities, who accepted Jesus (v. 42). That was not true of the mass of the people or of the authorities. They had reached their decision that he had to die. They were at that very moment making plans by which they could arrest him and bring him to his death.

The Logos had become flesh (1:14). He had been introduced as "the Lamb of God, who takes away the sin of the world!" (1:29) He had manifested himself through word and work in ways that were calculated to stimulate faith in his redemptive person and mission. Israel had from the beginning resisted him, and finally they rejected him. They were ready for the Romans to crucify him. He had come "to his own home, and his own people received him not" (1:11). So ended John's dramatic and graphic account of the Lamb and the old Israel.

Notes

1. Plummer, p. 250.
2. R. E. Brown, p. 469.
3. Robertson, *Harmony of the Gospels,* p. 157.
4. These are the tributary terms from all four Gospels; John does not have all of them.
5. Robinson stands alone in the authorities consulted in holding that these were Diaspora Jews who lived in Greek territory. See his "The Destination and Purpose of St. John's Gospel," pp. 124–127.
6. Pentecost was historically a harvest festival in Israel.

PART TWO

The Lamb
and the New Israel
13:1 to 21:25

IV. Introduction of the Lamb
13:1–38

In the Gospel of John, Jesus' public ministry spanned a possible period of three or three and one-half years. A more precise estimate would depend on identifying exactly the number of Passovers which Jesus attended. That does not seem possible (review the discussion of the identity of "the feast" in 5:1). His public ministry to the old Israel encompasses 1:35 to 12:36. John's conclusion of that ministry is very exact, "When Jesus had said this, he departed and hid himself from them" (12:36). The remainder of John's Gospel deals with Jesus' ministry to the small group of his disciples, the twelve apostles in the Synoptics, which we are calling the new Israel; this was the nucleus of what would come to be the new people for God's redemptive witness, the church. Approximately half of this Gospel is devoted to that ministry, and exclusive of the post-resurrection appearances in chapters 20–21, it covers a period of less than twenty-four hours. It begins with a supper which would have started after sunset on Thursday (13:1) and ends with the burial of Jesus before sunset on Friday (19:42). So much space and so important a part of Jesus' ministry and teaching for so short a period!

Chapter 13 opens with a problem which must be explored briefly, "Now before the feast of the Passover . . . ." (v. 1). That appears very naturally to identify the supper which followed (13:2 to 14:31) as the Passover Eve supper just as the Synoptics have the Passover Eve supper on that night, Thursday after sunset (Mark 14:12–26; Matt. 26:17–30; Luke 22:7–38). All four Gospels have the death of Jesus on the next day after this supper which is generally designated as the Last Supper.

The problem arises in John 18:28. During the course of Jesus' trial before Pontius Pilate early on Friday morning, the members of the Sanhedrin stayed outside of the praetorium while Pilate questioned Jesus on the inside. The reason was that they would become ceremonially defiled if they went into a room where Gentiles were present. They stayed outside, therefore, "so that they might not be defiled, but might eat the passover" (v. 28). That implies that the Passover Eve supper was yet to be eaten and that it would be eaten that day after sunset.

In that sequence, Jesus would be on the cross that afternoon at the very time the Passover lambs were being sacrificed at the Temple. It fits John's theological emphasis beautifully, the Lamb of God sacrificed at the same time as the Passover lambs. He would be in the grave while the Passover Eve supper was observed throughout Jerusalem. Passover day would be the sabbath when he would rest from his trials and suffering. On the first day of the week he would be raised in triumph over sin and death.

How does such a sequence relate to the Synoptic account? By this reckoning, the Synoptics would have the Last Supper on Thursday night after sunset, the beginning of Friday Nisan fifteenth in the Jewish calendar, and it would be the Passover supper. John, however, would have the last Supper on Thursday night after sunset, beginning Friday Nisan fourteenth, and it would not be the Passover supper. By John's reckoning, Jesus did not observe the Passover at all. He had a meaningful supper with the twelve on his last night with them, but the Passover supper would be the next night; he would be in the tomb; Judas would have committed suicide; the eleven would be hiding from the Sanhedrin.

Interpretive opinion is probably more fragmented over this question than any other part of the Gospel of John. Granting multiple variations within basic views, observe the following major divisions of opinion. First, there are many who hold that in both the Synoptics and in John, the Last Supper was the Passover Eve supper on Thursday evening after sunset beginning Friday Nisan fifteenth. The Passover lambs were sacrificed on Thursday afternoon the fourteenth beginning at three o'clock. The supper was observed after the fifteenth began when it was dark enough to see the first star, all in conformity with Jewish law and practice. Jesus was crucified the next morning at nine o'clock (Mark 15:25), still Friday by the Jewish calendar.

These interpreters find no conflict between John and the Synoptics. They offer good arguments in interpreting in harmony the five passages which are usually used to argue that John and the Synoptics are not in agreement (13:1; 13:27; 18:28; 19:14; 19:31). The most troublesome one of the five is 18:28. They understand "eat the passover" to refer to the observance of the entire festival week as it is used in 2 Chronicles 30:22, "and they did eat throughout the feast seven days" (KJV). From this viewpoint the Sanhedrin did not want to defile themselves so they would be ceremonially clean for the next festival meal. The most concise presentation on this view is by Robertson.[1] He grants that in the Synoptics, "eat the passover" referred to the supper itself. He argues, however, that since John uses the word "Passover" nine times and the other eight refer to observing the entire week, we may fairly infer that it does so in 18:28. What Robertson does not point out is that only in 18:28 is the word *eat* used with the word *Passover*.

Second, many other interpreters hold that the Synoptics accurately present the Last Supper as the Passover supper, but John presents it as a preliminary meal, not the Passover. They note that there is only one passage in John's account which is also in the Synoptic account, the role of Judas as the betrayer (13:21–30). This passage also contains the only possible Passover ritual, the dipping of the morsel in verses 26 and 30, and it is not at all certain that it was a Passover ritual. They hold that John's presentation is strictly theological. This is probably the prevailing opinion in scholarly circles today.[2] An interesting back-to-back article with that of Torrey cited above is by the Jewish scholar, Zeitlin.[3]

Third, out of respect for the scholarship of Plummer, we should note his rather unique view.[4] He was so certain that John is correct in his meticulous chronology of the events of Jesus' last week that he held that the Last Supper was not a Passover supper in John or in the Synoptics. He granted that in the Synoptics the Last Supper had in some sense the character of a Passover meal, but it is not a Passover meal. It is, in Plummer's view, the impression derived from the Synoptic accounts which must be modified and John was modifying it for his Jewish readers. He made it clear to them "that on the very day and at the very hour when the Paschal lambs had to be slain, the True Lamb was being sacrificed on the Cross."[5]

Fourth, not an entirely separate outlook, but an important modification of the second view already presented is that of Jeremias. His masterful review of evidences for and against opposing theories is an indispensable volume for serious consideration of this entire area of Gospel study.[6] His conclusion is that in the Synoptics the Last Supper is unquestionably a Passover meal but in John an *unquestionable decision* cannot be made *either* way. It must be left open because the Johannine report "is not uniform."[7] Two possible views stand beside one another. In 18:28, on Friday morning at Jesus' trial, the Passover supper was anticipated for that night. In 13:21–30, however, the Thursday night supper must be identified with the Passover supper of the Synoptics (Mark 14:17–21; Matt. 26:20–25; Luke 22:14–18). His argument is convincing and his scholarship is impeccable. It is from that stance that we will leave the question open and will proceed to examine John's account in search of his theological message for his readers then and now.

Jesus' parabolic action in washing the feet of his disciples introduced him to this new Israel in a new light, the Lord of all who made himself the Servant of all (13:3–20). Guests arriving for a formal meal would be met at the door by the lowest slave in the household staff. His duty was to wash the dirt of the street from their feet. Jesus assumed that role in the absence of such a slave and washed their feet in the lofty consciousness that he had come from the Father (vv. 1,3). He served them in sincere humility. He loved the Jews, "his own" (1:11; 13:1) right up to the end. He did not cease to love them even when they rejected him. Here were some of "his own" whom he had chosen, whom he loved, with whom he had lived and served in difficult days. They called him Lord; he saw himself as servant. Here was a needed and meaningful service which he could render for them, even for Judas who had already bargained to betray him.

To follow this event understandably in John's account, one must envision the table and the participants' positions about it. The table appears to have been the Roman style *triclinnium,* three tables joined at the ends to form the three sides of an open square or rectangle. The diners reclined on couches, resting on the left forearm, leaving the right hand for handling the food, and with their feet extended away from the table. For this supper it seems clear that Jesus occupied the center position at the head table. John was on his right. Judas was on his left. Perhaps two others were at the head table beside John and Judas. The others would be four each at the two wing tables. Of the others, only Simon Peter's position is important. He was too far from Jesus to speak to him secretly, but he was in sight of John to communicate by signs. Think of him at one of the wing tables and at the farthest position from Jesus and John.

All of the apostles were doubtless surprised and perplexed when Jesus girded himself like a slave and started washing their feet. Only Simon Peter's reaction is reported. What Jesus was doing was a degrading service. Not even a Jewish slave was required to wash his master's feet as a Gentile slave would. Rabbinical students rendered personal services to their teachers, but they were not required to wash their teachers' feet. They might on occasion do it as a jesture of devotion. Here, then, was Jesus doing the unheard of service of a teacher washing his disciples' feet!

When Jesus reached Peter (the last one in the line?), his emotions had reached the breaking point. "Lord, *you?* Do you intend to wash my feet?" (author's translation to preserve the emphasis of the text). His pronoun *you* was emphatic. One can imagine his drawing his feet up under his robe so Jesus could not wash them. Jesus stayed there, kneeling at the end of the couch, assuring Peter that someday he would understand clearly what he was doing and why he was doing it (v. 7). Unconvinced, Peter burst forth, "Never will you wash my feet forever" (author's translation preserving the structure of his words). Jesus responded that unless Peter allowed him to wash his feet, this would not be a sharing experience for them (v. 8*b*). Then Simon, impulsive and volatile as ever, responded that in that case he wanted Jesus to wash him wholly, feet, hands, and head (v. 9)!

Jesus' answer was another of his famous riddles (v. 10). One who had been bathed did not need another bath upon arriving at the host's house; he needed only to have the dirt of the street washed from his feet. He said that all of them except one had been bathed. They needed only the servant's washing of their feet.

Interpreting his riddle, to be "clean," bathed, meant to be spiritually clean through God's cleansing. To have the "feet washed" meant to receive the humble service which he was rendering for them. They were all "clean" except one; that one was still a sinner. Even that one had received Jesus' humble service. They should have understood all of it except his veiled reference to Judas. Judas doubtless understood it. The rest would understand it before the night was over.

Having finished his service, Jesus returned to his place at the table. He explained more fully and in plain language the significance of what he had done (vv. 13–20). He was their Teacher and Lord. He had performed for them a lowly but necessary service. That was for them a lesson in humility. If he their Teacher and Lord had so served them, there was no necessary service too menial for them to perform for one another or for any person. For them to understand the meaning of service to others and to perform it sincerely as he had done was to experience the blessings of God (v. 17).

He returned to the theme that for one of them what he was saying did not apply (v. 18). Apart from that divine knowledge which John frequently emphasized, Jesus had been with the twelve in travel and service for three years. He had come to know every one of them, their strength and their weakness. He had watched as Judas turned from the selflessness which Jesus practiced and taught to the selfishness of the world. He had doubtless observed Judas' capacity for greed (12:6). All three Synoptic writers report that after the supper at Bethany when Jesus had rebuked the apostles for criticizing Mary, Judas returned to Jerusalem to make his initial arrangement with the Sanhedrin for the betrayal of Jesus (Mark 14:10–11; Matt. 26:14–16; Luke 22:3–6). Even now at the Passover supper Judas probably had his thirty pieces of silver on his person.

Jesus drew from a page of Israel's history to speak of what was happening in Judas' treachery. He quoted from Psalm 41:9, "He who ate my bread has lifted his heel against me" (John 13:18). This was King David's lament over the treachery of his friend Ahithophel. To share bread was a token of friendship. Ahithophel had been David's friend, but he joined in a plot to destroy him. To lift up the heel meant either to kick one as a horse kicks or to crush one by stamping him beneath the heel. Jesus saw in Judas' treachery a more meaningful application of that lament than the original one. Ahithophel had kicked or stamped on

David; Judas was kicking and stamping on the Son of David, the Messiah.

In that highly charged emotional atmosphere Jesus said plainly, "One of you will betray me" (v. 21). "Betray" meant precisely "to give him over" to the authorities, to make the formal identification by which they could legally arrest him and bring him to trial. Mutually the apostles started looking at one another wondering which one it might be, wondering if anyone knew and could reveal the identity of the traitor. At that time no one had any grounds for suspecting any other one in the group.

Here Simon's place at the table becomes important again. He knew that he was not the traitor. He just had to know who it was. He was too far from Jesus to ask secretly. His close friend, John the beloved disciple, was close enough to ask. Translated literally verse 24 reads, "Therefore Simon Peter motioned with his head to that one, to learn by asking who it might be concerning whom he was speaking." Reclining on his left arm John leaned back close to the breast of Jesus and asked, "Lord, who is it?" Jesus could have answered in one word, "Judas," but he did not. Perhaps he did not want the group to know yet. He trusted John. He was holding a small piece of the unleavened bread in his hand. Before him was a dish containing some form of "dip" food, perhaps the bitter herbs, salt, and vinegar symbolic of Israel's bitter years of slavery from which they were freed in the original Passover and the Exodus. Jesus told John that the traitor was the one to whom he would give the morsel when he had dipped it in the dish. They were apparently speaking in whispers; no one seems to have heard; Judas probably could have.

When Jesus dipped the morsel he handed it to Judas. The action seems to have been immediately after his words to John. John alone knew the significance of the giving of the morsel. The rest of the apostles heard Jesus' words to Judas but they did not know what they meant (vv. 28–29). Interpreters vary in their view of when the apostles learned that Judas was the betrayer. Some think that John told no one what he had learned from Jesus. Some think that John missed the exchange of the morsel so that not even he knew; that seems very unlikely. Some think John told Simon Peter by some kind of communication. Others think that by the end of the supper all of them knew. That, too, seems unlikely since no one gave any evidence of suspecting Judas until he led the officers to Gethsemane to arrest Jesus.

Jesus dipped the morsel and gave it to Judas. When Judas took the morsel from the hand of Jesus, "Satan entered into him" (v. 27). This probably means that Satan assumed complete control of Judas; Judas would act under that control. Judas' journey into greed and treachery had almost reached its end. Knowing Jesus, one feels that he must have done everything he could to help Judas. The offering of the morsel may have been one last appeal to him for repentance and the renouncing of Satan's dominance. Undocumented speculation as to a custom in the exchange of such a morsel at the Passover supper is plentiful: a token of friendship; a token of good will; an assurance of love from a father to the one of his children who was the most wayward and needed most his care and guidance. That would have been most appropriate in this case.

Jesus' words accompanying the morsel left the decision to Judas, "What you are going to do, do quickly" (v. 27). The word which is translated "quickly" is comparative in form and may be translated "more quickly." Some interpreters think that Jesus was encouraging Judas to complete his contract with the Sanhedrin "more quickly" than he had previously arranged. Most interpreters reject that view and hold that Jesus was telling Judas that there was no reason to delay longer the final step in his contract. Was there not a deeper meaning in Jesus' words? The "hour" of his glorification through death was approaching (see 12:23; 13:1; 17:1). Nothing could hold that back. If Judas had decided to be the agent of the forces of darkness, there was no need for him to delay the action.

Judas took the morsel from Jesus' hand. How bitter was it in his mouth? He arose from his couch and went immediately from the room and from the presence of Jesus; "and it was night" (v. 30). Darkness is Jerusalem, but more than that, darkness in the heart of Judas. How different from that man who in the beginning of John's Gospel came *to* Jesus *out of the night* and its darkness in Jerusalem, and all of his life was turned to light—Nicodemus!

Judas is an enigma. He became a follower of Jesus. He must have been a man of ability to have come to his trusted position in the group. Yet he was a dishonest man. He pretended to be a committed follower of Jesus even when others were turning back (6:60,66,70–71). Still he was stealing from the group funds and plotting to get more money by selling Jesus like a slave. In it all, it was his decision. He was no robot controlled by a dark destiny in which he had no voice. Jesus said, "What you are going to do, do quickly." He had determined to do the black deed; he did it; "and it was night."

The departure of Judas to complete the plans for Jesus' arrest was the signal that the end was very near. Jesus spoke to the eleven remaining apostles about his glorification (vv. 31–32), his going away from them (v. 33), and a new principle for their community life together after he had gone (vv. 34–35). Two particles in verse 31 link Judas' departure to Jesus' glorification. "When" is temporal; "therefore" (erroneously omitted in RSV) is causal. With Judas already on the way to the authorities and because he had gone to them, Jesus could say, "Now is the Son of man glorified" (v. 31). All along his glorification had been identified with his coming death and resurrection. That was still true, but it was so imminent that he could speak of it with the reality of an accomplished fact, literally, "Now has been glorified the Son of man" (v. 31).

In Daniel and 1 Enoch, the "Son of man" is an exaltation concept. In the Psalms and the Synoptics, it is a humiliation concept.

In John and Hebrews, it is a concept of exaltation through humiliation. Through the humiliation of death, Jesus, the Son of man, would experience exhaltation, that is, glorification. The idea is similar to Paul's incarnation hymn in Philippians 2:5–11: Christ is exhalted *because* of his death. In the Philippian hymn, too, God the Father is glorified through the exaltation of the Son. In Jesus' words in this Johannine passage, the Son is glorified in his death and God is glorified in the Son's obedience unto death. In essence Father and Son are one; in Christ's redemptive sacrifice they mutually glorify one another. The glorification would be no distant Parousia in this case; it would be immediate, through the resurrection of Jesus.

Jesus began to prepare the apostles for his departure from them (v. 33). "Little children" is a Johannine term used only here in the Gospel but often in 1 John. It is a term of tenderness and love. He would be with them only "a little while." To the Jews who opposed him in Jerusalem he had said the same thing seven months before, "I shall be with you a little longer" (7:33). Months, weeks, and days had now diminished to hours before his departure to be with the Father. As he said to the Jews on that occasion, he said to the apostles at this time, "You will seek me . . . . Where I am going you cannot come" (7:34; 13:33). The Jews could not go to that place where he would be with the Father because they would die in their sins (8:21). The apostles could not go to it yet because of their continuing ministry after he had gone; they would join him there later (v. 36).

Although they would miss his physical presence and yearn for it, he gave to them a new principle for living the exercise of which would always give them a sense of his spiritual presence. The principle he called a "new commandment," and it was that they "love one another" (v. 34). In one sense it was not a "new commandment"; the Mosaic law included love for one's fellowman. In other respects it was new: (1) It was new in that its model would be the love which he had shown them in humble service (vv. 13–17) and in laying down his life for them (10:11). (2) It was new in that it was a principle of life for the new age, the age between his ascension to the Father and his return for his people in the Parousia. This would be the age of the new covenant promised from God through Jeremiah (31:31–34). In instituting the Memorial Supper, Jesus identified his blood as the ratification of that new covenant (Luke 22:20). (3) It was new in that it was the way people would know that the apostles were his people; the pronoun is emphatic, "By this all men will know that *my* disciples you are" (v. 35, author's translation).

Peter interrupted Jesus to go back to his statement about his going away and their not being able to go to him, "Lord, where are you going?" (v. 36). It was at that point that Jesus told Peter that he could not follow him then, but that he would follow him later. Peter did follow him. He followed in effective service for many years; he followed in death, the death of a martyr; he even followed in the manner of his death, crucifixion. Peter, however, was impatient with the idea of delay. He had sensed that in veiled language Jesus was talking about death. Peter asked impetuously, "Why cannot I follow you now?" He was not afraid of death. If following Jesus meant death, he was willing, "I will lay down my life for you" (v. 37). He was ready to do for Jesus what Jesus had said he was doing for them. Was he really ready? Jesus knew that he was not. With patience for a devoted follower who did not really know what he would do in a time of crisis, Jesus answered, "Will you lay down your life for me? . . . . the cock will not crow, till you have denied me three times" (v. 38). His reference was to the crowing of roosters about daylight. Essentially he said, "Before sunrise in the morning you will have denied three times that you know me." It was a word of caution to Peter. It was given in such way that when it happened, and it did, Peter would remember and be reminded of his frailty (John 18:15–27; Mark 14:54,66–72; Matt. 26:58,69–75; Luke 22:54–62).

Notes

1. A. T. Robertson, *A Harmony of the Four Gospels* (New York: Harper and Brothers Publishers, 1922), pp. 279–284. See also: Hendriksen and Lenski *in loco,* and C. C. Torrey, "In the Fourth Gospel the Last Supper Was the Passover Meal," *Jewish Quarterly* (January 1952) pp. 237–250.
2. With variations in details see Barrett, Brown, Hull, and others *in loco.*
3. Solomon Zeitlin, "The Last Supper as an Ordinary Meal in the Fourth Gospel," *Jewish Quarterly* (January 1952), pp. 251–259.
4. Plummer, pp. 263,359–360.
5. Ibid., p. 360.
6. Joachim Jeremias, *The Eucharistic Words of Jesus* (New York: The Macmillan Company, 1955), pp. 1–60.
7. Ibid., p. 56.

V. Manifestation of the Lamb
14:1 to 20:10

At this point in John we encounter a large block of material which the Synoptics do not contain—chapters 14, 15, 16, 17. Chapter 14 contains teachings of Jesus while he and the eleven apostles remained in the upper room after the departure of Judas. The point of their departure is marked at 14:31 in Jesus' words, "Rise, let us go hence." Chapters 15, 16, and 17 contain teachings (15—16) and prayer (17) between their leaving the upper room and their arrival at the garden of Gethsemane at 18:1. In this study the activities of those chapters will be placed at the Temple. To avoid total confusion in studying the record of all four Gospels on Jesus' activities that night, one must observe the divergence of John and the Synoptics between the triumphal entry of Jesus on Sunday and his arrest in the garden late Thursday night.

John closes the triumphal entry event with Jesus' teachings in the Temple in response to the request of the Greeks to see him (12:50). He has nothing else of Jesus' activities that week until the Last Supper on Thursday night.[1] At the close of the Last Supper, he has the activities of chapters 14 to 17, followed by the arrival at Gethsemane where Jesus was immediately arrested (18:1–11).

The *Synoptics* have a detailed calendar of Jesus' activities for that week. Sunday—At the close of his observing what was going on in the Temple, Jesus returned to Bethany. Monday—He returned to Jerusalem, blighting the barren fig tree on the way, and cleansed the Temple. Tuesday—He had a long day of teaching in the Temple and on the Mount of Olives, followed by the Bethany supper that night. Wednesday—There is no record of activities; it was probably a day of rest. Thursday—After extensive preparation the Passover supper was observed that night followed by the institution of the Lord's Supper; the long prayer agony in Gethsemane was followed by the arrest.[2]

Think of all of this in terms of comparative blocks of material in Matthew (representing the Synoptics) and John. Matthew's block is from 21:12 to 26:56. John's block is from 13:1 to 18:1. The only event which unquestionably is in both blocks is the announcement of Judas as the betrayer (Matt. 26:20–25; John 13:21–30). Each block makes its own tremendous and indispensable contribution to our total understanding of Jesus' actions and teachings of that fateful week. For our present purpose, John 14—17 must be treated as it stands and with even less reference to Synoptic materials than we have previously made. Recall the previously cited statement of Plummer, "In the large gaps left by each there is plenty of room for all that is peculiar to the others."

Manifestation as the Way to the Father
14:1–31

"Let not your hearts be troubled" (v. 1) begins a new emphasis in Jesus' table discourse, but it links directly to his foregoing words. He had said that shortly he would be leaving them (v. 33). He had said that they could not go with him (v. 33). He had said that one of the twelve was a traitor (v. 21). He had said that before the night was over, Simon Peter, the leader of the twelve, would deny that he even knew him (v. 38). Was that not enough to agitate them? The word which is translated "troubled" is the one used of Jesus' agitation at his announcement of his coming betrayal (13:21). The grammatical construction used prohibits the continuation of such agitation on their part: "Stop letting your hearts be troubled." He had passed the stage of agitation and moved into the realm of confident assurance (13:31). So, too, must they. His next statement (v. 1) may be understood in various ways. The two verbs "believe . . . believe" are identical in form. In the inflection of this verb to show tense and mood, this form may be either indicative mood (making a statement of fact or asking a question), or it may be imperative mood (giving a command). Several combinations are possible:

(1) "You believe in God, believe also in me."
(2) "Believe in God; believe also in me."
(3) "You believe in God, and you believe in me."
(4) "Do you believe in God? Believe also in me."

The King James Version translation follows the pattern of number (1), understanding the first verb to be indicative and the second imperative. The American Standard Version, Revised Standard Version and *Today's English Version* all follow the pattern of number (2), understanding both verbs to be imperative. That seems to fit the sense of the situation best. The force of the imperatives is clearer if we recognize the continuous action of the present tense—"keep on believing in God . . . keep on believing in me also." We do well, also, to note that the construction translated "believe in" is John's regular formula for expressing trust—"keep on trusting God . . . keep on trusting me also." Agitation in time of crisis may be a very natural emotion, but for God's people it must give way to trust.

Verses 2–4 contain the first of five reasons which Jesus gave to show the apostles that it was advantageous for them that he go away.[3] He was going in order that he might prepare for them a place of permanent residence in his Father's house. Jesus, a carpenter in this world, was going to prepare dwelling places for his people in the heavenly world! His Father has many children. In his house are sufficient dwelling places for all of them. How one punctuates verse 2 depends on how he interprets it. The Revised Standard Version makes it a question which refers to some previous time when he had told them about the many dwelling places: "if it were not so, would I have told you that I go to prepare a place for you?" The problem is that the Scriptures contain no such previous statement to them. The American Standard Version translates it, "if it were not so, I would have told you; for I go to prepare a place for you." This rather implies that "if it were not so, I would have told you" should be considered as a parenthesis like this: "In my Father's house are many dwelling places (if it were not so, I would have told you) for I am going to prepare a place for you." That meaning is clear; there are many dwelling places because Jesus is going to prepare them and otherwise he would have told them of the lack of sufficient space!

The King James Version translation simply omits the particle which is translated "that" in Revised Standard Version and "for" in American Standard Version and renders it: "if it were not so, I would have told you. I go to prepare a place for you." The omission of the particle has good manuscript support, but the retaining of it has better support. In spite of that, the simplified King James Version translation may be the accurate one. It fits perfectly the total sequence of: (1) the many dwelling places in the Father's house, (2) Jesus' going away to prepare some of them for the apostles, (3) his coming back to receive the apostles for eternal dwelling with him. John's eschatology is not so "realized" that it omits the second coming of Christ to consummate God's purpose for his creation (see 5:28,29; 6:39,40,44,54, and subsequent references to be noted). "I will come again" (v. 3) reflects so precisely the second coming of Christ, as it is reflected in the Synoptics, Acts, and the Epistles, that it cannot be ruled out as the primary reference here. So Christians throughout the ages have claimed this promise for themselves too. We must also recognize the validity of the view of some interpreters that the promise applies to Jesus' coming for his people at the point of their death, as in the case of Stephen (Acts 7:55–60). That would have been particularly meaningful for the apostles who themselves faced death at the hands of Jesus' opponents.

Again, variant manuscripts support the verse 4 readings of both Revised Standard Version ("And you know the way where I am going"), and King James Version ("And whither I go ye know, and the way ye know"). The former has better support, but a bit clearer phrasing of it may be, "And where I am going, you know the way." The genius of *Today's English Version* for simplicity and accuracy may have the best of all, "You know the way that leads to the place where I am going." Primarily he was going to the Father (or the Father's house in the immediate context) and the way to get there was through faith in him. That had been the theme of so much of his controversy with the Jews. Latent in his meaning was the fact that the way he was going to the Father was the way of the agony of the crucifixion and the glory of the resurrection. The way for his followers to go to the Father was by a faith acceptance of that agony and glory as God's provision of redemption. The apostles were still having a problem at that point and would have until they experienced his resurrection.

Thomas, so obscure in the Synoptics but so prominent in John, had a question: Since they did not know where he was going (13:33,36), how could they know the way to that place (v. 5)? Jesus' answer was another of his "I am" claims and a classic of beauty: "I am the way, and the truth, and the life; no one comes to the Father, but by me" (v. 6). That answered both parts of Thomas' question but in reverse—he was going to the Father, and he alone was the way to the Father. Subsequently in the spread of the Christian mission, his people would come to be known as "the people of the Way" (Acts 9:2; 22:4; 24:14).

Well has it been emphasized that he was not the way-shower; he was "the way." The word which is translated "way" is *hodos.* It was the word for road. In Greece today it is the word for highway and so appears on directional signs: the *hodos* to Athens, the *hodos* to Corinth. Jesus was the *road* to God, and he was

the *only* road and still is. That would be the message which the
Christian missionaries would proclaim as they preached in Jerusalem, Judea, Samaria, and to the uttermost parts of the earth—
Antioch, Cyprus, Galatia, Philippi, Athens, Corinth, Rome, and
every stopping place where anyone would listen: "Jesus Christ
is the only way to God." He came from God; he was the chain
to bind men to God; he returned to God; there is no other access
to God. So he taught; so they preached; so the first-century world
believed and was turned upside down (Acts 17:6). When will the
twentieth century learn?

Two other of Jesus' I-am claims are joined to "I am the way."
They are "I am the truth" and "I am the life." They have sometimes been made into modifiers in a clever claim, "I am the true
and living way." The statement cannot be challenged, but it weakens the force of Jesus' claim. All three words are nouns; all three
have the definitive article; and Jesus' pronoun is emphatic: *"I
alone* am *the* way, *the* truth, *the* life" (author's italics). Without
him men lose the way. Without him they walk in error. Without
him the end of thei   Way, he bridges earth
and heaven for ma   ter. As the Truth, he
is that by which all   e is the express image
of God's person (H   mage of the invisible
God" (Col. 1:15). A   stainer of all natural
life, as he is of all c   1:17) and the giver of
all spiritual life (Joh

If heretofore the   is in the full sense of
who he was and w   y would have known
his Father also (v.   comprehended Jesus'
redemptive mission   uld have known also
that the Father who had sent him was redemptive in character.
Henceforth, after his death-resurrection-ascension had become
an accomplished fact, they would know what God is like because
they would have seen him in his Son (v. 7*b*).[4] To know the Son
is to know the Son's Father. No one can know God as fully as

man is capable of knowing God if his back is turned upon the Son and his mind is closed to him.

Philip, another apostle, who is so obscure in the Synoptics but so prominent in John, had a request, "Lord, show us the Father, and we shall be satisfied" (v. 8). He had heard Jesus talk much in the last few months about the Father. Now Jesus had stirred his hunger to know the Father fully by seeing him. His request was the desire of sincere seekers, the longing to see God. He needed more than some sort of spiritual vision; he needed something of substance. Was it too much to ask for a theophany? *Show us; let us see the Father; that is all we are asking.*

Jesus' response was tender and compassionate. He had no rebuke for a sincere seeker who felt that he needed a bit more evidence. His response, however, had an air of weariness for the slow learner: So long, Philip, so long I have been with you and still you do not really know me (v. 9*a*)? Philip had known him since that first follow-me invitation more than three years before (1:43). But he still did not know Jesus in the way Jesus meant: to *know* him was to *see* the Father (13:7). Jesus, therefore, stated his position as clearly as it could be stated, "He who has seen me has seen the Father" (v. 9). Ah! There is the glory of the incarnation. Do we want to know what God is like? Let us look at what God incarnate was like. Do we want to know what God thinks about sin, salvation, and the redeemed life of love? Let us look at what God incarnate taught about them. That is the vision splendid, and it is the only way we can "see" God in the days of our flesh. Let us ask ourselves the question which Jesus asked Philip (v. 9). How can we say, "Show us the Father"? He *has* shown us the Father just by being what he is, the Son of the Father. Christ the God-like shows us God the Christlike. In that revelation, our search for God finds its treasure.

Jesus continued to speak of his revelation of the Father in terms of their mutual indwelling—he is in the Father and the Father is in him. The Son abides eternally in the Father (1:18). The Father dwelling in the Son does his work through him. Jesus asked Philip, "You believe that I am in the Father and the Father is in me, don't you?" (literal translation). We ask ourselves that question and our hearts respond, Yes; beyond our ability to understand it, we believe it. In its ultimate implications, it must remain a faith confession, a part of the mystery of the Trinity.

Jesus made to Philip two appeals for belief that there is a valid sense in which we may speak of Father and Son as dwelling in one another. First, he appealed to his words (v. 10). His teachings were not independent of the Father. It was through the indwelling Father that he taught. Second, he appealed to his works (v. 11). He no more worked independently than he taught independently. Long ago Nicodemus had said "No one can do these signs that you do, unless God is with him." (3:2). Jesus' emphasis would change that to "unless God is *in* him." The Father dwelling in him and working through him accomplished his works. Jesus did not hesitate to appeal to his works or words as evidence of his union with the Father.

Jesus made three promises to the one who trusted in him. One, the one who trusted in him would do works of the same quality as his works (v. 12*a*). Two, the one who trusted in him would do greater works than he had done because he was going to the Father (v. 12*b*). Three, as the trusting one did these works, Jesus having gone to the Father would grant whatever the trusting one asked in his name; he would grant it in order that the Father might be glorified in the Son (vv. 13–14).

Regarding the first promise, it was anticipated that the apostles, in continuing the work after Jesus had departed, would be empowered to perform miracles. This would validate their genuineness as his representatives. They had been so empowered when he had sent them out while he was with them (Matt. 10:1). So they would be empowered after he had departed. The Acts of the Apostles contains evidences of such work by some of the apostles (Peter, John, Paul later on). Regarding the second prom-

ise, the "greater works" that they would do is understood in the
sense of more works. It is not likely that in greatness they would
go beyond his raising Lazarus. They would do more works than
he had done because they would move out in an ever growing
circle of influence and ministry which would see thousands of
people brought to faith in him, Jews and Gentiles alike. This is
another of the advantages in his going away. (See the comment
above on verse three.) It involved not only his going away but
also his sending the Holy Spirit to empower and accompany them,
a theme to be introduced subsequently in this chapter and developed in John 16.

Regarding the third promise, his going away would not mean
that empowering prayer to the Father would cease. One of the
striking phenomena of Jesus' earthly life and ministry is the Gospel
record of his praying, particularly in times of crisis which called
for critical decision about where he was to go and what he was
to do.[5] Now that he was going away, his apostles would pray *as
he had prayed.* That is the meaning of "in my name" (v. 13,
and many other places). They would pray as his representatives.
They would pray as he would pray if he were on earth and in
their situation. To pray in his name, is to pray, "Thy kingdom
come. Thy will be done," as he had prayed and had taught them
to pray (Matt. 6:10). He would grant what they asked in that
spirit. He gave them full assurance, "I will do it" (v. 14). Such
praying on their part and granting on his part would glorify the
Father (v. 13) whom he had glorified by his words and works
throughout his life and in a short time would glorify through
his death.

The remainder of chapter 14 extends his manifestation of himself as the way to the Father, but it introduces another facet of
his manifestation which will be more fully developed in chapter
16, his manifestation as the giver of the Spirit. In these discourses
there is much overlap in back-and-forth references. Although his
giving of the Spirit is developed in chapter 16, there are anticipat-

ing references to it in 14:15–17; 14:25–26; and 15:26–27. In the
continuing exposition, we will note these references as they appear but for the most part will hold their development for the
major thrust in John 16.

In verse 15, Jesus linked his followers' love for him to their
obedience to him in a cause-effect relationship, "If you love me,
you will keep my commandments." "If you love" states the condition; "you will keep my commandments" states the result. The
former states the cause; the latter states the effect. Because they
love him they will keep his commandments. Love is the motivation for obedience. His word was "commandments," but the
meaning which he put into it was more of principle than of legal
stress. Precept may be a better translation. Look back to 13:34,
"A new commandment I give to you, that you love one another."
There and here in 14:15 the word is the same. That which is
involved is a controlling principle of life. The frequently quoted
contemporary ethical maxim is true, You cannot legislate love.
A principle of life, however, can be more compelling than legisla-
tion. Where responsibility to our children is concerned, love goes
far beyond law as a compelling force. Where obedience to our
Lord is concerned, love is more compelling than law.

In a dramatic emphasis, verses 15,21, and 23 form a striking
literary pattern of parallelism. Verses 15 and 21 are set in the
reversed parallelism of chiasmus. Verse 23 reverses verse 21 and
returns to parallel verse 15:

v. 15 "If you love me,   you will keep my command-
                                    ments."
v. 21 "He who has my com-
mandments and keeps
them,   he it is who loves me."
v. 23 "If a man loves me,   he will keep my word."

All three are stating the same basic relationship between love
and obedience in the believer's devotion to his Lord. Verse 21
adds to verse 15 the fact that the one who loves Jesus will be

loved both by the Father and the Son. More than that, the Son will manifest himself, will make himself clearly known to the obedient, loving believer. Verse 23 adds that the Father and the Son will make their home with the one who loves him—a three-way mutual indwelling of Father, Son, and believer.

The one who does not love him does not keep his words; his "words" in verses 23–24 are the same as his "commandments" in verses 15,21. Such a person is rejecting the very words (commandments) of the Father who sent the Son into the world. Verses 23–24 Jesus gave in response to a question by Judas (not Iscariot) as to how Jesus would manifest himself (make himself known) to his followers but not to the world (v. 22). To manifest means to show plainly. If he showed himself plainly to his followers, how was it that the world would not see him? His answer was that he would show himself plainly to them in that he and the Father would come and make their home with them. He would dwell with them not physically, as in the days of his incarnation, but spiritually, through the Spirit's presence with them.

Looking back to verse 16, note that it was to those who obeyed him out of love for him that he would ask the Father to send them "another Counselor" who would be with them forever. Jesus had been with them physically for three years. This Counselor would be with them spiritually forever. The Counselor is called "the Spirit of truth" in verse 17 and the Holy Spirit in verse 26. These passages will be explored fully in the theme of the Holy Spirit in chapter 16. Here we should note that the word which is translated "Counselor" means basically "one who comes to help." The adjective which is translated "another" means "another of the same kind." The Counselor would be another helper of the same kind that Jesus had been to them, and he would be with them forever. The nature of the help which he would give would differ from that which Jesus had given. That facet will be examined later.

So Jesus could say, "I will not leave you desolate; I will come to you" (v. 18). The word which is translated "desolate" is *orphanous* which we transliterate as orphans. It was used of those who were left alone, deprived of comforting support by the death of parents. In nonbiblical literature it was also used of disciples who were deprived of their teacher. Socrates' disciples were made *orphanous* by his death. By Jesus' death his disciples would be deprived of his comforting support, but he would not leave them in that state; he would come to them. Several "coming" sayings in this chapter are ambiguous (vv. 3,18,21,23,28). They are left so they may mean one or more of three "comings" to be with them. They may refer to his post-resurrection coming, to his Pentecost coming, or to his Parousia coming. Verse 19 suggests that in this instance the primary reference is to his post-resurrection coming—the world will not see him; they will see him; his life beyond death will be the guarantee of their life beyond death (v. 19c). Verses 16 and 26 suggest that his coming to them finds an additional application to the coming of the Holy Spirit at Pentecost.

In closing his discourse in the upper room, Jesus gave his peace to the apostles (v. 27). As his parting gift, he left them the peace that he alone can give. He gave it "not as the world gives." The world's peace is temporary; the peace he gives is permanent. The peace the world gives is too often a troubled peace; the peace which he gives quiets troubled hearts and removes their fears. So we sing, "Sweet peace, the gift of God's love." He reminded them again that he would come to them again (v. 28). He called upon them to rejoice because he was going to the Father. He was telling them that his death was not to be defeat but victory. He wanted them to hear it from him then, so when it happened they would believe that it would end in victory. With all of his preparing them for it (see the Synoptics, too), how little were they ready for it!

The time for his talking with them was brief (v. 30). Shortly he would do battle with "the ruler of this world" (Satan), but that one had nothing by which to defeat Jesus, not even death. Jesus, therefore, accepted the Father's purpose for him, death as sacrifice for sin, and by that the world would know of his love for the Father.

His words, "Rise, let us go hence" were the signal for them to leave the room, but by John's manner of interpreting words, they had solemn overtones. He went hence to meet "the ruler of this world" (v. 30). He went hence also to go to the Father (v. 28) in order that others might find in him the Way to the Father (v. 6).

Manifestation as the True Vine
15:1–27

The setting for this very graphic teaching of Jesus is uncertain. The last definable place in these discourses was the room of the Last Supper which presumably they left at 14:31. The next is the garden where he was arrested (18:1). Opinions vary on the setting for these teachings between those two points. Some interpreters do not even mention it. Some mention the question but dismiss it as unanswerable. Some think that when Jesus said, "Rise, let us go hence" (14:31), they arose from their couches, but stood around in the room while Jesus delivered the materials of chapters 15—17 before leading them from the room at 18:1. That seems highly unlikely. Some think that Jesus delivered the teachings of chapters 15—16 and the prayer of chapter 17 as he and the eleven walked through the narrow streets of Jerusalem on the way to the garden. That seems almost inconceivable.

The most plausible view is that on the way to the garden, Jesus led them by the Temple for one last visit. He stood there on the site of so much of his teaching, of Israel's opposition and final rejection, and where the Sanhedrin reached its decision that he had to be executed. The Passover moon made clearly visible the huge gold grapevine carved into the structure of the Temple entrance.[6] Its trunk was taller than a man's head and its branches reached out proportionately with their tremendous gold leaves and bunches of grapes covered by gold leaf. Historically the grapevine was a symbol of national Israel as God's fruit-bearer. John the Baptist, Jesus, Paul, and later the early church felt that Israel had failed in that mission. What more dramatic scene than one of Jesus and the new Israel in nucleus standing before that beautiful but tragic symbol under the light of the Passover moon with Jesus opening his teaching with the words, "I am the genuine vine . . ." (v. 1, author's translation)?

The form of the teaching is allegory, one of the many comparative or likeness categories of the *mashal* which Jesus used so much. He had used this form in his I am the good shepherd teaching in 10:1–18: the shepherd, the fold, the door, the thieves, the "other sheep" which he was to bring. The present *mashal* is not as fully worked out to the fine points of comparison by pure allegory, but the basic ideas are there: the vineyard, the vineyard owner, the vine, the branches both fruit-bearing and non-fruit-bearing ones. As in the allegorical method, much of the fine detail of application is left to the hearer or reader. At that point caution is always in order lest one lose sight of the central thrust of the allegory by pressing for spiritualizing beyond the intended scope of the original purpose.

The structure of the entire chapter is subject to much division of opinion. The great variety of such may be observed in scanning a shelf of commentaries on John. That which is followed here is admittedly subjective and results from accepting and rejecting different parts of many presentations. Verses 1–8 will be presented as the basic allegory. Verses 9–17 will be presented as exhortations based on the allegory. Verses 18–27 will be presented as Jesus' encouragement to the "branches" (the apostles) as they face the difficult days after his departure. The encouragement will close with a reference to the coming of the promised Counselor (v. 26) which makes the transition to chapter 16 and the manifestation of Jesus as the Giver of the Spirit.

Jesus' use of the vine has a solid background in Old Testament history. Many passages have been assembled by interpreters to indicate that background. Three very graphic ones seem sufficient for our purpose: Psalm 80:8–19; Isaiah 5:1–7; Jeremiah 2:21–22. In Psalm 80, Israel is looked upon as a vine which God brought out of Egypt and planted in a land which he had prepared for it. It grew until it covered the mighty cedars of the mountains and its branches stretched from the sea to the river. Then it came to judgment which left it crying for mercy. Isaiah 5:1–7 is an allegorical sermon in poetic form. Israel was planted as a vineyard to bear fruit for God. When God looked for good grapes from it, he found only wild grapes. The sermon, like the Psalm, ends on a note of judgment in which the vineyard would be brought to total ruin by "a nation afar off" (v. 26). Jeremiah 2:21–22 also looks upon Israel as a vine which God planted, "a choice vine, wholly of pure seed," but the vine turned degenerate and produced fruit only as a wild vine does. Lye and soap would not remove her guilt. Judgment lay ahead.

Jesus had thought much of Israel's failure to bear fruit for God. Luke 13:6–9 contains a parable of a barren fig tree. Matthew 21:18–19 and Mark 11:12–14 contain the miracle account of Jesus' blighting a barren fig tree. Mark 12:1–9, Matthew 21:33–41, Luke 20:9–16 all contain Jesus' parable of the vineyard and the wicked husbandmen. It ended with an emphasis on judgment: The owner of the vineyard (God) would destroy the husbandmen (the religious leaders of Israel) and turn the vineyard over to others (Jesus' followers) who would care for it properly. When the leaders caught on that Jesus was talking about them, their response was, "God forbid!" The blighting of the barren fig tree and Jesus' telling the parable of the vineyard had taken place that very week. He saw old Israel as a people who had forfeited their opportunity to be the people of God's redemptive witness (Isa. 40:9) and his followers, the church, as the new Israel to carry out that witness.

The basic allegory is simple and direct (vv. 1–8). In another of his I-am affirmations Jesus said, "I am the true vine," perhaps pointing to himself as he said it. The pronoun is emphatic, "I alone am the true vine." The word which is translated "true" is the word for that which is genuine. As he is the genuine Light (1:9), the genuine Bread (6:32), the genuine Witness (Rev. 3:14), so is he the genuine Vine. With all of its beauty, the gold vine in the Temple structure was but brass compared to him. It was a symbol only, a symbol of a people who had become fruitless. In contrast, all that a vine ought to be and to do, Jesus was. He was the perfect Vine, the ideal Vine.

"My Father is the vinedresser." The word "vinedresser" only partially expresses the Father's role in the allegory. The word which it translates meant basically the one who tilled the soil in the vineyard, but he did much more. He did everything that needed to be done to bring the vines to fruit-bearing—all of that God does in his vineyard. In dressing the vines to effect better production, he takes away the branches that bear no fruit and he prunes the branches that bear in order that they may bear more. Note that where Revised Standard Version has "prunes," King James Version has "purges" and American Standard Version has "cleanses" (v. 2). The King James Version and American Standard Version translations are more accurate, but the Revised Standard Version meaning is more accurate. It may be that the verb for cleanse was used because it rhymes with the verb for takes away thus forming the kind of pun which so often appears in Greek. It is more likely, however, that it was used to prepare the way for the clean idea in the next verse.

The meaning is clear. In order for a vine to be productive, some branches have to be removed because experience has demonstrated that they are not fruit-bearing branches. Such a branch was Judas who had just removed himself by his decision to betray Jesus. Jesus knew that; the eleven did not, but they would before the night was over. The vine's branches that were fruit-bearing would occasionally require the pruning away of matters which would prevent the most effective fruit-bearing. Such a branch might be Simon Peter who, before the night was over, would have some boasting pruned away by tears of shame and repentance. Or Thomas who would need a special encounter with the risen Lord to prune away his skepticism.

The apostles were the Lord's branches. That is clear by his statement in verse 5, "You are the branches." Lest the remaining eleven be too uneasy because of the language of pruning (or cleaning, to get back to the basic meaning of the verb), Jesus spoke words of encouragement to them in verse 3, "You are already made clean." The pronoun is emphatic; it sets them apart from someone. From whom? Judas? Perhaps so. If that is the case, it would mean more to them after Judas' betrayal and his resultant suicide became known. Their being "clean" and Judas' being not clean would be significant in view of Jesus' words when a few hours before he had washed their feet, "you are clean, but not every one of you" (13:10).

They had been cleansed by the word which he had spoken to them (v. 3). The word is a comprehensive reference to all of his teaching in the years of their association with him. It was a saving word which brought to them the spiritual cleansing of redemption (13:10). It was also a pruning word in the sense of its stripping from them many of their old fruitless ideas and practices. This did not mean that all which needed to be stripped away had been. The Vinedresser would continue to prune the branches progressively toward their most effective service.

To experience that preparation for and execution of effective fruit-bearing, they needed to "abide in" Christ and to have Christ abiding in them (v. 4). On the surface, "Abide in me, and I in you" is a strange statement. The first clause has an imperative (abide in me); the second clause has no verb at all. We look in vain for a variant reading with a future tense verb such as "I will abide in you." There is no such variant. *Today's English*

Version so understands it and translates, "Remain united to me, and I will remain united to you." One translation, which I have not found others suggesting, may be a valid one, "Abide in me; I also in you." This would understand the nonexistent future tense verb noted above and at the same time translate the Greek just as it stands. However we translate it, we know what it means. There can be no fruit-bearing apart from a mutual indwelling of the believer and his Lord. That mutual indwelling is at home in Johannine thought, and it is also very prominent under another expression in Paul ("in Christ"). More of Paul's theology can be organized under the "Christ in you—you in Christ" concept than any other of his many concepts.

Jesus explained this mutual indwelling of branches and vine in verse 4. The branch "by itself" (that is, cut off from the vine) can bear no fruit. Just so the believer can bear no fruit by himself, that is, cut off from Christ. Verse 5 repeats the entire proposition: Christ is the vine. The apostles are the branches. The one who abides in him bears much fruit. The one who is apart from him lacks the power to do anything. The dynamic for bearing fruit is not there. Such ones are as useless for fruit-bearing as a brush pile of withered branches. Was he thinking of Judas again?

On the other hand, if the apostles abide in Christ, and his words (teachings) abide in them, they may ask of him whatever they will, and he will grant it. The immediate application of this asking seems to be to the fruit-bearing. They may ask whatever they need in order to make fruit-bearing effective and it will be granted. Boldness? Wisdom? Persuasiveness? Power? He said, "Whatever you will"! Their bearing much fruit glorifies God and demonstrates that they are really his disciples (v. 8).

Jesus' exhortations based on the allegory are set out in verses 9–17. His first exhortation was that the apostles abide in his love (v. 9). It was based on his love for them, the model of which was the Father's love for him. For people devoted to him, that was strong motivation for their heeding the exhortation. To be loved by their Lord in the same way that his Father had loved him was an impelling reason for their abiding in him. To abide in him meant to be joined to him in a fruit-bearing union like that of a vine and its branches (v. 5). Keeping his commandments, following the directions which they had received from him, would assure such union, such abiding in him (v. 10). Their following his directions would be modeled after his following his Father's directions, abiding in the Father's love.

His motive for exhorting them in this way was twofold. First, by their heeding it, his joy would be in them. The joy which he had in his obedience to the Father in all things, including even the cross, would be in them, shared by them. Second, that would mean that their own joy would be made full. They could rejoice with him in the ultimate reach of his sufferings. When in their commitment to him they experienced suffering, they could rejoice in it. A dramatic fulfillment of this may be observed in the apostles' "rejoicing that they were worthy to suffer dishonor in the name" when they were in conflict with the Sanhedrin over their preaching (Acts 5:40–42).

A second exhortation was that they love one another (vv. 12–15,17). It was given in the form of calling them to remember the "new commandment" that he had given to them earlier that night (13:34). He urged them to keep on loving one another, to make loving one another their life practice (present tense). The model for their loving one another was his love for them. He was laying down his life for them; there was no greater demonstration possible. They in turn were emplored to lay down their lives, if necessary, for their friends. They were his friends, not his slaves. He had shared with them as friends everything the Father had told him. His love was that kind of love; so should theirs be for one another.

His third exhortation was that they "go and bear fruit," and it rested upon the fact that he had chosen them and appointed them for that purpose (v. 16). The record of that choice is in three of the Synoptic Gospels (Mark 3:13–19; Matt. 10:2–5; Luke 6:12–16). From all of his disciples (Luke 6:13) and after having prayed all night (Luke 6:12), he chose the twelve "to be with him, and to be sent out to preach" (Mark 3:14). All of the records stress his appointing them to preach. He chose them before they had chosen to follow him (v. 16). The purpose was that they go. That was true in the initial appointment, and after his resurrection it would be true in the Great Commission of Matthew 28:16–20, and the last commission of Acts 1:8.

Here we encounter a question which has been lurking beneath the surface in this entire talk of Jesus about "bearing fruit." What constitutes bearing fruit? Some interpreters identify fruit-bearing with godly living. Plummer specifically rules out "the missionary work of gathering in souls" and identifies it with holiness in life and "good works of all kinds." [7] Lenski states that it confuses and spoils the allegory to relate fruit-bearing to bringing "souls" to Christ.[8] The production of more branches, he states, "is wholly the business of Christ." He then identifies fruit-bearing with the fruit of the Spirit in Galatians 5:22–23: love, joy, peace, long-suffering, gentleness, goodness, faith, meekness, temperance, righteousness, truth. Hendriksen cites a long series of Scripture passages which, he holds, identify fruit-bearing with "good motives, desires, attitudes, dispositions (spiritual virtues), words, deeds, all springing from faith, in harmony with God's law, and done to his glory." [9] He adds that in view of such passages as 4:36 and 12:24, "It certainly is not amiss to point out that the good works of which Jesus is thinking are . . . a means unto the conversion of others."

Other interpreters think of godliness or holy living as an inevitable and natural result of being in union with Christ. They understand fruit-bearing to be the witnessing outreach of the new Israel in missionary activities and the winning of converts to Christ. Brown for example thinks that fruit-bearing implies the communi-

cation of life to others.[10] It involves a growth in love which binds
the Christian to Jesus and spreads life to others. He is positive
that the idea that there were others who had to be brought to
the flock (10:16) was too strong to have been left out of any understanding of what it meant to be united to Jesus. It is his view
that both the notions of going and of bearing fruit have connota-
tions of a mission to others. Strachan states that for the "new
Society," the new Israel, "The enterprise of spreading the Christian faith [and] the belief that Christianity is the absolute and
final religion are not humanly conceived." [11] In relation to fruit-
bearing, "The whole conception of a witnessing and missionary
church is Christ's."

Hoskyns notes that while Christ's work was geographically con-
fined, the apostles' work was to be worldwide.[12] "Their apostolic
activity will consist in bearing fruit, 'catching fish' (xxi:1 sqq.),
making converts . . . . Their converts . . . , those who believe
through the apostolic preaching, will *abide.*" Barrett understands
"go" in verse 16 to refer "to the mission of the apostles to the
world." [13] For him, "that your fruit should abide" in the same
verse was the Lord's assurance that, "The fruits of the apostolic
mission will be gathered in, and not lost." Hovey quotes G. W.
Clark (without further documentation) that "they were to go into
all the world and bring forth fruit, by their godly lives and earnest
teaching winning souls to Christ, founding churches, instructing
and confirming believers in the faith." [14] The fruit which they
gathered would be unto eternal life.

Their commission was to an awesome task. So he reminded
them of what he had told them earlier (14:13–14; 15:7), that in
their abiding in him and in their doing the work for which he
had appointed them, they had the assurance of answered prayer—
whatever they asked the Father in his name would be given (v.
16c). That promise has not been revoked.

Jesus' encouragement as they went out to bear fruit constitutes
verses 18–27. He did not begin on an encouraging note. He spoke

first of the anticipation of the world's hostility as they went out to represent him (v. 18). That was not to deter them. They were to remember that the world hated him before it hated them. Its hatred did not stop him from doing the Father's work. No more should it stop them. His example would encourage them in difficult days.

The world would persecute them (v. 20), acting out its hatred. It would persecute them because they represented him and because it did not know the God who had sent him (v. 21). Because God had sent him and because the world had rejected him, it was without excuse; it was guilty of the sin of hating the God who had sent him (vv. 22–24). It was hatred when they had no cause to hate (v. 25); God had offered only love, mercy, forgiveness, and salvation through regeneration. The world had rejected it all, and it stood self-condemned. The world meant the total of those who set themselves against God and his way, rejected the offer of his love, and determined to go their own way. As the apostles went out to bear fruit, they would encounter all of that. They were encouraged to look back to his example, to recall his triumph in the face of death itself, and to take heart.

The encouragement closed with a renewal of his promise to send the Counselor after he had departed. The Counselor would be "the Spirit of truth, who proceeds from the Father" (v. 26). He would take up the witness concerning Jesus and would lead the apostles in their witness. He would help them to witness out of all they had learned of Jesus in their ministry with him from the beginning. We may look into the Acts of the Apostles and read examples of that witness under the power and guidance of the Holy Spirit. Peter's sermon at Pentecost is a classic example (Acts 2:22–36). His subject was "Jesus of Nazareth" and his points were: his life, his death, his resurrection, his exaltation, his giving the Spirit, his lordship. The world heard, and the world responded—three thousand converts in one service! Their Lord had not left them desolate.

Manifestation as the Giver of the Spirit
16:1–33

This chapter, with supporting references from chapters 14 and 15, is the most comprehensive Gospel teaching on the Holy Spirit. In the total New Testament teaching, it stands with other great sections on this doctrine: the entire book of Acts; Romans 8; 1 Corinthians 12—14.

Introductory to the entire Gospel section, one must observe the basic and extended meanings of the word which Jesus used for the Holy Spirit—Paraclete, transliterated from the Greek *paraklētos*. Its translation varies in different versions: "Comforter" (KJV and ASV); "Counselor" (RSV); "Helper" (TEV). The preferred translation in contemporary use, Paraclete, avoids the ambiguity of these three terms. The verb from which the noun form is derived meant basically "to call to one's side" for help or assistance of some sort. That is very general. In nonbiblical use, two lines of help developed: to serve as an advocate; to serve as one who helps or consoles. Both ideas appear in its use in John.

The Paraclete idea is used five times in the Gospel: four times the noun is used (14:16–17; 14:25–26; 15:26; 16:7–11); once a pronoun is used (16:12–15, "that one"). In 1 John the noun form is used once (2:1).[15] In these passages in the Gospel, the Paraclete would help the apostles in many ways: he would teach them, guide them, explain Jesus' teachings, speak of things to come, bear witness on Jesus' behalf, recall to their memory things which Jesus said, console them in their grief. In relationship to the hostile world which does not believe in Jesus, the Paraclete would convict sinners, convince them of Jesus' righteousness, and judge them. In the one use of the word in 1 John, the Paraclete would be an advocate to plead the case of believers before God. It should be noted that in this passage it is Christ who is the advocate, not the Holy Spirit. The concept of advocate is a very fitting one in several of the Gospel references—those relating to witnessing, convicting, judging. Plummer uses it for all of the references in John.

Introductory to this Gospel section, too, is the different ways of referring to the coming of the Paraclete. In 14:16, the Father will send the Paraclete at Jesus' request. In 14:26, the Father will send the Paraclete in Jesus' name. In 15:26, Jesus will send the Paraclete from the Father. In 16:7, Jesus will send the Paraclete. These statements are not to be regarded as inconsistencies. They are very much in line with Jesus' teachings on his oneness with the Father. They do not act independently; what one does involves the other. In the same way, Jesus said that the Paraclete would not act independently, "on his own authority" (16:13). He would take the things which belonged to Jesus (16:14) and use them in his teaching. He would remind the disciples of what Jesus had told them. All of this working together of Father, Son, and Holy Spirit is a part of the mystery of the Trinity. We recognize the doctrine of the Trinity as biblical, and we confess it. We are more at ease with it when we are singing our beautiful and moving Trinitarian hymns than when we are trying to explain it.

Jesus' first reference to the Paraclete is in 14:16. It followed his discourse and dialogue with his disciples about his going to the Father. He promised them that having gone, he would ask the Father to give them "another Counselor." In contrast with Jesus' having been with them physically for a few years, this Counselor would be with them spiritually forever. Jesus identified him further as "the Spirit of truth" (v. 17). That identification is repeated in 15:26 and 16:13. As Jesus is "the truth" (14:16), the Paraclete is "the Spirit of truth." He would guide Jesus' followers into all truth (16:13); many interpreters prefer to translate "in all truth." A part of his work would be the communication of truth without error to the hearts of men. He would do that as the witness to and the bearer of the revelation of the Father in the Son.

The unbelieving world (14:17) could not receive the Spirit of truth because it had rejected that revelation. For them, the Paraclete's words fell on ears which were deaf to that witness. In 1 John 4:6, the world holds to "the spirit of error" in rejecting the incarnation of God in Jesus Christ. That "spirit of error" is set in contrast to the "spirit of truth" which characterizes those who accept that incarnation. In the Gospel reference, the disciples could receive the Spirit of truth, the Paraclete, because they had accepted the revelation. The Spirit of truth dwelt with them in fellowship and in them in power.

Jesus' second reference to the Paraclete is in 14:26. In this passage the Paraclete is identified as the Holy Spirit. He was to be sent by the Father in the name of Jesus. Recall from earlier references that "in the name" of one meant in that one's place. The Holy Spirit would take his place with the disciples as the spiritual presence of their physically departed Lord and Teacher. This is no Johannine denial of the doctrine of the second coming of Christ. In the exposition of 14:3 we noted that there is room in John's eschatology for that doctrine. His emphasis on the presence of the living Christ with his people in the here and now is distinctive. He wrote at a time when the seeming delay of the Lord's return had come to be a critical problem for many Christians.[16] John's emphasis is that such a "delay" from human perspective should not leave the Lord's people with a sense of desolation in his absence (14:18). Through the Holy Spirit, he is present now. His people, therefore, should not be discouraged and feel deprived of his presence. While the *now* of his presence and the *not yet* of his second coming is not a major emphasis in John as it is in the Synoptics, Acts, and the Epistles, it is a valid part of Johannine eschatology. (Review again 5:28–29 and 6:39,40,44, and 54.)

The Holy Spirit's presence viewed as the spiritual presence of Christ with his people (14:26) does not mean that he had no being as personality other than that spiritual presence of Christ.

References in verses 16 and 17 affirm the Spirit's personality apart from both the Father and the Son, just as the personality of the Son apart from the Father is elsewhere affirmed. Nor is this tritheism. God is one; he reveals himself to us and we know him and experience him as Father, Son, and Spirit—again, the mystery of the Trinity.

As the Spirit of truth/Paraclete was to be with the disciples for fellowship and in them for power (v. 17), so the Holy Spirit/ Paraclete was to be with them as their teacher (v. 26). Jesus' teaching of the disciples had been limited by their inability to grasp many of the things which he spoke. That was especially true of his teaching regarding his glorification through death, resurrection, and ascension. They just did not have the equipment for understanding it. The Synoptics record that the apostles resisted Jesus' teaching regarding his coming death on the first occasion of his giving it (Mark 8:31–33; Matt. 16:21–23; Luke 9:22), and on the second occasion, they did not understand it, were filled with sorrow because of it, and were afraid even to ask questions about it (Mark 9:32; Matt. 17:23; Luke 9:45). The coming of the Holy Spirit in his office work would be after those things were accomplished fact. He would call to the disciples' remembrance what Jesus had said and would lead them into an understanding of it all.

Jesus' third reference to the Paraclete is in 15:26. As he was in 14:17, he is identified again as the Spirit of truth, and Jesus sends him from the Father (v. 26). This is the clearest single reference in John to the three persons of the Trinity (*Jesus* sends the *Spirit* from the *Father*). In this instance, Jesus stated that the work of the Spirit of truth/Paraclete would be to witness. He would bear witness to Jesus. To bear witness is to give evidence. Through his recalling Jesus' teachings and his relating them to their fulfillment in Jesus' experience, he would give evidence of the truth of God's redemptive revelation in Christ. Through the disciples who had been with Jesus in his ministry, had observed his signs, had heard his teachings, and finally had experienced his death and resurrection, the Holy Spirit would bear witness. He would be witnessing through every testimony which they bore. He would be witnessing through every sermon which they preached. He would be witnessing through every act of their ministry. The "acts of the apostles" would in reality be "the acts of the Holy Spirit."

The Spirit and the world is the major emphasis in 16:1–11. This is a continuation of Jesus' discussion of the world's hostility for the apostles (15:18–25) and the Spirit's witness that the world is wrong in rejecting Jesus and the apostles (15:26–27). In pointing back to that theme of the world's hostility, Jesus told the disciples why he was giving them this warning. It was to prepare them for the persecution which they would face after his departure and to prevent their "falling away" from their appointed mission to witness (16:1). He warned them of the severity of the hostility which they would face. It would involve excommunication from the synagogue (v. 2). The official decision on that had already been made (9:22). It would involve martyrdom. The time would come when the killing of a Christian would be regarded as an act of service to God. That time came soon after Pentecost. When Paul looked back on his own persecution of Christians which involved killing them (Acts 7:54 to 8:3; 26:9–11; Gal. 1:13), he said that he did it because of his zeal for God. He thought it was what God wanted. There was precedent for such an idea in Jewish history. Based on the priestly honor bestowed upon Phinehas for killing Zimri and his Midianite harlot, an ancient rabbinical interpretation of Numbers 25:10–13 held that the shedding of the blood of a blasphemer was the offering of a blood sacrifice to God. Jesus attributed the hostility of the Jews for his followers to the fact that they knew neither the Father nor the Son (v. 3). They did not have the fatherhood of God because they rejected the sonship of Jesus.

Jesus had not previously spoken so plainly of future persecution of his followers because, up to this point, the hostility had been against him and because he had been with them personally to help if any hostility arose (v. 4). Now that he was going away and would not be present with them when hostilities arose, he thought it proper to warn them (v. 5). In his absence, however, they would not be without help. He was going to send the Paraclete in his place, another of the advantages to them in his going away (v. 7). In relation to the world, the mass of the unbelievers who were rejecting Jesus and would persecute his apostles, the work of the Paraclete/Spirit would be the convicting of the world of sin, of righteousness, and of judgment. This convicting work of the Spirit could not be done in the complete sense until Jesus' death, resurrection, and return to the Father had become a matter of history, an accomplished fact. That was Jesus' reason for saying that the Spirit would never come unless he departed to the Father (v. 7). The sequence of Jesus' going and the Spirit's coming was encompassed within the redemptive work of God.

What English word best conveys the meaning of the word which is used for the Spirit's work? It is translated "reprove" (KJV), "convict" (ASV), and "convince" (RSV). An entire clause is used instead of one word in *Today's English Version,* "he will prove to the people of the world that they are wrong." That is very exactly the meaning of the passage regardless of the single word which one chooses in translation. "Reprove" (KJV) seems the least desirable of the three major version translations. In common use it conveys the idea of rebuking, but much more than rebuke is involved here. "Convict" (ASV) seems to be the best choice for expressing the idea of the Spirit's work with reference to sin. In common use "to convict" one of sin seems more precise than "to convince" one of sin. On the other, "to convince" (RSV) one of the righteousness of Jesus Christ and of judgment involved in rejecting him seems a bit better than "to convict."

This threefold work of the Spirit in relation to the world is defined more precisely in verses 9–11. He will convict the world of the sin of unbelief in rejecting Jesus as God's Redeemer (v. 9). While the basic sin of rebellion against God and the acted out sin of disobedience to God are not excluded, the ultimate sin in John's Gospel is unbelief—the active, conscious disbelief in Jesus Christ as the one whom God has sent as the Redeemer. He will convict (or convince) the world of Jesus' righteousness (his rightness) because of his going to the Father. That involved his death and his resurrection. Jesus died—a death of sacrifice on an altar built in the form of a cross. It was the sacrifice of the Lamb slain in the purpose of God before the foundation of the world (Rev. 13:8, KJV). But it did not end there. He was raised from the dead, and in the process, he was so transformed that he could never die again. More than that, having completed his redemptive work, he returned to the Father who had sent him. The work of the Spirit included the use of his death-resurrection-ascension to prove to the world that Jesus was right in his claim that he had been sent by the Father for that very purpose. Read Peter's sermon at Pentecost (Acts 2:22–36) as a sample of apostolic witness to that total event. Read the result of that witness empowered by the Holy Spirit (Acts 2:37–42) as an example of what Jesus was predicting of the Spirit's work.

The Holy Spirit would convict (or convince) the world of judgment because at the cross of Jesus, "the ruler of this world" was judged (v. 11). Jesus was not the defeated one in that struggle with the power of evil, the forces of darkness. He was the victor. The one who was defeated was Satan. The cross was God's judgment on sin and Satan. At the cross, the redemptive righteousness of God and the sin of the world met on collision course. Where the vertical line of God's righteousness meets the horizontal line of man's sin there is what the Greeks called *krisis*. Our word for it is "judgment," and toward that goal moves every man apart from faith in Jesus Christ.

The Spirit and the apostles is the emphasis of verses 12–15. In the long range of history this may well be called "the Spirit and the Church." What the apostles did through the power of the Spirit following Pentecost has been the mission task of the church through the ages. Jesus could have told them much more about what faced them for the remainder of that night and for the days and years ahead. They, however, would not have understood (v. 12). They were burdened down with sorrow and perplexity over his veiled talk about his departing to be with the Father. They needed the background of his death and resurrection as an aid to understanding. To help them at that point was a part of the work of the Spirit of truth who was to come after those events had transpired.

The Spirit would be their guide "into all the truth" (v. 13). "In" is a better translation than "into." The word which is translated "guide" is a compound verb meaning to lead along the road. The Spirit would guide them by leading them along the road of total truth. Truth is the realm or the sphere in which he would be their guide. Redemptive truth, related to Jesus' death and resurrection, is the major emphasis; but it is only a part of the total truth in the study of which the Spirit of truth would guide them. He would not speak independently, "on his own authority" (v. 13). He would speak what he heard in union with Father and Son (another emphasis on the mutual indwelling of Father, Son, and Spirit). The Spirit would glorify the Son because he would take the Son's teachings and explain them to the apostles (v. 14). More than that, these teachings were not the Son's alone; the Son had received them from the Father (v. 15). Just as the Son glorified the Father in his teachings, so would the Spirit glorify the Son in his.

The Spirit's leading them in all truth would include his aiding them to understand the things that were to come, future developments (v. 13). Two large areas of future events may be envisioned in this ministry. One, there would be the enlarging ministry of the church in its missionary outreach. The Gospels contain some teachings of Jesus regarding the worldwide scope of his redemptive witness and the responsibility of his followers to get that message out to all men. That was particularly true in his teaching between his resurrection and his ascension. Evidences of it are especially clear in Luke 24:46–29; John 20:19–23; Matthew 28:18–20; Acts 1:8. That was small, however, compared to the emphasis on world witness after the Spirit came at Pentecost. Under his guidance, they came to see that the one God had provided one Way of salvation, and it followed naturally that the one Way was for all people—Jew and Gentile. It was the responsibility of the apostles to take that message to all people. Through their witness, the Spirit would bring to harvest the seed which they would sow. He would convict. He would convert. He would judge.

Two, another large area of understanding would be in eschatology. In that area, too, the Gospels contain some teachings of Jesus. The disciples, however, were handicapped in their understanding. As long as he was with them in the flesh, his talk about coming again did not mean as much as it would after his going away in the ascension. Too, they were handicapped in understanding his teaching about resurrection until they had experienced his resurrection. The foundation for New Testament eschatology is in Jesus' teachings. The superstructure of the tremendous emphasis on eschatology, God's ultimate purpose for his creation, is in the remainder of the New Testament. It grew as the Spirit of truth led them along the road of truth in teaching them of the things that were to come (v. 13).

When Jesus had finished his teaching on the ministry of the Holy Spirit to the apostles, he returned to the theme of his going to the Father (v. 16). He seemed reluctant to drop the subject. He had spoken of it on Sunday, the day of his triumphal entry (12:35–36). During the activities of this Thursday evening, he had brought it up and then dropped it several times (13:33–36; 14:1–6,12–14,18,27–28; 16:4–7). As he renewed the subject, he said that in a little while they would see him no more and then in a little while they would see him again (v. 16). From the perspective of history, we know that he was speaking of his death on Friday and his resurrection on Sunday. We think that the apostles were being very dull because according to the Synoptics he had talked to them on at least three occasions about his death and his resurrection on the third day afterward (Matt. 16:21–23; 17:22–23; 20:17–19 and parallels in Mark and Luke). We need to recall that on the first occasion they argued the question with Jesus, and on the other two they simply refused to consider it. Now they greeted his statement by indicating to one another that they did not understand what he meant (vv. 17–18).

Jesus sensed their need for further explanation (v. 19) and answered their question before they asked it. He spoke of their coming experience of sorrow in not seeing him and their subsequent joy in seeing him again (v. 20). The time of their sorrow in not seeing him would be a time of the world's rejoicing in not seeing him. Again, we know that this was a veiled reference to his death and burial. He tried to lift their sorrow a bit by an analogy of the suffering of a woman in childbirth and her subsequent rejoicing in the baby who is born of those sufferings (vv. 21–22).

In verses 23–24 Jesus used two different verbs for asking. Each one may mean either to ask questions or to ask in prayer. In this context Jesus appears to use one for asking questions and the other for asking in prayer. First, when they saw him again, there would be no need for their *asking questions* (Where are you going? How can we know the way? What do you mean by a little while when we will not see you?) as they had been doing (v. 23*a*). Then they would have knowledge which would require no such questions. Second, changing to the idea of *asking in prayer*, there would always be a place for them to ask in his name that the Father grant their needs as they did his work (v. 23*b*). Jesus assured them that they would receive whatever they asked in that spirit (v. 24) and that it would make their joy full. Thus his going away and return would mean for them fullness of knowledge (v. 23*a*), fullness of confidence in prayer (v. 23*b*), and fullness of joy (v. 24).

Granting that he had been speaking to them "in figures" (v. 25), a word for likeness sayings similar to parable, he spoke to them very plainly in a beautifully phrased chiasmus (v. 28): "I came from the Father and have come into the world . . . . I am leaving the world and going to the Father." Their response in verses 29–30 is a bit perplexing. There is an almost frivolous air of relief about it: (1) they know that he knows all things; (2) they know that there is no need for anyone to question him; (3) they believe that he has come from God. Let us examine the three. Number (1) seems to indicate that since he knew that they wanted to ask him for further explanation even though they did not ask (v. 19), they concluded that he knew everything; that is, he had supernatural knowledge. He had read their thoughts as he had read the character of Simon Peter (1:42), Nathanael (1:47), Nicodemus (3:3), the Samaritan woman (4:17–18), Judas Iscariot (6:70–71). They seem to have gone back to his responding to their unasked question and to have simply dismissed the matters of their not seeing him and then their seeing him again (v. 16) and his coming from the Father and his returning to the Father (v. 28).

Number (2) seems to indicate that they had concluded that there was no need for anyone to question a person who had the kind of knowledge he displayed. Number (3) indicates that they had decided to accept his statement that he had come from God. There was an air of self-pride in their making that confession. How could they have been so nonchalant about his statement that he was going to leave the world and return to the Father? Were they thinking of a departure like that of Elijah? They could hardly have been thinking of departure by Roman crucifixion.

Jesus called them back to the reality of their situation (v. 31). His response to their blithely given confession was a question, "Do you now believe?" (v. 31), and a sobering prediction (vv.

32–33). He said that when the hour of crisis came, the apostles would scatter to their own homes (or affairs) and leave him alone. The words of Zechariah 13:7 would be appropriate; when the Shepherd was smitten, the sheep would scatter.[17] Mark's short but graphic report of their conduct at Jesus' arrest is a word of fulfillment, "And they all forsook him, and fled" (14:50). His words, "You . . . will leave me alone" were fulfilled. None of them stood by him. Judas had already departed to arrange the betrayal. Peter and John observed a part of his trial (18:15–16), and that nearness led to Peter's denial of the charge that he was one of Jesus' followers (vv. 17–27). John was at the crucifixion (19:26–27). There is no record of the others during his trial and death.

Another word of prediction was, "Yet I am not alone, for the Father is with me" (v. 32). He was fully confident of the Father's sustaining presence because he was doing the Father's will even in death. There would be that one terrible moment when he would feel that even the Father had abandoned him to suffer alone, when out of the darkness, wrung from his lips, would come the words of the wretched psalmist, "My God, my God, why hast thou forsaken me?" (Matt. 27:46; Ps. 22:1). His closing words spoke to them in terms of assurance, "I have said this to you, that in me you may have peace" (v. 33). The translation "this" is misleading. The demonstrative pronoun is plural and should be rendered "these things" (as in KJV and ASV). "These things" may refer to his teachings regarding the coming of the Holy Spirit to help and comfort them. Most likely it refers to the discourses of the entire evening, at least those of chapters 14—16. He had made it an evening of preparation for them in view of his going away and of their continuing his ministry. In union with him they would experience peace. Even when it was peace under pressure, it would stabilize them in their service. "Tribulations" is the translation of a word for pressure. It was the word for grinding grain or pressing grapes in the winepress. Ahead of them "in the world" were crushing, grinding tribulations (v. 33*b*). In

Christ, by contrast, there was peace, the total integration of the person who is committed to him. He admonished them, therefore, to "be of good cheer" because he had conquered that world. Most of the standard versions render this verb "be of good cheer." Does that really convey the Lord's meaning in a word which means "to be courageous?" The *Today's English Version* translation fittingly is, "Be brave." They were going into battle with the forces of evil. He bade them be brave because he had conquered those forces. In the purpose of God, the defeat of those forces of evil could be viewed as an accomplished fact. By his death and resurrection, he was dealing the conquering blow to sin and death. The Spirit whom he was giving would be with them and would assist them in taking that message of victory to all the world.

Manifestation as the High Priest
17:1–26

In chapter 17 we move into the inner sanctuary, the very holy of holies, of the Gospel of John. "When Jesus had spoken these words" (v. 1) refers to the discourses of chapters 14—16 and indicates that Jesus had finished his teaching. "He lifted up his eyes to heaven" (v. 1) signals the beginning of a closing, farewell prayer. Where else in John or in all the Scriptures would one go for the combination of simplicity of language and profundity of meaning which follows in this prayer in which Son talks to Father with complete candor and confidence in the very shadow of tragedy and triumph?

In seeking for an appropriate title for the prayer, Hoskyns (p. 494) calls it "the Prayer of Consecration." Hovey (p. 333) prefers "the Lord's Prayer." In slightly varying terms, Brown (p. 747), Plummer (p. 297) and Strachan (p. 398) refer to it as "the Prayer of the High Priest." Barret (p. 417) recognizes both the "consecration" and "high priest" terminology but thinks that neither one does justice to the full range of the material in the prayer.

Both Brown and Hoskyns cite the reference to John 17 as "the high-priestly prayer" by the sixteenth-century Lutheran theologian, David Chytraus. Brown goes on back to the early fifth-century Cyril of Alexandria and his reference to Jesus in John 17 as a high priest making intercession on behalf of his people. Brown notes that if Jesus is interpreted as a high priest here, it must be understood that it is more in the role of intercession than in making sacrifice.

The following exposition will be made from the stance that Jesus is properly viewed as high priest in John 17 and that as such he both offers sacrifice and makes intercession. The sacrifice which he offers is himself in death on the cross. To that end he consecrates himself (RSV) or sanctifies himself (ASV,KJV) as stated in verse 19. Here is a striking similarity between John and the letter to the Hebrews. In vocabulary, grammar, and rhetorical structure the two books are poles apart, but in Christology, particularly at the point of high priesthood, they are very much alike. In Hebrews the sacrifice which Christ as high priest offers is his own blood (9:11 to 10:14), and through it he secures eternal redemption for sinful humanity (9:12).

In Hebrews, as an eternal high priest, Christ also makes intercession between man and God (7:23–25). Likewise in John he makes intercession, pleading for his disciples and for all believers. That is plainly marked out in the structure of the prayer. In verses 1–5, he prays for himself as he faces the cross. In verses 6–19, he prays for the disciples whom he is leaving to witness to a hostile world. In verses 20–24, he prays for believers through the ages, beginning with those who will become believers through the witness of the disciples. Verses 25–26 breathe the spirit of commitment as Jesus sums up the incarnation event in two sentences. What more fitting time for such a prayer than between the Last Supper in the upper room and the arrest in the garden? What more appropriate place for a high-priestly prayer than in the Temple?

Jesus prays for himself (vv. 1–5). Yet in the final sense, his prayer was for the glorification of the Father through the Son more than for his own glorification. In the continuing consciousness of sonship, he addressed God as "Father." In the agony prayer of the Synoptics the same is true—"My Father" in Matthew 26:39, and the tender Hebrew family word *"Abba"* followed by the Greek *patēr,* "Father" in Mark 14:36. Throughout this high-priestly prayer, the spirit is that of the beautiful simplicity of a son's confident talking with his father. It was on that confident basis that Jesus made his first petition, "glorify thy Son." He prayed thus in the recognition that the long-anticipated "hour" had come; review the comments on "the hour" in 2:4 and 12:23. Now had come the last in a series of crisis points in his earthly life. He prayed that in it, his death, he would be glorified by the Father. If death was to be the end of this crisis point, there would be no glory for Son or Father. Death was not to be the end. He looked beyond the cross to the empty tomb and his ascension to the Father. He would be glorified by that return to the glorious presence of the Father and the glorious relationship which he had with the Father before the incarnation. Literally translated, the verb indicates "which he was having."

His prayer for the Father to glorify him was not a selfish prayer. His glorification would mean the glorification of the Father, and it was for that ultimate result that he prayed "that the Son may glorify thee." In Paul's "hymn of praise" to the redemptive work of the Trinity (Eph. 1:3–14), each of the three stanzas (the work of the Father, of the Son, of the Holy Spirit) closes with the refrain "to the praise of his glory." [18] All that God has done in providing redemption for sinful man redounds to his glory and his praise. It was that for which the Son prayed as he prayed for himself that even in the agony and shame of a Roman crucifixion, he would bring glory to the Father.

The Father had entrusted to the Son the authority to give eternal life (v. 2; see comments on 5:25–26). He had given that eternal life to those whom the Father had given to him; the disciples were the ones who were in the immediate focus, but the gift was not to them alone. Eternal life consists in knowing the Father, "the only true God" and in knowing the Son whom the Father sent (v. 3). Here is repeated the theme which Jesus had frequently discussed—redemption through faith identification with Father and Son. Only those who accept the sonship of Jesus Christ may have the fatherhood of God.

In granting that eternal life, the Son had glorified the Father while he was on earth (v. 4), or as it is expressed in Hebrews, "in the days of his flesh" (5:7). He had accomplished what the Father had appointed him to do. Now he prayed that the Father would glorify him by receiving him into that glory which he had with the Father "before the world was made" (v. 5). The glory which he had with the Father was not just before the incarnation; it was before the world came to be. In fact, John begins with the preexistence of Christ—the affirmation that "in the beginning" the Word was with God and that he was the agent of God in creating everything which was created (1:1–3). It was not, however, just to that same state of being that he would return to God. He would return in his glorified humanity as an eternal indication of his redemptive work in incarnation, death, and resurrection. That, too, would be to the glory of both Father and Son. It would also be to the advantage of the redeemed because he would be an understanding and merciful High Priest. He had shared man's humanity: his temptations, his needs, his sorrow, his pain, even his death, as well as his joys (Heb. 4:14–16). To such a High Priest the redeemed can go in full confidence that they will find help right at the time they need it, the precise meaning of Hebrews 4:16.

Jesus prays for his disciples (vv. 16–19). It is at this point that his role as an *intercessory* High Priest comes into focus. As his work and witness had glorified God, so would their work and witness glorify God. To that ultimate end he prayed for them and dedicated them to the Father and for their service to him.

Verses 6–8 are introductory in stating the *basis* for the intercession. He had manifested the name of the Father to the disciples whom the Father had given to him (v. 7). "Manifest" is a favorite Johannine word. It is used frequently in this Gospel and in significant places in 1 John and Revelation. It is a word for revealing or making clear. His manifestation was made to people who were prepared to receive it. "Thine they were" indicates that in some sense the disciples, for whom he prayed in that tender moment, had belonged to the Father before he gave them to the Son. In what sense? It must include the strong predestinarian emphasis of this Gospel that in the infinite foreknowledge and purpose of God, these were a part of the redeemed by God's election.[19] It may also include the fact that at least some of them were committed to God as disciples of John the Baptist before they ever met Jesus (1:35–42) men who in the language of Luke 2:25 were "righteous and devout, looking for the consolation of Israel." In any case, they also belonged to God through their belief in his Son, and he had "given" them to the Son as apostles.

To them, Jesus had manifested the "name" of God. That name is not given explicitly in the Gospel. Plummer (p. 70) suggests that it may have been *Logos.* Brown (p. 764) thinks that it was I AM. In either case its application as a title for Jesus in this Gospel would emphasize his oneness with God and his full expression of the will and nature of God. Of one thing we can be fully certain—in Hebrew thought and use the *name* commonly stood for the *character* of the one who bore it. It was regarded as an index for telling not only *who* one was but *what* he was like. So the Son, visible as the incarnate Logos, had made known the character of the invisible God (1:18; 14:7,9); the Son manifested to the disciples the redemptive nature of the Father. They, in turn, became obedient to the Father's word (v. 6*c*); they came to understand that the teachings which Jesus had given them had been given to him by the Father (v. 7); they came to believe

that God had sent him into the world (v. 8). Through their knowledge of God as he was revealed in Jesus, they had come to the
faith that his redemptive work in its entirety had originated in
God. The God of creation is the God of redemption; that truth
is the foundation for *all* biblical theology.

Verses 9–19 contain the *content* of Jesus' intercession for the
disciples, "I am praying for them" (v.9), making request for them.
This was to be a highly specialized prayer; its circle was reduced
to exclude everybody except the eleven and their need. It is
spiritual nearsightedness which borders on blasphemy to suggest,
as some have, that "I am not praying for the world" (v. 9) indicates
that Jesus had no concern for the world. He had many concerns
other than his concern for the eleven. He had other followers
who believed in him; he had family members who were dear
to him. He would have been less than human, to say nothing of
less than divine, to have had no concern for them. If his Father
loved the world enough to give his only Son for its redemption
(3:16) and if the Son loved it enough to lay down his life for it
(10:17–18), he was concerned about it. Even from the cross he
would pray for those who had nailed him to the cross and were
rolling dice to divide his clothing while he died (Luke 23:34).
There was room in his heart for *all* the world, but at the moment,
his expressed concern was for a very special group in a very
special situation.

In praying for those who belonged to him, he was praying for
ones who belonged to the Father also; indeed, they had been
given to him by the Father (v. 9). As he had glorified the Father
through his life of love and obedience, his disciples had glorified
him through their life of love and obedience (v. 10). He had given
them the Father's word (teachings), and because of their acceptance of it and committment to it, the world was hostile to them
(v. 14). As their Lord was not "of the world," neither were they
"of the world," and for that reason the world hated them and
their Lord (v. 16). To be "of the world" meant to share its sense

of values, its life-style, its practices. To be "not of the world" meant to believe and to live a life which was founded upon a sense of values and life-style that was diametrically the opposite of that of the world. For that, the world hated them. It was preparing at that very moment to kill their Lord. It was only natural to anticipate that it would vent the same destructive wrath on the disciples.

In a few hours Jesus would be leaving the world. It was so near and so real that he could speak of it as already accomplished, "I am no more in the world" (v. 11). Beyond the shame and agony of the cross there was blessedness, "I am coming to thee." He would be returning to the glory he had known with the Father before the incarnation, before there was a world of sin, suffering, and death (v. 5). That was not true of the disciples; he was leaving them in the world to continue the work which he had been doing (v. 11). While he had been with them, he had "kept them" (v. 12), meaning to look carefully to their welfare. He had kept them as the Father's representative, "in thy name." It was a sacred trust and he had fulfilled it. "I have guarded them," a stronger expression than "I kept." He had absorbed the world's hostility so it did not get to them to injure them. The world had been able to get to only one of them, Judas. Judas was responsible for all of his actions. he chose to do what he did. Still his treachery could be set in the pattern of the fulfillment of Scripture. "That the scripture might be fulfilled" is a reference to Psalm 41:9. Review the comments on Judas' action in the exposition of 13:18 and the other references to his actions in 6:71; 13:2,18,26,30; 15:2,6.

Near the time when he would leave the world, but while he was still in the world, Jesus as their High Priest prayed for the apostles. He prayed in their hearing. He prayed that the joy which he knew even in the midst of hostilities and in the shadow of the cross might be fulfilled in them too (v. 13). For him it was the joy of a life of conformity to the Father's will; of love for the Father and for his disciples; of communion with the Father;

of confidence in the Father; of commitment to the service of the Father. All of that joy he desired for them. In the difficult days which were ahead, they would remember that he had prayed for them, and they would be stronger for it. How exhilarating to hear one whom we love and trust say, "I am praying for you"— and even more, to hear the prayer itself. How exhilarating for them to hear their Lord praying for them.

> Holy Father, keep them
>   in thy name (v. 11)
>   from the evil one (v. 15).
> Holy Father, consecrate them
>   in thy word (v. 17)
>   for thy service (v. 18).
> Holy Father, I consecrate myself
>   for their sake (v. 19a)
>   for their own consecration (v. 19b)

While "Father" was Jesus' customary address in prayer in both the Synoptics and John, it does not appear elsewhere with the adjective *holy*. It is important here because it relates to the nature of God, and that nature will be involved in Jesus' first petition for the disciples, "Keep them in thy name." God as holy is a major concept in the Old Testament and it carries over into the New. The two join in attributing holiness to God when the four living creatures surrounding his throne in Revelation 4 borrow from the seraphim above his throne in Isaiah 6 to sing, "Holy, holy, holy . . . Lord God Almighty."

Jesus prayed first that God would "keep" the disciples as he had kept them while he was in the world (v. 12). Already he was looking back on that phase of his work as finished. He was committing them to his Father's care. He asked, "Keep them in thy name" (v. 11). As previously noted, the name stood for the nature of God as Jesus had revealed him. The prayer was that God would keep the disciples true to a life which was consistent with the character of God as revealed by the Son. They would be God's own cherished possession, worshiping him, living for him, serving him.

The prayer was, too, that under God's keeping care, these disciples would be molded into a unity, "that they may be one." They were a diverse lot: Matthew, formerly a social outcast as a tax collector for Rome; Simon the Rock, who could sometimes be more like shifting sand; James and John, the thunderstorm brothers with their volatile tempers; Thomas, who was always a bit slow to catch on. Jesus was not praying for their *uniformity;* he was praying for their *unity,* a unity like that of the Father and the Son. He prayed for a vital unity which inwardly would be characterized by love for one another, as in the case of the Father and Son. Outward tokens of that vital inner union would be a oneness in ideals, thoughts, purposes, and goals. The more they possessed that oneness, the more effective would be their work.

As Jesus prayed that the Father would keep the disciples *in his name,* he prayed that he would also keep them *from the evil one* (v. 15). This grammatical structure, like the identical one in Matthew 6:13, is ambiguous. It may mean to keep them from evil, or it may mean to keep them from the evil one, Satan. Of all of the commentary interpreters who have been regularly cited in this exposition, one omits any reference to this expression and all of the others understand it to mean "the evil one," Satan. They recognize the ambiguity of the Gospel passage but feel that the very clear use of the idea in 1 John settles the question (1 John 2:13; 3:12; 5:19). That understanding is supported by the American Standard Version, Revised Standard Version, and *Today's English Version.* The King James Version translation retains the ambiguity by translating "keep them from the evil."

The easiest way to keep them from the evil one would be to take them out of his realm of operation, the world, and to take them to heaven with the Father and Son. Jesus pointedly did not pray for that, "I do not pray that thou shouldst take them out of the world." The very opposite was true; they were to be sent into the world. Under the guidance of the promised Holy Spirit, they would continue the work which Jesus had started. That was a part of the redemptive plan of God. It was his appointed method of getting the message of redemption to the world, the whole world. Jesus' prayer was that they would be so kept by the Father that, as they did their work in the world, they would not fall into Satan's snare and forfeit their apostleship as Judas had. For Judas the trap had been baited with greed and ambition. Satan would have other baits for other people. Jesus' prayer was that the apostles would find in the Father's wisdom and power their source for victory in all of their battles with evil and the evil one.

Jesus prayed next that God would consecrate the disciples (v. 18). It is difficult to choose the English verb for translating this Greek verb. It is the verb from which the adjective translated "holy" in verse 11 was derived. When the verb was used in reference to things, it meant to set them aside for religious use, as the vessels of the Temple were set aside for use in divine worship and were called "holy." Lexicographers list three English verbs to translate the word when it is used in reference to persons: consecrate, dedicate, sanctify. In this passage in John, the verb is used once in verse 17 and twice in verse 19. Here are the translations of the versions which we have been citing:

Verse 17	Verse 19
(KJV) Sanctify them	I sanctify myself . . . might be sanctified.
(ASV) Sanctify them	I sanctify myself . . . may be sanctified.
(RSV) Sanctify them	I consecrate myself . . . may be consecrated.
(TEV) Dedicate them	I dedicate myself . . . may be dedicated.

In the following exposition, the word *consecrate* will be used in all three instances. It is a subjective choice based on the "inner feeling" we often have about the precise meaning of a word in a speaker or writer's use.[20]

Jesus' petition was in effect that God would consecrate the disciples in his word (v. 17) and for his service (v. 18). "Consecrate them in the truth; thy word is truth" (author's translation). "Truth" in the first clause is identified with the Father's "word" in the second clause. In these discourses, God's "word" had been his teachings which he had given to the Son and which the Son had imparted to the disciples. Jesus, in leaving the world and that ministry of teaching, had sent the apostles out to carry that teaching to the world (v. 18). Again, he spoke of future event as accomplished fact. So the *realm* in which he prayed for the Father to consecrate the disciples was God's word, and the *service* for which he requested the consecration was the teaching of that word. To consecrate was to set them aside for (or to dedicate them to the purpose of) a permanent, irrevocable ministry of imparting the truth of God's word just as Jesus had been imparting it. How sacred was that task! How weighted with responsibility was that stewardship of the word, God's word, "the truth"!

Jesus prayed the prayer of self-consecration as a part of his prayer for the disciples (v. 19). He prayed it "for their sake" and that their own consecration might be all the more significant. In Jesus' controversy with the Jerusalem authorities over his relationship to the Father, he stated that the Father had consecrated him and had sent him into the world (10:36). That consecration was in the Old Testament pattern of the consecration of Jeremiah as a prophet (Jer. 1:5) or Aaron as a priest (Ex. 40:13). Jesus' self-consecration differs from that in that he is both the sacrifice and the High Priest who makes the sacrifice. On numerous occasions in the Gospel his death as redemptive is stressed (10:11; 11:50–51; 15:13). The most striking one is his own words in 10:17–18: "For this reason the Father loves me, because I lay down my life, that I may take it again. No one takes it from me, but I lay it down of my own accord." In the introduction to this unit, we discussed the similarity of the Gospel of John and the letter to the Hebrews, in both of which Jesus is presented as both the sacrificial animal and the High Priest who sacrifices the animal. Here, then, was his prayer as he set himself apart as a sacrifice for sin. He is, therefore, an *intercessory* High Priest (vv. 9–18; 20–24) and a *sacrificing* High Priest (v. 19). The atoning blood which he offers in sacrifice is his own blood (Heb. 9:11–15; 10:11–22). In his own self-consecration, he went far beyond the consecration of his disciples which he asked of the Father.

Jesus prays for believers through the ages (vv. 20–24). Expanding the dimensions of his intercession, Jesus reached out to draw into the circle of his high-priestly ministry all believers of all ages. In reality that is the perspective. As he prayed for the apostles in their ministry of witnessing, he envisioned all of those who would become believers through their witness (v. 20). In the sense that the faith of all future believers could be traced in chain-link fashion back to the witness of the apostles after Pentecost, Jesus prayed for the believers through the ages. It is in that sense that believers since Pentecost, even in our own day, have been able to say, "Jesus prayed for us."

Granting that the claim has validity beyond sentimentality, believers need to observe what it was that Jesus prayed for them— "that they may all be one; even as thou, Father, art in me, and I in thee" (v. 21). He prayed for a relationship of oneness among all believers, the kind of oneness which existed between Father and Son. He had prayed for the same sort of oneness to characterize the apostles (v. 11). In this petition for all believers, he envisioned a similar inner, vital unity characterized by mutual love after the model of the unity of Father and Son. It was to be a unity of faith and life in oneness with the Father and the Son (v. 21*a*). The ultimate purpose of this union was to challenge an unbelieving world to come to faith in Jesus Christ (v. 21*b*). Only a genuine and vital union of believers could make a valid challenge of that sort.

As a means of bringing about that unity of all believers, that they might be one as Father and Son are one (vv. 22*b*,23*a*), Jesus stated that he had given to the believers the "glory" which the

Father had given to him (v. 22*a*). This must refer to the glory which he asked of the Father in verse 1. That glory was to be realized through his death and resurrection. So in verse 22 he spoke of future event (his death and resurrection) as historically accomplished fact—"I have given to them." He had shared with them the glorious experience of his triumph over sin and death. Of course at the time this book was written, that "glory" was an accomplished fact and the believers of that time could look back to it as we can and could be conscious of sharing with Christ in that glorious triumph. That triumph and the consciousness of sharing in it are at the very core of Christian unity. The perfected oneness to which believers would come through sharing in that glory would convince the world that God had sent Jesus into the world and that God loved those believers in the same way he loved the Son (v. 23).

In the words of verse 24, Jesus turned to another aspect of his glory, that glory for which he had prayed in verse 5. There he had prayed that in heaven the Father would glorify him with the glory which he had known with the Father before the world was created. Going back to that petition and with full confidence in the Father's granting it, Jesus stated his desire that all believers might ultimately be with him to witness that glory. The form of the statement was not that of a *request*. It was an expression of his *will* in the Father-Son relation of the Godhead. The verb is that of willing or desiring an object. The ultimate, complete union of Jesus and his people in heaven is a prominent part of New Testament eschatology. Here Jesus looked upon it as a time when his former and eternal glory will be witnessed by all who believe in him.

Summation and commitment constitute verses 25–26. Jesus addressed God as "righteous Father." Of all the terms that have been named as the most basic concept of the nature of God, *righteousness* may be the best. His righteousness encompasses other choice terms such as *holiness* and *love.* Continuing, Jesus summarized the incarnation event, his mission in the world in a few brief but meaningful statements so simple and so clear that they need no comments: the world did not know the Father; Jesus did know him; the disciples who were with him as he prayed had come to know that God had sent Jesus into the world; he had made known to them the name of God; he was committed to continue to make that name known, in order that the love with which the Father had loved the Son might continue to be in them, and that he, the Son, might continue to be in them. The prayer of the High Priest had begun with a request for himself. It ended with a request for his disciples. Truly did John say, "having loved his own who were in the world, he loved them to the end" (13:1).

Manifestation as the Lamb Slain
18:1 to 19:30

Chapter 18 begins with the statement that when Jesus had finished the prayer, "he went forth with his disciples across the Kidron valley, where there was a garden" (v. 1). There is no indication of the place from which they "went forth." The most natural suggestion is that they went from the Temple courts where they had stopped after leaving the upper room at 14:31. The garden of Gethsemane was at the foot of the Mount of Olives, just across the Kidron valley from the Temple. Mark and Matthew supply the name of the garden, Gethsemane. John does not have the long, agonizing prayer experience of Jesus and the apostles in the garden before Judas' arrival with the arresting officers. So in dealing with John's account, we come to the arrest immediately after they entered the garden. His account of the betrayal and arrest is much shorter than that of the Synoptics. He omitted many details which the Synoptics included. He included some details which the Synoptics lack. His account has some statements which cannot be clearly and fully understood apart from a full account of a background event in the Synoptics. As an example of this feature, Jesus' question in 18:11, "Shall I not drink the cup which the Father has given me?" presupposes an acquaintance with the experience and prayer of Jesus in the garden relative to his drinking the cup, a symbolic reference to his death. In the following comments, consideration will be restricted to the account of John with cross references to the Synoptics only as necessary. We search in John's account for his theological interest and emphasis.

The betrayal and arrest is presented in verses 1–12. Judas had completed his arrangements with the Sanhedrin. They in turn had arranged for official Roman assistance. Judas knew or suspected that Jesus and the other apostles would be in the garden (v. 2). He led the arresting officers to the place. Interpreters of the different Gospels debate over the identity of the arresting officers—Jewish or Roman? John's account is very specific; the answer is both. There was a cohort *(speira,* v. 3) of Roman soldiers under their captain *(xiliarxos,* v. 12) and there were officers *(supēretai,* v. 3) from the Jewish Sanhedrin. There is no indication of the combined number. A cohort was normally a tenth part of a Roman legion (6000); hence, 600. Whether the entire cohort was present or only a number deemed adequate for the task is a matter of speculation. If the entire cohort had been called out for the task, it indicates the apprehensiveness of the Sanhedrin over the possibility of resistance by the crowds of people who had staged the remarkable welcome when Jesus entered Jerusalem that week. No such resistance developed.

It seems a bit strange that Judas played so minor a role in the betrayal account in John. John had emphasized the coming betrayal by Judas since 6:70–71. He had brought it up over and over, particularly in events of that week: at the supper in Bethany; at the Last Supper; in the account of Jesus' teachings. Now when the time arrived, he indicated Judas' leading the arresting officers to the garden (v. 3) and his standing with them as they talked with Jesus (v. 5), and that is all. Judas appears to have no more part in the action than a spectator, and he is never mentioned in John's account again. Further comments on this will be made in the details of the arrest. Readers, who feel that John was unduly harsh in his treatment of Judas, need to read carefully the Synoptic account of Judas' role from his original contact with the Sanhedrin to his suicide when he saw the real result of what he had done! They are more severe than John.

Anticipating the possibility of difficulty in finding, identifying, and arresting Jesus, the officers came well equipped with torches, lanterns, and weapons (v. 3). Their precautions proved to be unnecessary. Well aware of what was to follow, Jesus "came forward" and asked, "Whom do you seek?" The word means precisely, "came out." It may mean that he came out of the garden to meet them; or that he came out a bit from the apostles to distinguish himself clearly. He was very eager to shield them from danger by association with him (v. 8). For the same reason, to keep the records clear, he asked, "Whom do you seek?" They answered according to the instructions which had been given to them, "Jesus of Nazareth." Their orders included nothing about his disciples.

Jesus answered, "I am he" (v. 5). There is a fine point of interpretation possible in his answer. The word "he" in our translations is supplied for English clarity. The Greek text has only "I am." It is an expression of major importance in John's Gospel. It relates to Jesus' theological identity: I am the light of the world, I am the resurrection and the life; I am before Abraham; I am the one whom God has sent; I am the Good Shepherd who lays down his life for his sheep, and so on more than a dozen times it is so used. Jesus' answer, "I am" could have had no such overtones for the Romans, but it could have had them for the Jews. Especially would that have been true if in the group there were priests and Pharisees who had heard him teach and had argued with him about his claims. Again assuming that Jesus was speaking in Aramaic, the equivalent of "I am" would have been to Jewish ears the name of God, *Jehovah* in English, which was so sacred that they would not pronounce it. The Romans would have made no such association, but the Jews would.

How are we to explain the reaction of the arresting group to Jesus' answer? If they understood it simply as self-identification, "I am Jesus of Nazareth," why did they retreat and fall to the ground (v. 6)? Was it because of what he had said or because of his entire conduct in the situation or both? The Jews could have acted in reverence or in horror at Jesus' speaking the sacred name of God. The normal action, however, would have been prostration rather than falling backward. The Romans would have had no cause for such action, and John's indication is that all of the group stumbled backward from Jesus and fell to the ground; literally, "they went from [him] backward and fell to the ground." As he had *come out* to meet them, they *went back* from him.

Some interpreters treat this as a miracle performed by Jesus' spoken word as some of his other miracles had been performed (the lame man at the pool, ch. 5; the raising of Lazarus, ch. 11). Others do not attribute their action to a deliberate miracle of Jesus, but they do attribute it to the majesty of his presence, his words, his total conduct. Judas had come to identify Jesus; the officers had come to search out his presence, to overcome by weapons any resistance, to arrest him and take him to trial. Instead of their carrying out their plans, Jesus had taken charge. He went out to meet them; he took over questioning; he made his own identification. He was in complete control of the entire situation. There was a majesty in his conduct and in his *"I am"* which overcame and dazed them. They were awestruck and as helpless to arrest him as had been his fellow villagers to throw him over the precipice in Nazareth (Luke 4:28–30).

If John had written that Nazareth episode, he would probably have added that the villagers could do nothing because his hour had not yet come! Now, however, his hour had come, but no one was going to take his life from him. He was laying it down of his own will in accordance with the Father's will. John was very eager to show that, hence, the negligible role of Judas when the betrayal time came, and the helplessness of the Roman cohort and the Temple guard. They could not take him until he was ready to go, and he was not ready to go until he had assured the safety of his disciples. When the officers had recovered their composure, Jesus resumed the questioning:

"Whom do you seek?"
"Jesus of Nazareth."
"I told you that I am he; so if you seek me, let these men go" (vv. 7–8).

John commented that in securing the safety of the eleven, Jesus fulfilled his own word of prophecy, "Of those whom thou gavest me I lost not one" (18:9).

As the officers approached to make the arrest, Simon Peter drew a sword to defend Jesus in the face of the entire Roman cohort and the Temple police (v. 10). As far back as the Caesarea Philippi confession and Jesus' first prediction of his death, Peter had resisted the idea. On that occasion, his "This shall never happen to you" (Matt. 16:22) had an implication of "if I can prevent it." Earlier on this very night he had vowed, "I will lay down my life for you" (13:37). Now he was ready to do all he could to prevent the arrest. From some concealed place on his person, he drew a "sword." The word may mean a short dagger-like sword or a butcher knife. Was it a sword, or was it the knife Peter had used that afternoon to prepare the Passover lamb (Luke 22:7–13)? It has no real importance, but it was unusual that Peter would have a "sword" and that he would be carrying it during holy week. He attacked the slave of the high priest, and by a very literal translation of John's precise account, "he cut from him the ear, the right one." That, too, is not of great importance, but it is of interest that it is the sort of detail which eyewitnesses remember and tell and retell until it becomes a part of the living

oral account. Luke, too, noted that it was the slave's right ear
and he added the detail of Jesus' healing the ear (22:50–51). Another such remembered detail was the name of the slave, Malchus.

In different ways, Matthew, Luke, and John report that Jesus
stopped Peter's fighting and rebuked him. Luke has only, "No
more of this!" (22:51). Matthew reports Jesus' statement that if
fighting were the way to accomplish God's purpose, he would
have asked and God would have sent "twelve legions of angels"
to do battle and prevent his death, a legion of 6000 fighting angels
for each of the eleven and one for Jesus! But that was not God's
way of bringing about that which was prophesied in the Scriptures
(Matt. 26:53–54). John's account quotes Jesus as telling Peter to
put away his sword and then as asking, "Shall I not drink the
cup which the Father has given me?" (v. 11). The "cup" was
his death, and he had accepted it as the will of the Father for
him (Matt. 26:39). The Roman captain led his cohort and the
Temple police in seizing and binding Jesus. Mark reports that
at that point the apostles "all forsook him, and fled" (14:50).

The Jewish phase of Jesus' trial is set out in verses 13–27. At
this point a few comments are in order regarding the accounts
of Jesus' trial as they are presented in all four Gospels. Viewed
from that perspective, there were six phases of Jesus' trial, three
in Jewish hearings and three in Roman.[21]

One, John alone gives the hearing before Annas (18:12–24).
Two, all four Gospels give a hearing before Caiaphas and the
    Sanhedrin, though John has only a statement that there was
    such a hearing; he gives no details (Mark 14:53–65; Matt.
    26:57–68; Luke 22:54–65; John 18:24).
Three, the Synoptics present a second hearing before Caiaphas
    and the Sanhedrin after dawn on Friday (Mark 15:1; Matt.
    27:1; Luke 22:66–71).
Four, all four Gospels report the hearing before Pilate (Mark 15:1–
    5; Matt. 27:2,11–14; Luke 23:1–5; John 18:28–38).

Five, Luke alone reports that the hearing before Pilate was interrupted by Pilate's sending Jesus to be tried by Herod Antipas (23:6–12).

Six, all four Gospels contain the remainder of the hearing before Pilate; in fact, apart from Luke's account of the interruption, the Gospels have one lengthy hearing before Pilate. That hearing is the main feature of John's account (Mark 15:6–15; Matt. 27:15–26; Luke 23:13–25; John 18:39 to 19:16).

The four Gospels are as one in reporting that the charge against Jesus in the Jewish hearings was *blasphemy,* and in the Roman hearings it was *treason;* that is, that Jesus' claim that he was the Messiah constituted a threat against Caesar.

As noted above, John is alone in indicating that the arresting officers led Jesus directly to Annas (v. 13). That affords an insight into the power and influence of this man in both Jewish and Roman affairs. Under the Romans, the previously honored office of high priest became a political plum more civic than religious. For more than fifty years, Annas built what amounted to a dynasty. He was high priest in A.D. 7–14. After he was deposed, his son Eleazar was high priest in A.D. 16. From A.D. 18–36, his son-in-law Caiaphas held the office. After him, four more of Annas' sons held the office; the last one who also was named Annas was high priest in A.D. 62 and was responsible for the martyrdom of James of Jerusalem. Historians are divided as to whether the elder Annas was a good man or only a good politician. The fact that the Roman cohort took Jesus to him rather than to Caiaphas is an indication of his political power. The Jews also preferred him to Caiaphas. One modern Jewish scholar, author, and professor of history has characterized Caiaphas as "unworthy leader," a part of "a harsh and arrogant priestly oligarchy" who was "no more worth defending" than the Catholic bishop at the time of Joan of Arc.[22] For John's statement that Caiaphas was "high priest that year," review the comments on 11:49–52.

Jesus' hearing before Annas was entirely unofficial, even though in verses 19 and 22 he was called "high priest." There were many former high priests active in the priestly affairs; they were likely referred to loosely as high priests as we refer to a former president as "president." The episode probably does not warrant the title hearing, but it is so designated because it is the only one in John which includes any details of what took place (vv. 19–23). The only indication is the summary statement that Annas questioned Jesus "about his disciples and his teaching" (v. 19). We can assume that he was interested in the claim of Jesus' disciples that Jesus was the Messiah and how their views might be evaluated politically. In other words, were they revolutionaries? Too, he probably wanted to hear from Jesus himself some of the ideas which had so upset the Sanhedrin and the Pharisees. Was Jesus really a blasphemer? Jesus did not accomodate him. He responded in a very direct way that he had done nothing and taught nothing secretly; it was all a matter of public knowledge. Let Annas ask the Jews what he had actually said. His attitude may reflect his realization that this was an unnecessary delay which could have no bearing on the outcome of his arrest. Annas knew that, too, and he sent Jesus still bound as a prisoner to Caiaphas (v. 24).

Annas' attempt to get information from Jesus may have covered more time than the brief account suggests. Woven into it is the account of Peter's denials. Peter and another unidentified apostle had secured entrance into the court where the hearing was in progress. Speculation has often identified the disciple as John. Peter was out on the edge of the activities, warming himself by a charcoal fire which the "servants and officers" had made.[23] In that situation he was accused three times of being one of Jesus' followers. One of the accusers was a kinsman of Malchus whose ear Peter had cut off (v. 26). Each time he denied the charge (vv. 17,25,26–27). The third denial was followed by the crowing of the cock just as Jesus had predicted earlier that night (13:38). Surprisingly, perhaps, it is not John but Luke who has the most dramatic account of the third denial and of Peter's distress when Jesus turned and looked at him, and Peter remembered the words of Jesus (22:59–62). It was for Peter a bitter experience.

Annas sent Jesus to Caiaphas. He was still bound by ropes or chains and in the custody of the Temple guard. That guard is mentioned three times during the trial of Jesus (18:18; 18:22; 19:6). The Roman cohort is not mentioned after Jesus was delivered to Annas (18:13). It appears again, in charge of the crucifixion (19:23). It is difficult to understand why John omitted the actual hearing before Caiaphas. In the Synoptics it is one of the most graphic and dramatic accounts of the trial: the attempts of the Sanhedrin to get witnesses against Jesus; their success in getting witnesses who testified in half-truths and outright falsehoods; the high priest's putting Jesus on oath to testify as to his claim to be the Son of God; Jesus' testimony under oath that he was; the histrionics of the high priest in ripping apart his gorgeous robe in feigned horror at Jesus' testimony; his call for the Sanhedrin to vote Jesus guilty of blasphemy; their affirmative vote followed by their uncivilized treatments of Jesus—spitting in his face and playing a child's game of blind-man's bluff with him (Matt. 26:57–68).

All of that John omitted, reporting only that "they led Jesus from the house of Caiaphas to the praetorium" (v. 28), the official residence of the Roman governor. "They" in verse 28 naturally refers to the Temple guard. We know from the procedure of the hearing under Pilate that the Sanhedrin went with the guard to make and to press the charges against Jesus.

The Roman phase of Jesus' trial is set out in 18:28 to 19:16. "It was early" (v. 28) agrees with the Synoptic indication that the Sanhedrin's hearing was in the morning hours before dawn and that after dawn they assembled again for a second vote before taking Jesus to Pilate (Luke 22:66–71, brief references in Mark 15:1 and Matt. 27:1). The praetorium was the word for the official residence of a Roman governor. Some opinion has identified the

Jerusalem praetorium with the Palace of Herod in the western part of the city. Prevailing opinion today identifies it with the Antonia fortress adjoining the Temple area on the northwest. To the chagrin of the Jews, one of the four Antonia towers was built high enough to make it possible for the Romans to see into areas of Temple activity where they as Gentiles were not permitted to go. It was the tower which was nearest the Temple, and from its 115-foot height the Romans could see into every part of the Temple except the inner sanctuary.

For a Jew to go into a room where Gentiles were present was to be ceremonially defiled and banned from official religious activities for a day or until he had been purified by a ritual bath. For that reason the Sanhedrin members stayed outside the courtroom lest they be defiled and not be able to "eat the passover" (v. 28). We have discussed earlier the importance of this statement in determining whether John regarded Saturday as Passover day that year, whereas the Synoptics regarded Friday as Passover day.[24] If he did so, his view would be that the Passover Eve supper was not eaten until after sundown on the day of Jesus' trial and death. From that viewpoint, Jesus was being sacrificed on the cross as the Passover lambs were being sacrificed in the Temple. Jeremias has demonstrated from Philo and rabbinical writings that in Jesus' day the sacrificing of the lambs started at 3:00 P.M.[25] Brown, however, argues for the beginning of the sacrificing just after 12:00 noon.[26] According to the Synoptic account, Jesus died at 3:00 P.M. (Mark 15:33–37; Matt. 27:45–50; Luke 23:44–46). The view fits precisely John's theology of Jesus as a sacrificed lamb, but the problem of the date is still unsolved. Not all of the evidence is clearly on either side of the debate.

The Sanhedrin demanded the death penalty for Jesus (vv. 28–32). While Jesus waited inside the courtroom, Pilate went out to get a clear understanding of the Sanhedrin's reason for bringing Jesus to him for trial. Ordinarily the Sanhedrin very jealously guarded its right of trial and resisted any effort at encroachment by the

Romans. This case, however, was not an ordinary one. What they wanted lay outside their jurisdiction. When Pilate asked what charge they were making against Jesus (v. 29), they reacted as if Pilate was already predisposed to find Jesus innocent. They made no specific charge but insisted that Jesus was "an evildoer" or they would not have brought him to Pilate (v. 30). To do evil normally referred to religious or moral matters. Since all matters of religious nature were within the jurisdiction of the Sanhedrin, Pilate told them to try Jesus themselves and by their own religious law (v. 31*a*). The Jews then stated plainly what they wanted; they wanted Jesus to be put to death and that would require Roman court judgment and execution (v. 31*b*).

In a prophecy and fulfillment motif, John linked Jesus' own teaching about the manner in which he would die to the demand of the Sanhedrin that the Romans try him and execute him (v. 32). The primary reference is doubtless to Jesus' teachings about his being "lifted up" (John 3:14; 12:32). We cannot, however, exclude the Synoptic teachings which, by the time of John's writings, would have been well known. From Jesus' first two Synoptic teachings about his death, the natural assumption would be that death would be at the hands of the Jewish religious authorities, and, hence, by stoning (Matt. 16:21; 17:22–23, with parallels in Mark and Luke.) It would also have been illegal, mob violence by Roman law. In the third of his Synoptic teachings, however, it is very clear: He would be betrayed to the Jews, tried and condemned to death by them, turned over to the Romans, executed by crucifixion (Matt. 20:17–19 and parallels in Mark and Luke).

Pilate questioned Jesus (vv. 33–38*a*), but the entire episode indicates that it was to appease the Jews and that he felt that from the viewpoint of Roman law, there was no reason for Jesus to be condemned. From John's Gospel alone, Pilate's first question seems to be abrupt and without background, "Are you the King of the Jews?" (v. 33). It appears to suggest that the Sanhedrin had made that charge, and Jesus seems to have interpreted it in that way. He answered, "Do you say this of your own accord, or did others say it to you about me?" (v. 34). There is such a background for the question and the answer, but it is in Luke, not in John. In Luke's account of the initial request by Pilate for charges against Jesus, the Sanhedrin accused Jesus of three things: (1) leading Israel astray; (2) forbidding the payment of taxes to Caesar; (3) claiming to be Christ, a king (Luke 23:2). Pilate could have related that to the crowd's welcoming Jesus to Jerusalem as "the King of Israel" on the preceding Sunday (12:13–15). He could have, that is, if he had heard that report.

For Pilate, as a Roman judge, it was an important question. If Jesus' was claiming to be a king, he could be regarded as a revolutionary, and to the Romans, that was a serious matter. In neither Luke's account nor in John's is Jesus' answer a clear one. In Luke his answer literally translated was, *"You* are speaking" (23:3). Some interpreters understand that as an affirmation, such as, "You are saying that because that is what I am." Others understand it as a denial. The pronoun is emphatic. So they understand Jesus to mean, *"You* are saying that; I am not." In John's account, Jesus did not really answer the question. At first he turned the question into another question to ask if Pilate was himself the source of the question or if others, presumably the Sanhedrin, had said that (v. 34). Pilate's response was an emotional mixture of indignation at Jesus, anger at the Jews for this early-morning court session, and just plain perplexity (v. 35). *He* was no Jew; how was he to understand this "Christ, a king" business of the Jews? *Jesus* was a Jew; what had he done to cause the Jews to want him executed as a threat to Rome? Normally they would have praised such a person.

In his second response to Pilate's questioning, Jesus' used his *mashal* approach: He had a "kingdom," but it was not a "this-world" kind of "kingdom"; if his "kingdom" were a this-world kind of "kingdom," he would have servants (the word for the

Temple guard) to fight for him against the Jews (v. 36). Pilate handled the riddle rather well. He understood from Jesus' use of "my kingdom" three times in one sentence that he was some kind of king. But how can one be a king with no territory to rule and no army to help him if he had the territory? He responded with a question which reflected his perplexity. It was introduced by a compound particle which is both inferential and interrogative in force; it is used only this one time in the New Testament, *oukoun*. The *oun*, meaning "so" or "therefore," goes back to the original question of verse 33. The *ouk* introduces a question which anticipates the answer yes. Very freely rendered it was. "So then, you are a king, aren't you?" (v. 37). The tone of the question suggests that he could have added, "But what kind of a king are you?"

Jesus' answer was in two sentences. First, "You say that I am a king." The pronoun "you" is emphatic. With its verb alone, it is the same expression cited above in Luke's account of Jesus' response to Pilate's first question (23:3). We noted there the ambiguous nature of the statement, *"You* are saying [that]," by which some interpreters understand Jesus to answer affirmatively ("You say that because that is what I am,") but others understand him to answer negatively (*"You* are saying that; I am not"). Here in John's account (v. 37) the expression does not stand alone. The remainder of Jesus' answer reflects that his response to the word "king" is more tentative than ambiguous, *"You* say that I am a king." By the emphatic use of the pronoun, he stressed that the word "king" was Pilate's choice, not his.

The second sentence in his answer reflects *his* choice of terms, "For *this* I was born, and for *this* I have come into the world, *to bear witness to the truth"* (author's emphasis). Pilate used the word "king" to identify Jesus' role; Jesus preferred the word "witness." He did not reject the word "king." At his triumphal entry, he had accepted it from those who were acclaiming him a messianic King. By his own definition of "king" and "kingdom," he could accept the terms. By man's common definition of the terms, a worldly kingdom, established by worldly means, for worldly aims and purposes, he could not accept the terms. Essentially what he said to Pilate was, *"You* say that I am a king; *I* say that I am a witness"—both pronouns are emphatic in the Greek text. "I was born" and "I have come into the world" are parallel expressions. The demonstrative pronoun "this" in both clauses refers to the *purpose* clause "to bear witness to the truth." That claim is consistent with the thematic purpose of the incarnation in John and is not inconsistent with the Synoptics. From the viewpoint of Jesus' purpose in the world, "to bear witness to the truth" (John 18:37) is basically the same as "to give his life a ranson for many" (Matt. 20:28) or "to save the lost" (Matt. 18:11). Throughout his teachings in John, Jesus' record was one of witnessing to the truth: the truth of man's sin, the truth of God's love, the truth of God's redemptive provision for man's sin through the gift of his Son. Jesus not only witnessed to the truth, he was the very embodiment of truth (14:6). True seekers for the truth heard his witness, understood his witness, and accepted his witness. With no inclination to discuss philosophy or theology with Jesus, Pilate terminated the questioning by asking the philosopher's question, "What is truth?" (v. 38). He did not, however, seek an answer to that question from Jesus.

Pilate found Jesus to be not guilty of any crime where Roman law was concerned (vv. 38*b*–40). he went outside and made that announcement to the waiting Sanhedrin, "I find no crime in him" (v. 38). His word for "crime" was a legal term meaning "a cause or reason for pronouncing one guilty of the charge against him." It is used only three times in the New Testament. In Acts 19:40 the town clerk at Ephesus used it to tell the silversmiths under Demetrius' leadership that the Christians were guilty of no crime against Roman law. The other two instances are here in Pilate's statement to the Sanhedrin (John 18:38*b* and Luke 23:4). Since they had charged Jesus with a crime which demanded the death sentence in a Roman court, the thrust of Pilate's statement was that he found Jesus guilty of no such crime. Jesus had broken no Roman law; he did not deserve to die.

When all of the Gospel accounts are considered together, it is clear that Pilate did not want to have Jesus executed. He unsuccessfully tried three different ways to avoid having to pronounce the death sentence.[27] First, he gave the Sanhedrin the right to make the decision to release Jesus (vv. 39–40). The Synoptic account of this action is much more complete than John's. Pilate referred to a custom of releasing some outstanding Jewish prisoner at Passover to help the Jews to symbolize release from bondage which characterized the original Passover. Borrowing from the Synoptic records, we know that there were two notable Jewish prisoners whose cases would make them very fitting choices. Jesus of Nazareth was on trial on the charge of treason against Rome. Pilate had tried him and had pronounced him not guilty. Barabbas, a highway robber, had led a revolution which resulted in several deaths. He had been tried, pronounced guilty, and was waiting to be executed. Pilate proposed that the Sanhedrin make the choice. Should he release Barabbas who was guilty as charged as a revolutionist? Or should he release Jesus who had been so charged but whom Pilate had found not guilty? Pilate may have added fuel to their anger by asking the Sanhedrin if he should release Barabbas or "the King of the Jews." [28] Their response was unanimous (Synoptic accounts), loud, and angry. "Not this man, but Barabbas." The verb means to shout or cry loudly. The word "again" (v. 40) does not necessarily mean that Pilate had already asked once and they had replied as they were now. It probably means that Pilate had shouted his question loudly so all could hear, and they were responding by shouting back at him. The scene reflects the temper of the Sanhedrin and their determination that Jesus had to die. John's account represents only the action of the Sanhedrin in this and subsequent events. The Synoptics report the presence of crowds of people whom the Sanhedrin had stirred up to demand Jesus' death. The implication of Pilate's actions is that he had hoped that the Sanhedrin would agree to release Jesus. One wonders if he was surprised when they refused to do so. The Synoptics indicate that he did release Barabbas as they had requested. It is clear, however, from John and Luke that he was not yet ready to grant their request that Jesus be executed.

Pilate questioned Jesus a second time before yielding to the Sanhedrin's demands (19:1–11). He decided to try to appease the Jews by having Jesus scourged (Luke 23:16).[29] The Roman scourge was so cruel and extreme that prisoners frequently died under it. After the scourging, the Roman soldiers played a mocking game of "King" with their victim (vv. 2–3). A king should have a crown; they made one out of thorns and pushed it down on his head. A king should have a royal robe; they robed him in one of the royal color, purple. A king should have subjects to do him honor; in mockery they greeted him with what they must have considered the greatest of insults, "Hail, King of the Jews!" To show how helpless this king was, they struck him with their bare hands.

He must have been a wretched sight when Pilate presented him to show the Sanhedrin that he had been punished. He came out as a mock king who had been subjected to the Romans' most cruel punishment next to crucifixion. To the Sanhedrin, Pilate said, "Behold the man!" (v. 5). (*Ecce Homo* in Latin, the theme of so much Christian art on the death of Jesus.) It is as if Pilate appealed to them, "Look at him. Isn't that enough punishment?" Surely the supreme court of the nation would drop prejudice in favor of justice. Not so. The Sanhedrin members and their Temple guard joined in a rabble chant, a one-word, second-person-singular imperative hurled at Pilate at full volume: "Crucify, crucify!" In exasperation Pilate responded with a second-person, plural imperative, "Take him, *you* crucify him, for *I* do not find in him cause for crucifying" (author's translation preserving the emphasis of the constructions). The Sanhedrin responded with similar emphasis, "We have a law"—Jewish law *versus* Roman law now. According to their law, Jesus deserved to die for blasphemy, "because he has made himself the Son of God" (v. 7). This was their interpretation of Leviticus 24:16 which decreed death by stoning for anyone who blasphemed the name of God. They were forbidden by Roman law to carry out the Mosaic law of congregational stoning of the guilty. They were demanding that the civil law of Rome give way to the religious law of Israel.

When Pilate heard that Jesus claimed to be the Son of God, "he was the more afraid" (v. 8); *Today's English Version* has "even more afraid;" Brown (p. 873) has "more afraid than ever." In John's account alone this could refer to some heretofore unmentioned fear or awe of Pilate in the presence of a man who talked about being king of a kingdom of another world ("not of this world," 18:36). In Matthew 27:19 there is another incident which could have increased such fear. While the Barabbas event was in progress, Pilate's wife had sent a message to him urging him to have nothing to do with the case against Jesus ("that righteous man") because that very day she had experienced a very distressing dream about him. To these bases for superstitious fear was now added the fact that Jesus claimed to be the Son of the God of Israel.

Pilate went back inside the praetorium to ask Jesus one more question, "Where are you from?" Whence are you? What is your source? If Jesus had answered, "I am the Son of the Creator of the universe," it likely would not have bothered Pilate as much as Jesus' refusal to answer the question at all. One who answered in such way as here suggested might be written off by a Roman judge as an incompetent. But what does a judge do with one who faced such charges as Jesus did but refused to cooperate with the one person who was trying to help him? Pilate reminded Jesus of that, "I have power to release you, and power to crucify you" (v. 10). His implication was that Jesus should fear him rather than the mob outside, even if that mob did include the high priest and the supreme court of Israel. The word which is translated "power" is the one for "authority," power which grows out of the power of position.

Jesus answered that question. His reply was that only an authority (or power) "from above" made it possible for Pilate to have any authority over him at all (v. 11). The only higher authority which a Roman governor recognized was the emperor of Rome, but that was not what Jesus meant. His reference was, of course, to the eternal God. Pilate received his authority from God in the sense in which Paul argues in Romans 13:1–7 that the very principle of human authority in law and order is God's gift to his creation. In this matter of Jesus' destiny, there was a higher authority than a Roman governor or a Jewish high priest. And because that authority from above was working, Pilate had less "sin" than the one who had delivered Jesus to him. The personal reference indicates that Jesus was referring to the high priest, though the Sanhedrin as a body was involved in what was going on. From the perspective of degrees of wrongdoing, "sin," it was wrong for Pilate, a Gentile judge, to protect his own position by permitting a man whom he had judged innocent to be put to death (vv. 12–13). It was a greater wrong for Caiaphas, a Jewish high priest of the God of Israel, to reject the Son of God and to secure his death on false charges.

Pilate finally bowed to the demands of the Sanhedrin and sentenced Jesus to die (vv. 12–16). His efforts to release Jesus through the Barabbas event and the scourging event had failed. The imperfect tense of the verb in verse 12 indicates that because of his dialogue with Jesus over the "Son of God" matter (vv. 7–11), Pilate still was seeking a way to release Jesus. While he was seeking it, the Sanhedrin brought their clinching argument. They threatened his position as governor by Caesar's appointment (v. 12*b*). They argued that anyone who posed as a king was setting himself up as a rival to Caesar. Though Pilate was convinced that Jesus did not pose as that kind of king, it was a forceful argument. He might not be able to convince Caesar that such was the case. Tiberias, the reigning Caesar, was known for the severity of his punishment for any who were disloyal to him or to the position which he had given them. When the Jews said, "If you release this man, you are not Caesar's friend," they were striking Pilate at his most vulnerable spot. The title *Philokaisar,* friend of Caesar, was a coveted title received by official conferral. Pilate may have held the title, or he may have been seeking it; we have no evidence one way or the other. Loyalty to Caesar was an absolute necessity whether one held the title or only acted the part convincingly. When the choice lay between protecting his own position and protecting a Jewish teacher of religion whose own people had rejected him, Pilate's decision was an easy one.

He led Jesus out of the room where the hearings had been conducted and to a place which the Romans called *lithostrōtos,* stone pavement, and the Hebrews called *gabbatha,* probably meaning an elevated place. He sat down at the *bēma,* judgment seat for the official announcement of his decision.[30] He could not resist the opportunity to tantalize the Jews a bit before announcing the decision. He began by saying, "Behold your king." By then Jesus was a wretched spectacle of a man to say nothing of looking like a king. Their shouted clamor was, "Away, away, crucify him" (v. 15, literal translation). They had not changed their view or their demand. Pilate infuriated them even more, *"Your* King shall I crucify?" (literal translation preserving the emphasis). Only the response of the chief priests is indicated, "We have no king but Caesar." Although the Sadducees, the priestly party, were more friendly to Rome than the remainder of the Jews, those are still strange words to come from the lips of first-century Jews under Roman dominance. They reflect how very determined they were in their rejection of Jesus as the Messiah. "Then" (v. 16), when every effort to release Jesus had been exhausted, "he handed him over to them to be crucified." That sounds as if he handed Jesus over to the Sanhedrin for crucifixion. That, of course, was not John's meaning. Pilate handed Jesus over to the *will* of the Sanhedrin as Luke 23:25 states, but it was the Roman soldiers who carried out the execution (vv. 23–25*a*).

"Like a lamb that is led to the slaughter" (Isa. 53:7) was the death of Jesus (vv. 17–30). This lamb symbolism of Isaiah's suffering servant is fitly joined to John's Passover lamb symbolism. John's account of the crucifixion of Jesus is brief. As in other areas previously noted, it adds details which the Synoptics lack, and it lacks many details which the Synoptics provide. All of the Gospels are in agreement that the crucifixion of Jesus was on Friday and that death came about 3:00 P.M. There is a question of agreement as to when the crucifixion began and the length of time that Jesus was on the cross. Mark 15:25 records that "it was the third hour, when they crucified him." By all reckoning that would be 9:00 A.M. Matthew and Luke do not mention the hour of the crucifixion but they follow Mark in his report (v. 33) that the darkness started at the sixth hour (12:00 noon) and in his report (v. 34) that Jesus' death came at the ninth hour (3:00 P.M.). That means that Jesus spent six hours on the cross.

John, however, indicates that the end of the trial before Pilate and the beginning of the crucifixion came "about the sixth hour" (v. 14). The problem of the reckoning of time in the Gospel of John is a recurring one. (Observe this in commentary discussions on 1:39; 4:6; 4:53; 19:14.) No way has yet been found for equating the "third hour" in Mark with the "sixth hour" in John. Falling back on one Gospel using Jewish time and another using Roman time will not work. Not even the theological-purpose approach is satisfactory in this case. Brown (pp. 882–883) uses it. He holds that John set the beginning of the crucifixion to coincide with the beginning of the sacrificing of the lambs at 12:00 noon. Jeremias' argument, however, for beginning the sacrificing of the lambs at 3:00 P.M. is stronger than Brown's argument for 12:00. Too, Jeremias' view is just as theological as Brown's since by it the point of Jesus' death would coincide with the sacrificing of the lambs. Beyond that, both of them argue from the view that in John 19, Friday was Passover Eve, the day of the sacrificing of the Passover lambs, and that position lacks much of having a QED solution!

In the final analysis, whether Jesus was on the cross six or three hours is not of major importance. Either one would be mercifully brief. Normally death on the cross took from thirty-six to forty-eight hours, and much longer periods were not rare. The brevity and simplicity of John's account of the crucifixion minimizes the drama and lurid details of the longer Synoptic accounts. It does not minimize the importance of the event, and no other account quite reaches the emotional peak of John's report of the very end and Jesus' words, "It is finished" (v. 30).

The soldiers led Jesus to the place of the crucifixion, Golgotha. He followed them "bearing his own cross." There is no reference to another helping him as in the Synoptics. Jesus was still in charge, laying down his life; no one was taking it from him, a Johannine distinctive. John included the two who were crucified with Jesus; but in contrast to the Synoptic account, they had no other part in the event. Isaiah's suffering servant song comes to mind again, he "was numbered with the transgressors; yet he bore the sins of many" (53:12). Pilate composed a title for him and affixed it to the cross, "Jesus of Nazareth, the King of the Jews" (John 20:19). John alone reports that it was written in the three languages of the Roman world: Hebrew (for the Jews); Latin (for the Romans); Greek (for the Greeks). Even the title on the cross radiated its message for the whole world. The government's reason for such titles was to warn anyone who could read any of the languages not to commit the crime for which the person on that cross was hanged. John's account indicates that Pilate was at the crucifixion. The chief priests requested him to change the title to read, "This man said, 'I am King of the Jews'" (v. 21). Pilate not only honored a Roman aversion for changing any

decree after it had been written, he also gratified his own ego
in having the last word with the Jewish court which he loathed.
"What I have written, I have written" (v. 22). In reality what
he had written was more accurate than what the Sanhedrin requested. Jesus had not said, "I am the King of the Jews," but
he was. He was the Son of David, messianic King whom God
had promised Israel through his prophets. But Israel rejected him,
"his own people received him not" (1:11).

All four Gospels report the disposal of Jesus' clothing. Under
a centurion (Luke 23:47), four Roman soldiers had done the actual
crucifixion. The clothes and any other possessions on the persons
crucified belonged to the soldiers as a part of their pay. By Roman
custom, crucifixion was in the nude; the condemned one had
no further use for clothes. The soldiers divided Jesus' clothes into
four equal parts and "cast lots" to determine which part each
one would get. John mentioned an infrequently used, general
word for casting lots; it did not indicate the method used. All
three Synoptic writers used a word which indicated the tossing
of small stone or wood pieces, similar to dice today. John added
the detail of their casting a separate lot for Jesus' outer robe,
considering it too good for ripping into four parts (v. 24). Luke
added the detail of Jesus' praying for his executioners, "Father,
forgive them; for they know not what they do" (23:34). To the
modern mind, their action appears calloused to the point of vul-
garity. To their mind, they were doing their job. They did not
know that they were crucifying the Son of God. Was their action
any more calloused than that of those who, after nearly two thousand years of historical demonstration that he *was* the Son of
God, still reject him? John (v. 24) related the entire clothes-divid-
ing episode to the Scriptures. He used the same Psalm (22:18)
which Jesus quoted in the hours of agony and darkness, "My God,
my God, why hast thou forsaken me?" (Ps. 22:1; Matt. 27:46).

As the end of his life drew nearer, Jesus committed the care
of his mother to the beloved disciple (vv. 25–27). Near enough

to the cross for identification and conversation stood the beloved
disciple with Jesus' mother and three other women: his mother's
sister; Mary, the wife of Clophas; Mary Magdalene (v. 25).[31] There
is intriguing speculation that "his mother's sister" (19:25) is the
same as "Salome" in Mark 15:40 and "the mother of the sons
of Zebedee" in Matthew 27:56. In that case James and John were
cousins to Jesus; Mary Magdalene is known from other Gospel
events; nothing more is known of Mary, the wife of Clophas;
there is much conjecture about her identification, but that is all
that it is.

Jesus put his own agony into the background long enough to
comfort and provide for his mother. There is much of emotion
and tenderness in the scene. His words, "Behold, your son!" and
"Behold, your mother!" have the sense of, "Look, *he* is your son
now!" and "Look, she is *your* mother now!" He apparently felt
better about leaving his mother in the care of his beloved disciple
than in the care of his four unbelieving half-brothers.[32] The statement that the disciple took Mary to his own home "from that
hour" means that thereafter she made her home with him. It
does not mean, as some suggest, that they left the cross at that
point and did not observe the remainder of that sad experience.

Jesus knew that the end was very near, but he was also conscious
of intense thirst (v. 28). The loss of blood and the exposure to
the sun resulted in the dehydration of the body and intense thirst.
Earlier Jesus had refused a drink which included a sedative which
would have eased his suffering (Mark 15:23; Matt. 27:34). Now
in the intensity of his suffering he cried out, "I thirst." How quickly
do we respond to any person's saying, "I am thirsty"? With so
much water in our world, why should anyone thirst? They did
not offer Jesus water. There was a jar there containing what is
translated as "vinegar" (v. 29). It was the lowest form of cheap
wine, the very dregs of wine, which was provided for the executioners. No sedative had been mixed with it as in the earlier
case. Using a reed and a sponge, they offered the filthy liquid

to him who had offered to the world the Water of life. It may be that in the mystique of John we are to recall that in the beginning of his ministry at a happy wedding occasion Jesus had provided for men the best wine (2:10); now at the end, men offer him the worst.

Having tasted the filthy drink Jesus cried out, " 'It is finished'; and he bowed his head and gave up his spirit" (v. 30). All of these words are packed with theological overtones and meaning. The verb which is translated "bowed" is the one from which we derive our word for a couch for sleeping. Jesus in raising Lazarus and the daughter of Jairus had spoken of death as sleep. Now even on the cross, he inclined his head as on a couch for going to sleep. The verb which is translated "gave up" is a compound one meaning "to give over," he gave over to the Father, the spirit which the Father had given to him. The emphasis in John on Jesus' own voluntary action in his death is still present. Even on the cross, he is still in charge. No one takes his life from him: not Judas, not the Sanhedrin, not Caiaphas, not Pilate, not the Roman soldiers. *He* lays down his head. *He* gives over his spirit. Recall his words in the Good Shepherd teaching. "I lay down my life for the sheep" (10:15); "No one takes it from me . . . I have power [authority] to lay it down" (10:18). And let us never forget that he also said, "I have power to take it again" (v. 18). The "glory" event did not end on Friday. We must wait till Sunday to see his triumph!

Although that is true, his last words on Friday took the form of a cry of triumph, "It is finished"! The Latin versions have *Consummatum est,* it is consummated. Actually the Greek expression is in one word *Tetelestai*—perfect, passive of *teleō,* "it is ended." Luke includes that Jesus said, "Father, into thy hands I commit my spirit!" (23:46). Mark (15:37) and Matthew (27:50) have only that Jesus uttered a piercing cry. Only John provides this theological cry of redemption triumphant, "It is finished."

Let us not be restrictive in Jesus' understanding of what was finished. The agony of the hours on the cross? Yes, but more than that. The suffering of this entire week of Israel's renunciation? Yes, but more. The agony of a sensitive soul in a lifetime of rejection by the people that he loved? Yes, but far more. All that was symbolized in the sacrificial system of the Temple of Israel was finished. All that was promised through the prophets of ancient Israel was finished. All that was symbolized in the tabernacle in the wilderness was finished. All that was started by God's call of Abraham from Ur of Chaldea was finished. All that was latent in that simple sentence from the Garden of Eden was finished—the serpent has bruised the heel of the seed of woman; but the heel of the seed of woman has bruised the head of the serpent (Gen. 3:15). And it doesn't stop there. It reaches back to the place where man can speak of it only in terms of "before the foundation of the world" and in terms of "the lamb slain before the foundation of the world." "It is finished" embraces the total of what contemporary theologians call "salvation history." God would not see man in sin and do nothing about it. Even when it cost him his Son, he moved into man's experience redemptively. Shout it above the din of the crowd on that skull-shaped hill; shout it from the darkness when the sun refused to look on what man was doing to the Lamb of God—*"It is finished!"*

In summary, why did Jesus die? Who was responsible for his death? According to the New Testament, from the viewpoint of the Jewish Sanhedrin, he was guilty of blasphemy in claiming to be the Son of God (Matt. 26:65–66 for example). From the viewpoint of the Roman court he was guilty of treason, a threat against Caesar (John 19:12,21). From the viewpoint of the Christians he died as a sacrifice for the sins of man. His death demonstrated the enormity of man's sin and the enormity of God's love.

Who then was responsible for his death? In his book previously cited, the Jewish scholar Isaac argues unconvincingly that the primary, almost the total, responsibility for Jesus' death must be attributed to the Romans. Nevertheless, he can say that Caiaphas and the high priests have their share of the responsibility.[33] But he can say further that from the viewpoint of theology, "Jewish responsibility is subordinated to the collective responsibility of sinful humanity . . . the human race, the whole of sinful mankind."[34] And in striking similar tone the Southern Baptist, A. T. Robertson, could name the major participants and their roles in the event, Pilate, the Sanhedrin, Pharisees, Sadducees, Judas, and comment, "There is guilt enough for all the plotters in the greatest wrong of the ages."[35] Granting all of that, we cannot in good conscience stop until we have confessed that it was *our* sins, the sins of all of us which nailed the Lamb of God to the cross. Let modern man in his spirit of independence react as he will against the vicarious death of Jesus of Nazareth, such as "I do not want anyone dying for me." The doctrine is still there in the Scriptures. In some sense, beyond our power to grasp, but in the economy of God's redemptive work, Jesus of Nazareth as Suffering Servant (Isa. 53:5) or as Lamb of God (John 1:29) died for our sins.

Manifestation as Victor over Death
19:31 to 20:10

The burial of Jesus, according to John's account, was carried out strictly in accordance with Jewish custom and requirement (vv. 31–42). His followers were anticipating no resurrection; he was buried with the same sense of permanence that would have marked the burial of any other person. Even though it had to be done in haste, it was done in the lavish manner which was sometimes displayed in the burial of royalty. It was preparation day of Passover week. *Preparation* was the Jews' term for the day before the sabbath. On it all necessary work in business or in the home would be done to assure that no labor took place from sunset on preparation to sunset on sabbath. Recall that Jesus died about 3:00 P.M. Everything in his burial would have to be completed by about 6:00 P.M., to be very exact, when the light of the first star could be seen.

Two requests were made of Pilate regarding the disposal of the body of Jesus, one from his enemies and one from his friends. First, the Sanhedrin requested that the legs of the executed men be broken and the bodies removed from the crosses before the sabbath began (v. 31). No indication is given as to their thoughts as to whether the bodies would be buried or simply discarded as garbage. Further comments on this matter will be made in the following pages. Second, a member of the Sanhedrin who was also a disciple of Jesus, Joseph of Arimathea, requested permission to receive the body of Jesus from the cross and to bury it. Pilate granted both requests.

By Mosaic law, bodies of criminals which had been hanged could not be left on "the tree" over night; to do so would have been to defile the land (Deut. 21:22–23). John's verse 31 is commonly interpreted to mean that this prohibition applied only to the sabbath. It applied to every day. They may have been more concerned in cases in which the sabbath was involved because of their honor for the sabbath above other days. In Jesus' case the matter was of double importance because the sabbath of a holy week was of special importance. John termed it "a high day"; the Greek text has it "great was the day of that sabbath." To assure the observance of that law, the chief priests made their request. Roman custom in crucifixion was to leave bodies on the crosses for the vultures or until they decayed. In cases like this, when bodies had to be taken from the crosses before death came, they were probably cast on the garbage dump in the valley of Hinnom, Gehenna. Breaking the legs would prevent their crawling away and recovering; it was also regarded as a means of hastening death.

Jewish custom permitted relatives or friends to bury the body of one who had been executed, but the burial place had to meet Sanhedrin regulations; outside the city, for example. In Jesus' case, it was two friends who provided all the work and supplies for burial, including the tomb. Both friends were members of the Sanhedrin. When the soldiers had finished their gruesome task with the two robbers, they saw no reason for breaking Jesus' legs because he had already died. Most interpreters take it as an added touch of spite that one of the soldiers thrust his lance into Jesus' side. A subjective opinion is that he wanted to be very sure that after so brief a time Jesus was really dead. He wanted no negligence in the performance of duties charged against him when he reported to his centurion or to Pilate who would want positive proof. John alone reported this incident of the piercing of Jesus' side.[36] The text reflects a keen interest of John in the phenomenon of both blood and water coming from the sword wound (v. 34). Traditionally, Christian art has placed the wound on the right side. The left side would be more natural since the spear seems to have pierced both the pericardium and the heart.

The phenomenon of the blood and the water has resulted in lengthy speculation regarding its physical significance, as well as some possible spiritual significance, in John's mind. Brown has devoted twelve pages to a meticulous review of opinion on the passage.[37] From the standpoint of the physical aspect, how long had Jesus been dead? Noting in verse 30 that death had already come to Jesus before the Sanhedrin made its request (v. 31) and that blood ceases to flow after the heart stops pumping, some interpreters deny the physical possibility of what John reported and, hence, reject the authenticity of the account. Other interpreters counter that the Sanhedrin's request could have been made even before the execution; they knew that the men would not die before sunset. Too, some blood could issue from the upward thrust of a spear into the heart of one who was in an upright position as Jesus was; there is no indication of the amount of fluid which issued, little or much. The "water" was likely the water-like serum from the pericardium. Some interpreters regard the phenomenon as a miracle for some special purpose. John, however, does not report it as a miracle. It is possible that he welcomed it as a very natural matter which indicated the reality of the incarnation; Jesus was really a man and his death showed it. That would show the error of the Gnostic doctrine that Jesus only *seemed* to be a man but really was not. The Docetic Gnostics denied the reality of the incarnation. Recall that in 1 John those who denied the reality of the incarnation were called "antichrists"; John regarded them as heretics of the worst sort (1 John 2:18,22–23; 4:1–3).

Other than this anti-Gnostic view, there are many theories of the significance of the blood and the water. Some see it as an indication that Jesus did not die from the physical sufferings of the cross, but that he died of a ruptured heart brought on by extreme emotional and spiritual suffering. They speak of him as dying of a broken heart. Some think John interpreted the blood as teaching the sacrifice of Jesus and the water as teaching baptism.[38] Some think he understood the blood to teach the Eucharist (the cup of his death) and the water to teach baptism. Another thinks that John saw the work of Jesus in the blood and the work of the Holy Spirit in the water (making use of 3:5–8; 7:38–39). These are some of the less extreme theories! In all honesty we must recognize that John explicitly gave only one interpretation of the piercing of Jesus' side—it was the fulfillment of Scripture (Zech. 12:10). For that reason or for whatever other reason he may have had, the author saw great importance in the event. That was the reason he was so emphatic about the eyewitness nature of the report (v. 35). The beloved disciple is rather generally accepted as that eyewitness.

We are not left to wonder about John's view on the significance of Jesus' legs not being broken (v. 33). That, too, he understood as fulfillment of Scripture (Ex. 12:46; Num. 9:12). In the initial Passover, the instructions for the sacrificing of the lamb included, "you shall not break a bone of it." In the first chapter of this Gospel, Jesus was identified as "the Lamb of God, who takes away the sin of the world" (1:29). Now in the end of his ministry in his sacrifice of himself for the sins of the world, he so fits the

Passover lamb pattern that his bones were not broken. Even in that detail, he was the Passover Lamb to which all previous Passover lambs had pointed.

John's theological theme develops the Passover lamb nature of Jesus' sacrifice, but as indicated in the introduction to this volume, the sacrifice is not restricted to that. John understood a rather total sacrificial lamb significance in Jesus' death:

In this same body of Johannine writings the Living Christ is presented in Revelation 5:6 as a Lamb that had been sacrificed in religious worship; he was alive; he ultimately would defeat all evil and lead God's redeemed servants into the New Jerusalem. So rather than seeing one particular sacrificial idea here, we may more properly see all the sacrifice of the Hebrew religion epitomized. Much in the same way, the writer of Hebrews sees Jesus in total sacrifice but presents it in a "Day of Atonement" setting.[39]

In his death, Jesus was the Passover Lamb whose sacrifice effected freedom from spiritual bondage and launched a *new Exodus* through which God would create a *new Israel* for his redemptive witness. The early Christians called that body *ecclēsia,* church.

The second request to Pilate was from Joseph of Arimathea. He asked permission to bury the body of Jesus. Pilate granted that request too. He may have been impressed that a man of Joseph's position would make such a request. Putting together bits of information from all four Gospels, we know that he was a rich man from Arimathea. He had probably moved to make Jerusalem his home. He owned a garden there containing his personal burial cave which he had carved out of the stone. He was a good and righteous man who was a member of the Sanhedrin but had voted against their action in condemning Jesus. He was a man who had an active hope in the promised kingdom of God. He had become a disciple of Jesus but kept it secret because of fear of his fellow Jews. Recall that they had voted to ban from the synagogue anyone who confessed that Jesus was the Christ (9:22). He summoned courage, however, to brave their wrath in order to bury Jesus; Mark 15:43 records that he "took courage and went to Pilate" and made his request.[40]

John alone adds the detail that he was joined by Nicodemus, whom he would have known as a fellow member of the Sanhedrin. From Nicodemus' siding with Jesus on other occasions, it would be safe to assume that he had joined Joseph in voting against the Sanhedrin in Jesus' case. They brought linen, powdered aloes, and gum of myrrh; all of these items were materials commonly used in burials. The quantity of the spices was extravagant (v. 39). As indicated above, such lavishness was sometimes displayed in the burial of one of royal standing. As Mary of Bethany had preanointed his body lavishly before his death, so did Joseph and Nicodemus anoint it after his death. John noted that their preparation of his body was according to "the burial custom of the Jews" (v. 40). This was to distinguish it from the Roman custom of cremation and the Egyptian custom of total embalmment.

The body would have been washed. The spices and linen would have been applied in either of two ways. The myrrh could have been spread over the body and the aloes sprinkled among the folds of the linen as the body was wrapped. Or the myrrh and aloes could have been mixed in a neutral oil base and placed either on the body before the wrapping or on the cloth before the wrapping. Uncertainty is present because the three Synoptics used one word for linen and it is singular, "a linen cloth"—sheet-like. John used a different word and it is plural, "linen bandages" or strips of linen. It is not a matter of great importance. Either one would fit the description of the grave clothes after Jesus' resurrection. That matter was very important to John. When Peter and the beloved disciple entered the tomb after Mary's report that the tomb was empty, they found the grave clothes intact, holding the form of the absent body in such way that the beloved disciple "believed" that a miracle had taken place (20:2–8).

Other details which were important to the Gospel writers were

that the garden was near the place where Jesus was crucified
(19:41–42); the cave had been carved out of stone by Joseph as
his own burial place (Matt. 27:60); it had never been used before
Jesus was buried there (John 19:41; Luke 23:53, probably another
touch of royal honor); when the burial was completed, the cave
was closed by a great disk-like stone door (Matt. 27:60; Mark
15:46). John and Luke note that when the burial was finished,
it was almost time for the sabbath to begin (19:42; Luke 23:54).

Had any of Jesus' family or friends ever spent a sadder sabbath?
His life on earth was destined to change the world, but for them
it was a life that had ended in unbelievable and indescribable
tragedy. With Jesus' death, all for which they had hoped had
ended. In what is perhaps the greatest choral music of the Christian
liturgy, Bach's *The Passion According to St. Matthew*, the
burial of Jesus ends at the tomb with the tender and heart-rending
"Fare Thee well, Lord Jesus" and "In tears, Dear Lord, we leave
Thee." Bach could close it in that way because the music was
written for Good Friday services. But that climactic event of the
ages did not end on Friday. And we live *this side* of Friday;
yea, we live this side of *Sunday*. And that makes all of the difference
in this world and beyond this world.

Sunday came (20:1) and with it the first evidence of what theologians
refer to as the Easter event—Jesus' body was no longer in
Joseph's tomb (20:1–10).[41] The New Testament records contain
two major facets of that Easter event, the empty tomb and the
resurrection appearances of Jesus. Both were of tremendous importance
to the recorders of the event and apparently to the
early church. John's account has a selective but masterful blending
of the first into the second to demonstrate the *fact* of the resurrection
and that the fact was perceived by *faith* before it was perceived
by *sight*. From this point to the end of this Gospel, both
implicitly and explicitly, the role of the beloved disciple is a major
one.

With varying details as to numbers and names, all four Gospels report that early on the first day of the week women went to the tomb and found it open and empty.[42] Mary Magdalene, the only one who is named in all of the accounts, saw the open cave, inferred that the body had been taken away, and fled to find the apostles to report it. The other women lingered at the tomb, entered to find that the body was not there, encountered angels who told them that Jesus had been raised, and subsequently saw the Lord himself before they went to report their experience (Matt. 28:1-10; Mark 16:1-8; Luke 24:1-11). While all of that was taking place at the tomb, Mary found Simon Peter and the beloved disciple and reported, "They have taken the Lord out of the tomb, and we do not know where they have laid him" (v. 2). Several points may be noted. Readers of the New Testament who want a "Gospel quartet" that sings in *unison* must in these accounts settle for one which sings only in *harmony,* and the harmony is not always simple! The Synoptics make no mention of Mary's leaving the tomb before the events mentioned above, and Luke implies (24:10-11) that it was in response to the report of all of the women that Peter (no mention of the beloved disciple) went to the tomb to check up on the womens' report (v. 12). John was not a careless reporter; he was driving for one theological purpose and the line went directly from the report of the empty tomb (v. 1) to the faith of the beloved disciple (v. 8). Other details he neither included nor denied; implications must always be recognized for what they are, implications.

Another point of interest and, perhaps, importance is Mary's statement, "They have taken the Lord out of the tomb." John's record does not indicate that she even looked into the tomb until much later (v. 11). Seeing the tomb open, she inferred (rightly) that the body was not in it. Her only thought was that someone had taken it away. Who was the unidentified antecedent of her pronoun "they" (v. 2)? Neither the Romans nor the friends and family of Jesus would have had reason for moving it. Grave robbers would not have taken it away for reburial as Mary's words "where they have laid him" suggest. That would leave only the Jewish religious authorities. What reason would they have had? Strachan charges that their request for the breaking of the legs and the removal from the crosses was to "have Jesus buried in a nameless or dishonored grave." [43] He is not alone in seeing their request as another indication of hostility. Other interpreters have seen their hostility reaching out through the request to inflict additional suffering. All of this is, of course, speculation, but it is not unreasonable speculation.

Another additional point of interest in Mary's action and report was her saying, "we" do not know. To whom did she refer? The natural answer is that she referred to the other women who accompanied her to the tomb, women absent from John's account but present in the Synoptics. She was, therefore, assuming that their thoughts were the same as hers, that all of them shared the same bewilderment. She had not waited to find out!

Peter and the beloved disciple may have started walking toward the tomb (v. 3). If so, they found the pace too slow for their eagerness so they ran, with the beloved disciple outrunning Peter and arriving first (v. 4). The writer was so interested in the beloved disciple's arriving first that he used more words than were really needed, "The two were running together, and the other disciple ran ahead faster than Peter and came first unto the tomb" (literal translation). Interpreters divide as to whether the beloved disciple outran Peter because he was younger or just a faster runner. Such questions interest readers who would like to determine relative ages of the apostles, especially the age of the beloved disciple. John's interest, however, was much more serious and theological. He wanted to establish that the beloved disciple was not only the first of the apostles to "see" the empty grave clothes (v. 5) but he was also the first of the apostles to "believe" that Jesus had been raised (v. 8). The primacy of the faith of that apostle was an important part of the authenticity of his witness (19:35; 21:24).

Stopping and stooping to peer into the semigloom of the cave, the apostle could see the empty grave clothes. Why did he hesitate to enter the cave? Reverence? Bewilderment like Mary's? Was his grief-numbed mind beginning to remember words of Jesus about death, resurrection, their seeing him no more, his going to the Father? Was a glimmer of light about to break into the abysmal darkness in which he had walked for three days? Nothing slowed the impulsive Simon. He stopped for no look from the outside. He entered the cave immediately and looked at the empty linen bandages that had enclosed the body of Jesus and the headpiece rolled separately (or folded) and unattached to the others (v. 6–7). John's account makes no mention of Peter's reaction to what he saw. Luke, who reports Peter's going to the tomb but omits the presence of the beloved disciple, states that he went away "wondering at what had happened" (24:12).[44]

The beloved disciple followed Peter into the cave. He observed at close range that which he had seen from the outside. The linen bandages were just as Joseph and Nicodemus had left them about the body of Jesus. The turban-like headpiece was separate from the others as it might have fallen when the body went out of the cloths (or the translation may be "folded," as if carefully done). The impression is that there was no evidence that anyone, friend or foe, had disturbed the clothes or that Jesus had unwrapped himself from the bandages. Everything was in perfect order except that there was no body. The scene was one to produce total mystification. Any mystification which it may have held for the beloved disciple disappeared in faith, "he saw and believed" (v. 8).

The affirmation of the New Testament is that the body of Jesus did not decay in the cave but was made to live again and in the process was so transformed that it could never again be limited by time, space, material, or death.[45] The first manifestation of that was present there in the cave and its undisturbed contents. So the only apostle who had gone through the trials of Jesus and even to the foot of the cross stood in the empty tomb and "saw and believed." The exact number of people who saw the tomb and the grave clothes before Jesus' appearance is not clear. Luke does not indicate the number of "other women" whom he mentions in 24:10 or the number of men (plural masculine pronoun) who went to check on the women's report (24:24). A very conservative estimate would be eight to twelve. There was plenty of *seeing,* but except for the beloved disciple, there was no *believing* until the appearances began. He *saw* that the body was not there and that no human hands could have taken it away. He *believed* that Jesus had been raised from the dead, though he had not yet seen the risen Lord.

From that moment the apostolic faith in the resurrection of Jesus Christ from the dead was a matter of history. It was not a static faith. It would grow; it would become clearer; its base would be enlarged. One facet of that enlarging would be their relating it to their Scriptures, the Old Testament. Verse 9 reflects that need "for as yet they did not know the scripture, that he must rise from the dead" (v. 9). Their belief that Jesus was the Messiah whom God had sent was well anchored in their Scriptures. He had spoken to them often about his death and resurrection. They did not have a clear concept of that as anchored in their Scriptures. They at first debated the matter with him (Matt. 16:21–23; Mark 8:31–33) and later refused even to discuss it with him or ask for more information about it (Matt. 17:22–23; Mark 9:30–32; Luke 9:43–45).

If they lacked that foundation where his death was concerned, how much greater was their lack of a foundation for accepting the idea that he would be raised on the third day? (Review Jesus' teaching after his resurrection in which he used all three sections of their Scriptures [Law; Prophets; Hagiographa—Psalms] to show the scriptural foundation for his resurrection [Luke 24:27,44–48].) We do not have a record of the precise passages of the Hebrew Scriptures which Jesus used. From the perspective of history, Christian faith looks at the Old Testament and finds many predictive references to Jesus' death and resurrection. We are limited in our knowledge of which Scriptures the apostles came to use. In Paul's four verb statement on the content of the apostolic gospel, he included "raised . . . in accordance with the scriptures" with "died for our sins in accordance with the scriptures." [46] The two stood together or fell together in the witness of the early church. There is one classic passage which we know they used— Psalm 16:8–11. It was the heart of Simon Peter's sermon at Pentecost, the sermon which launched the witness of the new Israel: Jesus of Nazareth *lived* (Acts 2:22); he *died* (2:23); he was *raised* from the dead (2:24–32, God did not abandon him to the powers of death, v. 27*a*, nor permit his body to decay in the tomb, v. 27*b*); he was exalted to the right hand of God (2:33–36). Ordinarily in John the singular construction "the scripture" refers to one definite passage from the Old Testament rather than to the whole body of writings. It appears very likely that it is to this Psalm that he referred in verse 9.

The beloved disciple left the tomb with the firm faith that Jesus was victor over death; somewhere, in some form, he was alive. Before that day had ended, to his *faith* would be added *sight,* in the appearance of the risen Lord.

Notes

1. Recall that for theolgoical reasons John used the cleansing of the Temple in 2:13–25 and that he placed the supper at Bethany at 12:1–11 before the triumphal entry.

2. For a more detailed calendar including Scripture divisions for these days of activity, see Summers, *Commentary on Luke,* pp. 232–289.

3. Note 14:2–4; 14:28; 16:7; 16:16; 16:20–22.

4. Luke 24:44–49, Jesus spent the forty days between his resurrection and ascension appearing to the apostles and explaining the redemptive significance of his death and resurrection.

5. This record is more pronounced in Luke's Gospel than in the others. I have traced it throughout my *Commentary on Luke.*

6. Josephus' account of this vine in his *Antiquities* XV 11.3 is substantiated by the Roman historian, Tacitus, as well as by rabbinical references.

7. Plummer, p. 286.

8. Lenski, p. 1030.

9. Hendriksen, pp. 298,308.

10. R. E. Brown, pp. 676–682.

11. R. H. Strachan, *The Fourth Gospel, Its Significance and Environment* (London: SCM Press, Ltd., 1917), p. 291.

12. E. C. Hoskyns, ed. F. N. Davey, *The Fourth Gospel* (London: Faber and Faber Limited, 1947), p. 478.

13. Barrett, p. 399.

14. Hovey, p. 303.

15. Two specific works on these passages may be helpful: R. E. Brown, "The Paraclete in the Fourth Gospel," *New Testament Studies* (January 1967), pp. 113–132; Hans Windisch, *The Spirit-Paraclete in the Fourth Gospel*, trans. James W. Cox (Philadelphia: Fortress Press, 1968).

16. Review Luke's presentation of Jesus' Mount of Olives discourse from this same perspective (Luke 21:5–26) as discussed in Summers' *Commentary on Luke*, pp. 252–266. Compare also 2 Peter 3:3–10.

17. In Mark's account Jesus quoted that passage in predicting the flight of the apostles (14:27).

18. See Ray Summers, *Ephesians: Pattern for Christian Living* (Nashville: Broadman Press, 1960), pp. 6–25.

19. This approach to election in terms of God's foreknowledge and purpose is a part of the total scriptural doctrine. For example, note Romans 8:28–30 and Ephesians 1:3–6.

20. Since my earliest years in leading students in the study of the Scriptures, I have defined translation as "the effort of one mind to follow the thought processes of another mind through the medium of language." By that definition, all translation is interpretation.

21. This summary is from my *Commentary on Luke*, p. 289.

22. Jules Isaac, *The Teaching of Contempt* (New York: Holt, Rinehart and Winston, 1964), pp. 145–146.

23. Consistently in these accounts, John used the word for "slave" (18:10,18,26). Some interpreters accept the term "slave"; others understand it as a reference to household servants.

24. Above, exposition of chapter 13.

25. Jeremias, *The Eucharistic Words of Jesus*, p. 8.

26. R. E. Brown (pp. 883,895) really makes no argument. He cites the research of Bonsirven in rabbinical writings as the basis for his view.

27. His efforts are analyzed and explained in my *Commentary on Luke*, pp. 295–299.

28. An ancient tradition, known by Origen (A.D. 235–240) but supported only by one ninth-century Greek manuscript and some Latin, Aramaic, and Syriac

sources, held that Barabbas was also known as Jesus. By that reading of Matthew 27:16–17, Pilate asked, "Shall I release the Jesus called Barabbas or the Jesus called Christ?" When they cried out for Barabbas to be released, Pilate asked, "What then shall I do with the Jesus called Christ?" It makes dramatic preaching but it has poor textual support! Review the textual evidence in the American Bible Society edition of *The Greek New Testament,* eds. Aland, Black, Metzger, and Wikgren, p. 109, footnote on Matthew 27:16–17.

29. This is the second of his three efforts to avoid sentencing Jesus to die. The third one is in Luke only: Pilate attempted to get Herod Antipas to take over the trial of Jesus (Luke 23:6–12).

30. It is possible that the Aramaic *gabbatha* was a reference to the stone structure known as the *bēma* in Roman court practice. It may also refer to the knoll on which the Antonia was built.

31. See R. E. Brown, pp. 904–906, for a detailed discussion and chart on identifying the Galilean women who are named in the different Gospels and in different phases of Jesus' death, burial, and resurrection.

32. See above for comments on John 7:5, regarding Jesus' brothers' unbelief until after his resurrection.

33. Isaac, p. 146.

34. Ibid.

35. Robertson, *A Harmony of the Four Gospels,* p. 225, footnote.

36. See Revelation 1:7 and Zechariah 12:10 and comments in Summers, *Worthy Is the Lamb,* pp. 63–64.

37. R. E. Brown, pp. 944–956.

38. Compare 1 John 5:6–8 in which the threefold witness to the deity of Jesus is given by water (baptism), blood (death), and Spirit (the Holy Spirit).

39. Ray Summers, "The Death and Resurrection of Jesus, John 18–21," *Review and Expositor* (October 1965), p. 480.

40. These details are assembled from Matthew 27:57–60; Mark 15:42–46; Luke 23:50–53; John 19:38–42.

41. For a review of all four Gospel accounts on (1) the empty tomb and (2) angelic announcements that Jesus had been raised (Synoptics only), see Summers, *The Life Beyond,* pp. 32–37.

42. Matthew: Mary Magdalene; the other Mary. Mark: Mary Magdalene; Mary, mother of James; Salome. Luke: Mary Magdalene; Mary, mother of James; Joanna; "other women." John: Mary Magdalene.

43. Strachan, p. 40.

44. Although the place of this verse is secure in the best of third-, fourth-, and fifth-century manuscripts of Luke, RSV omits it, preferring the sixth-century Codex Bezae which omits it.

45. Summers, *The Life Beyond,* p. 33.

46. 1 Corinthians 15:3–5: Christ died; Christ was buried; Christ was raised; Christ appeared numerous times.

VI. Acceptance of the Lamb
(20:11 to 21:25)

An interpretive principle of this exposition has been that just *as the old Israel's ultimate rejection of Jesus as the Christ grew out of the raising of Lazarus from the dead, so the new Israel's ultimate acceptance of him as the Christ grew out of his own resurrection from the dead.* We have looked carefully at the phenomenon of the empty tomb with the main focus on the Johannine account. In doing that, we have noted only in passing the angelic announcements that he had been raised; John has none of the announcements though he does report the presence of angels at the tomb (20:12–13). We come now to the post-resurrection appearances of Jesus, an area of great importance in John as well as in Matthew, Luke-Acts, and 1 Corinthians.[1] A brief scanning of all of the recorded appearances is in order before giving comprehensive attention to the four appearances which are in John's Gospel.

We noted earlier the affirmation of the New Testament regarding the nature of Jesus' body in the resurrection accounts. That claim is so stupendous that it can be accepted only on the basis of the best evidence. These appearances of Jesus are a part of that evidence.[2] In the forty days before his ascension, Jesus appeared from ten to thirteen times depending on problems of identification. No precise location is possible for some of them. Observe this list; numbers are for subsequent comparative comments:

Appearances the First Day

1. To a group of women (Matt. 28:9–10)
2. To Mary Magdalene (John 20:11–18)
3. To two on the road to Emmaus (Luke 24:13–32)
4. To Simon Peter (Luke 24:34; 1 Cor. 15:5)
5. To a Large group, Thomas absent (Luke 24:36–43; John 20: 19–25)

Appearance One Week Later

6. To the apostles, Thomas present (John 20:26–29)

Appearances Unidentified as to Time

7. To five hundred at one time (1 Cor. 15:6)
8. To the apostles in Galilee, Great Commission given, (Matt. 28:16–20)
9. To James (1 Cor. 15:7)
10. To seven by the Sea of Galilee (John 21:1–23)

Appearance at End of Forty Days

11. To an unspecified number, Mount of Olives, last commission, ascension (Acts 1:9–12)

Appearances of Uncertain Identification

12. To the twelve (1 Cor. 15:5)
13. To all the apostles (1 Cor. 15:7)

Comparison Comments: Robertson identifies number 7 with number 8. There is no textual evidence for doing so, and his stated reason is unconvincing.[3] Number 12 may be a separate appearance, or it may be one of the preceding ones, number 5, perhaps. Paul's use of twelve is a round number sort of group reference to the apostles; it cannot be literal because Judas' suicide apparently was before Jesus' death. In similar fashion "all the apostles," number 13, is a group reference which could be a separate appearance, or it could be one of the preceding ones, number 11, perhaps.

The choices of the Gospel writers were selective in support

of their theological emphases. Matthew's two appearances (nos. 1 and 8) combine to present Jesus' meeting the apostles in Galilee and giving them the Great Commission. Luke's four (nos. 3,4,5, and 11) emphasize Jesus' teaching during the forty days of his appearances. The teaching majored on the theological significance of Jesus' death and resurrection and the responsibility of the apostles to get that message out "to the end of the earth" (Acts 1:8, the last commission in popular reference). John's four (nos. 2,5,6, and 10) stress the reality of the resurrection of Jesus and its affect on certain individuals: Mary Magdalene, Thomas, Simon Peter, and the beloved disciple.

All of the appearance reports focus on the historicity and nature of Jesus' resurrection. Two words characterize the total impact: tangible and transcendent. His body was *tangible;* they saw him, talked with him, walked with him, ate with him, and touched him. Yet it was *transcendent;* it was no longer subject to the limitations of time, space, material, suffering, or death. The basis of the new Israel's acceptance of him as the redeeming Lord of life and death was not resuscitation; it was resurrection!

Acceptance by Mary Magdalene stands first in the Gospel of John (20:11–18). Two definite purposes were served by it. It affirmed the reality of Jesus' resurrection, and it helped to prepare Jesus' followers for his appearance to them that night. Mary followed Peter and the beloved disciple back to the tomb. If she arrived before they finished their inspection and left, either the beloved disciple did not share with her his belief that Jesus had been raised, or she did not believe it. Peering into the cave she saw two angels; if she saw the grave clothes, it is not mentioned. The angels asked why she was weeping, and she gave to them the same report which she had given to the two apostles; someone had taken away the body of the Lord, and she did not know where they had buried it (v. 13). The angels offered no information and gave her no comfort. Turning from the cave she saw a man whom she supposed to be the gardener. He asked the same question which the angels had asked and added another one, "Woman, why are you weeping? Whom do you seek?" (v. 15). Mary did not respond directly to the question. Her answer implies that she thought that as the gardener he would know who had been buried there and that he may have been the one who moved the body. Her pronouns were emphatic, "if *you* have carried him away . . . *I* will take him away." Apparently she meant to assume responsibility for reburying the body in some known and appropriate place.

Seeking not a risen Lord but a misplaced corpse, looking through tear-blurred eyes, hearing only a very commonly used address, "woman," she did not recognize Jesus (v. 14). Then he spoke her name, "Mary" (v. 16). Something in that personal address, implying sympathy in the knowledge of her grief, called up recognition on her part. The Good Shepherd calls his sheep by name, and they know his voice (10:3,14,27). Turning directly to Jesus and in tones of at least joyful surprise, she spoke, "My Teacher" (author's translation). Here emerges another facet of the resurrection appearances. In some cases, those to whom Jesus appeared recognized him immediately: the women of Matthew 28:9–10; the disciples of Matthew 28:16–20; the disciples (and others?) who witnessed his ascension (Acts 1:3–9). In other cases, the ones to whom he appeared did not recognize him at first but came to do so through some word or action on his part: Mary Magdalene in this passage; the two disciples on the road to Emmaus (Luke 24:13–32); the gathered group in Luke 24:36–43 and John 20:19–25—they "recognized" his likeness but thought he was a "ghost"; Thomas in John 20:26–31, a similar reaction; the seven disciples by the Sea of Galilee (John 21:1–13). For whatever reasons were involved, some cases demonstrated instantaneous recognition by the beholder; other cases required a combination of self-revelation on the part of Jesus and apprehension on the part of the beholder. There is no uniform, stylized pattern. That fact, with many others, speaks to the authenticity of the differing accounts and the refusal of subsequent copyists to force them into one pattern.

Although Mary recognized Jesus, her understanding of his being there was incomplete. Her reaction leads the reader to think that she saw him as one who had returned to life as Lazarus had, that is resuscitation, a return to the former physical life. She seized his robe, or fell to clasp his feet, as if she would never let him get away again. His tender but firm rebuke was to inform her that his case was very different from that of others who had returned to life through his power: Lazarus; the daughter of Jairus; the son of the widow of Nain. The King James Version's and American Standard Version's translations of his words are misleading, "Touch me not" (v. 17). The Revised Standard Version's translation is better, "Do not hold me," and the *Today's English Version* is the best of the four, "Do not hold on to me." The grammatical construction is one which prohibits the continuance of an action which is already in progress; she was already holding him. Recognizing that, the interpreters regularly cited in this work use such expressions as: "stop holding me"; "you must not hold me like this"; "do not continue holding me"; "stop clinging to me"; "do not cling to me." Such expressions accurately catch the real meaning of Jesus' words.

He wanted Mary to understand that his entire relational situation had changed—to the world, to the apostles, to all of his followers. His next words were meant to clarify that. In the hands of interpreters, however, they have sometimes confused rather than clarified: "for I have not yet ascended to the Father; but go to my brethren and say to them, I am ascending to my Father and your Father, to my God and your God" (v. 17). The word "for" has been a troublesome one. It suggests some sort of causal connection between "do not hold me" and "I have not yet ascended to the Father." But what is it?

It should be noted that there is not in John one definite ascension event as there is in the Luke-Acts account (Luke 24:50–51 and Acts 1:9–11). Rather, the tense of Jesus' words "I am ascending" (v. 17) suggests a not-yet-completed process of ascension including death, resurrection, and return to the Father. It is as if the period of the appearances (forty days according to Acts 1:3) was a going-to-the-Father and a coming-to-the-disciples sort of ascension joining his incarnation presence with them to his Paraclete/Spirit presence with them as he had promised in chapters 14 and 16. In the beautiful metaphor of his words to Nathanael in the beginning of his public ministry, he had become that Jacob's ladder connecting heaven and earth (1:51) and so indicating that he was "the Son of God . . . the King of Israel" of Nathanael's confession (1:49).

In wrestling with this passage, interpreters have sought for some reason for Jesus' rebuking Mary for touching him that morning but inviting the gathered group to touch him that night (John 20:20 and Luke 24:40) and Thomas to do so the next Sunday night (20:27). Some have suggested that Jesus was not to be touched after his resurrection until he had ascended to the Father and had presented the evidence of his having completed his work of redemption. The implication would be that it would be all right for his followers to touch him after he had done that. The implication would also be that Jesus made such an ascension and presentation to the Father in the interim between his appearance to Mary and his appearance to the gathered group that night. Two questions may be asked of these interpreters. First, if they use all of the appearances of Jesus, how do they relate this one to the appearance to the group of women in Matthew 28:8–10? Had Jesus ascended to the Father before they "took hold of his feet" in worship when he met them as they were going from the tomb to make their report to the apostles? Second, whether one uses all of the appearances or only those in John, what is the foundation, biblical or conjectural, for the view that Jesus was not to be touched between his resurrection and his ascension but could be touched after that?

Other interpreters have understood Jesus' words to Mary in relation to his words to the apostles at the Last Supper, "I shall not drink again of the fruit of the vine until that day when I drink it new in the kingdom of God" (Mark 14:25; also Matt. 26:29; Luke 22:18). In both instances, they understand Jesus to speak of some future date when the messianic kingdom was to be established at which time there would be renewed the joyous fellowship which Jesus had known with his followers before the cross. Then he could be touched but not until then. This view faces the same question as the preceding one, plus an additional one: Was the anticipated messianic kingdom fulfilled in Jesus' appearance to the group that night, thus making it all right for them to touch him?

A much more simple interpretation may be the correct one: Jesus was not rebuking Mary for touching him but for her manner and attitude in so doing. For days Jesus had been talking about his death, his resurrection, and his ascending to the Father. Now his death and resurrection had been accomplished. He appeared to Mary. Forgetting his talk about ascending to the Father, if she knew about it, she was overcome with joy to find him not dead and in some unknown tomb, but alive, standing before her, calling her by name. Her thoughts were not of the future; they were of that indescribably joyous moment. She laid hold of him as if to prolong that realization: He is not dead; he is alive; he is here!

So he was, but that did not mean that he was there *just as he had been before the cross*. He was to be with them for all of the future but in a different way. On that last night with the apostles, he had told them that he was going to the Father, that he was going to send the Holy Spirit to be with them. That presence would result in a far more meaningful work and fellowship than had been possible in the days of his incarnation. It was thus to their advantage that he ascend to the Father. It was in that spirit that he said to Mary, in free translation, "Stop clinging to me like this. I have not yet ascended to the Father; but go to my brethren and remind them, I am ascending to my Father and your Father, to my God and your God." That dramatic reminder should turn their thoughts to all he had said about his death, his resurrection, his going to the Father. It should prepare them for his appearance at the end of that very day to assure them of his resurrection, to begin to prepare them for the work they were to do, and to impart to them the Holy Spirit. Without reference to any of the previously cited interpretations, Strachan states that in this Gospel the ascension of Jesus to the Father took place after the appearance to Mary, so that when he met the apostles that night, he went not from the empty tomb, but from "the glory he had with the Father." [4]

We cannot know how much of all of that Mary understood. We know that she obeyed Jesus' command. She reported to the disciples that she had seen him, and from John's account at least, she was the first of the new Israel to see, to accept, and to obey the risen Christ.

Acceptance by ten of the apostles, with Thomas absent, came on that same day (20:19–23). This topic specifies ten of the apostles because in John the focus is on the apostles with Thomas absent (vv. 24–25) in relation to the appearance to the apostles with Thomas present one week later (vv. 26–29). Although the details differ, it is very certain that John's report of Jesus' first appearance to the apostles is the same one which Luke reports in 24:33–43.[5] Luke included the presence of the apostles, the presence of the two to whom Jesus had appeared on the road to Emmaus, and the presence of an unspecified number of "those who were with them" (v. 33). This may be a reference to the Galilean people who were mentioned in Luke 23:49,55. John restricted his reference to the apostles and to what happened to them.

The apostles were in a house with both exterior and interior doors locked "for fear of the Jews" (v. 19). They had good reason to anticipate the Sanhedrin's hostility against them. That hostility

developed, but it did not come until after Pentecost when the
Christian movement became so strong that the Sanhedrin took
official means for stopping it. Acts 4—9 and 12 record the hostility
and persecution which covered several years. Their locked doors
on this night probably would not have kept the Temple guard
out if it had chosen to enter. The interest of Luke and John is
that locked doors did not keep Jesus out!

Suddenly they were aware of his presence in their midst. Modern popular reference to Jesus' walking through walls and closed
doors is the magic language of television; it is foreign to the language of the Bible. Jesus was simply *there* without walking
through anything; there were no barriers to his post-resurrection
presence. Compare Luke's account (24:33–36). While they were
talking excitedly about Jesus' appearance to Simon Peter (v. 34)
and to the two on the road to Emmaus (v. 35), they were suddenly
aware that he was there with them. In both Luke and John's
accounts he demonstrated to their satisfaction that he was not
a ghost (vv. 37,39)—one of the few places in the Scriptures where
pneuma [spirit] may be properly translated "ghost." To prove
that he was not a ghost he said, "See . . . that I am myself" (v.
39, literal translation). His *egō eimi,* "I am," sounds more Johannine than Lucan!

His first word to their disturbed hearts was the beautiful *shalom*
of the Hebrews, "Peace" (John 20:19). He opened his hands that
they might see the scars from the nails. He bared his side that
they might see the scar from the spear (v. 20). Luke included
that he invited them to put their hands on his body to be convinced that it was real (24:39). While the possibility was there
and the invitation was sincere, neither Gospel indicates that anyone actually touched him. Both Gospels emphasize their joy in
seeing him. They may have remembered his words from the preceding Thursday night, "You will be sorrowful, but your sorrow
will be turned into joy" (16:20). Luke's statement that they "disbe-
lieved for joy" (v. 41) sounds very much like our "too good to

be true" when we encounter something which we know to be true but can hardly believe it.

Beyond the point of verse 41 in Luke and verse 20 in John, the accounts diverge. Some of the ideas in the two are similar; some are different. The language differs greatly. Since the major interest of this exposition is in the area of John's theology, we will follow his account from this point. Probably after joyous demonstrations by the apostles had subsided, Jesus repeated his "Peace be with you." Then he commissioned them for their continuing work with the mind-staggering words, "As the Father has sent me, even so send I you" (v. 21). The particle is modal, "just as." It meant that the model of his sending them was the Father's having sent him. The verb means basically "to send with a message"; the noun *apostle* is derived from it. The perfect tense of the verb emphasizes the permanence of his commission from the Father. Is it reading too much into the passage to think of his commission to proclaim the message of God's redemptive love as extending beyond the incarnation and continuing through the work of the Holy Spirit?

So, "Just as the Father has sent me to proclaim the message of his redeeming love, I also am sending you" (author's translation). The parallel may be extended in detail. He was sending them for the same purpose that the Father had sent him. He was sending them with the same support. He was sending them with the same spirit of compassion for a lost world. He was sending them with the same divine authority to undergird them. He was sending them with the same assurance of ultimate triumph through God's power.

Having commissioned them after the model of his own commission, he breathed upon them and said, "Receive the Holy Spirit" (v. 22). Here is one of the most dramatic differences in the accounts of Luke and John who alone reported the promise and the giving of the Holy Spirit. Observe the basic differences. In John, the Holy Spirit, was *promised* by Jesus in the Thursday night discourses of chapters 14 and 16. The Holy Spirit was *given* on the first appearance of Jesus to the apostles after his resurrection (20:22). They were empowered to forgive and to retain sin. On the other hand, in Luke Jesus *promised* the Holy Spirit near the end of the forty days of appearing and instructing the apostles before his ascension (24:49); he told them to wait in Jerusalem until the power came. He repeated the promise on the occasion of his last commission and ascension (Acts 1:5,8). Then the Holy Spirit was *given* at Pentecost (Acts 2:1–4). They were empowered to preach the message of redemption.

How are we to understand these two accounts of one of the most important tenets of the Christian faith, the giving of the Holy Spirit? In the history of the interpretation of the passage in John, two basic approaches have emerged. As usual there are variations of opinion among the interpreters in each group. First, Brown may be looked upon as representative of the view that the two accounts are independent reports (or interpretations) of one event—the bestowal of the Holy Spirit to empower the apostolic witness.[6] The Johannine account of the giving of the Spirit in 20:22 is to be understood as the total fulfillment of the promise in the earlier Gospel passages (chs. 14—16). He holds that *functionally* John 20:22 is describing the same event as Acts 2:1–4, the giving of the Holy Spirit by the risen and ascended Lord; only the descriptions are different. From the viewpoint of *content,* he understands the two accounts to have the same meaning— the task of the Holy Spirit to take the place of Jesus, to continue Jesus' work, and to constitute Jesus' presence in the world. He confesses that in a symbolic sense he can refer to John 20:22 as "the Johannine Pentecost" though he dates it at the time of Passover-Unleavened Bread festival rather than fifty days later at Pentecost.

Second, look at Plummer as representative of the view that the Johannine and the Luke-Acts accounts are two separate bestowals of the Holy Spirit—one at Jesus' first post-resurrection appearance to the apostles (John 20:22) and another on the day of Pentecost fifty days later (Acts 2:1–4).[7] By his interpretation, the New Testament presents a Passover bestowal of the Holy Spirit in preparation for the Pentecost bestowal. The first one Plummer characterizes as "an anticipation and earnest of Pentecost" (p. 343). This is similar to the language of Ephesians 1:14 in which the sealing of the believer in (or by) the Holy Spirit is characterized as an earnest (KJV) or guarantee (RSV) of the inheritance which will ultimately be possessed by the believer. The two are of the same quality, but the second is more comprehensive than the first. Jesus' bestowal of the Holy Spirit on the day of his resurrection (20:22) is not, then, to be identified with his bestowal of the Holy Spirit at Pentecost (Acts 1:1–4). Plummer speaks of the two in the language of analogy: the Johannine bestowal anticipated the Pentecostal one just as Jesus' bodily return from the grave and temporary presence with them for forty days anticipated his coming in the Spirit at Pentecost to be present with them to the end of the world. Conceptually, such reasoning is at home in the theological patterns of the Gospel of John. Here, as often in other theological areas, our thought patterns are in their expression limited by our language. We can give expression to our thoughts only to the extent that the language which we have permits it. Our language is never adequate in giving full expression where the doctrine of the Holy Spirit is concerned.

One other matter in verse 22 calls for attention. Jesus "breathed" on the apostles in bestowing the Holy Spirit. It is elementary knowledge that in Greek the word for spirit *(pneuma)* also means "breath" or "wind"; the same is true of *ruach* in Hebrew. The *ruach* (wind or Spirit) of God blew upon Ezekiel's valley of dry bones bringing them to life (Ezek. 37:1–10). So also the *pneuma* (wind or spirit) of God moved to bring to Nicodemus spiritual life (John 3:8). It is instructive, however, that in 20:22 the verb which is translated "breathed" is not the ordinary one from which the noun *pneuma* (spirit) is derived. Nowhere else in the New Testament is John's word for "breathed" used. It is used in the Greek translation of Genesis 2:7. In God's creation of Adam, he "breathed into his nostrils the breath of life." In the opening words of John's Gospel, "In the beginning" (1:1), God's initial creation through the Word was recalled. So in the end of his Gospel (20:22) the incarnate Word having become the risen Lord breathed upon God's new creation imparting the life-giving Spirit to empower them for the work to which he was appointing them.

Verse 23 establishes the apostles' task in the realm of the forgiveness of sin, "If you forgive the sins of any . . . if you retain the sins of any. . . ." There is a similar saying of Jesus in Matthew 16:19. In that setting, Peter had just voiced the apostles' confession, "You are the Christ, the Son of the living God." Jesus responded with his much disputed statement about his giving "the keys of the kingdom of heaven" for the apostles' use in binding and loosing. In that setting, the keys of the kingdom appear to relate to the idea of the authoritative action of the apostles as they would ultimately carry on the Lord's work. Peter was likely addressed as the representative of all of them, just as he had confessed as representative of all of them. In rabbinical use "binding and loosing" related to the interpretation of the Scriptures. By analogy, then, Jesus spoke of giving to the apostles the authority to interpret the terms of kingdom citizenship, the terms of salvation. How they acquited themselves of that responsibility would determine how men entered or failed to enter the kingdom. The saying involved no judgmental "I loose you of your sins," or "I bind you to your sins." While heaven's ratification would be upon their work, only God could pronounce forgiveness or condemnation.

Is this post-resurrection saying of Jesus about forgiving or retaining sin different from that earlier one? Note that it was definitely addressed to the apostolic group, not just to a representative one. Note also that it focused specifically on the forgiveness or the retention of sin. While agreeing in a general way that the meaning of the two sayings is the same, interpreters disagree on what the meaning is. Two rather basic views are expressed. Some hold that Jesus gave to the apostles, as a group acting under the guidance of the Holy Spirit, the authority to declare sins forgiven or sins retained. These interpreters hold, too, that the same authority resides in the church through all of its history as the redeemed community under the guidance and power of the Holy Spirit. With the inevitable variations in emphases and ideas, Barrett, Brown, Dodd, and Hoskyns are recommended as representatives of this group. Many of the interpretive energies of these scholars have been dissipated through debating whether the sins so pronounced as forgiven are sins committed before baptism as the entrance into the redeemed body or sins committed after baptism. Brown doubts that there is enough evidence in John to settle that question.[8]

He questions, too, the validity of attempting to determine the meaning of John 20:23 *by appealing to the meaning* of Matthew 16:19. He thinks that the Johannine passage must be interpreted in the larger context of the Gospel of John with a major emphasis on the immediate context of verses 21–22. The apostles can with authority declare sins forgiven or retained because Christ sent them *as the Father had sent him,* and that involved his declaring sins forgiven or retained. For example, in John 9:39–41, Jesus indicated that his coming into the world resulted in both forgiveness of sin and retention of sin. The blind man was willing to see, and he came to forgiveness. The religious leaders held on to their blindness refusing to see, and their sins remained (v. 41). Since Jesus was sending the apostles into the world as he had been sent, they were to continue that discriminatory judgment between good and evil, sins forgiven or sins retained. So Brown can say, "The disciples both by deed and word cause men to judge themselves; some come to the light and receive forgiveness; some turn away and are hardened in their sins." [9] While

that statement has a very evangelical sound, one assumes that
Professor Brown is writing within the framework of the dogma
of his confession and that a declaratory judgment on forgiveness
or retention of sins could be made by the church in relation to
the sacraments of the church.

Other interpreters think that John 20:23 *must be interpreted
in association* with Matthew 16:19. This would mean that the
forgiving and retaining of sin is realized in the apostles' proclamation of the message of God's forgiveness of sin or judgment upon
sin. These interpreters would hold with the previously discussed
scholars that such action was not given for the apostles alone
but that it is the responsibility of the redeemed community
through all of its history to make such proclamation. As the message of redemption is proclaimed and God's offer of forgiveness
is made, based on the genuineness of a faith acceptance of the
offer or of a willed rejection of the offer, God alone can make
the declaratory judgment, "I forgive your sins," or "I retain your
sins." The redeemed community, however, can make its encouraging declaration of opinion that on the basis of the faith acceptance God has forgiven or its warning declaration of opinion that
on the basis of willed rejection of God's offer one's sins are retained, still held in judgment against the sinner.

Within variations of vocabulary and emphases, the following
are recommended for further study as representatives of this general approach: Hendriksen, Hovey, Hull, Lenski, Plummer and
Strachan. Hovey has the most incisive presentation.[10] He points
to the fact that in the early church very little exercise of authoritative declaratory judgment of sin is in evidence. These were of
such extraordinary character as that of Ananias and Sapphira (Acts
5:1-11), Simon Magus (Acts 8:9-24), or the incestuous member
of the church at Corinth (1 Cor. 5:1-5). He summarizes by writing:

We do not believe that Jesus referred, in these words, to any formal
judicial action of his disciples. To what then did he refer? To the work
of the disciples as qualified by the Holy Spirit to declare without error

the conditions of forgiveness or condemnation under the reign of Christ.[11]

This interpretation is consistent with the remainder of New Testament teachings of sin, salvation, and judgment.

Acceptance by all of the apostles, with Thomas present, came on the following Sunday (20:24–29). Verses 24–25 contain an explanatory background to prepare the reader for Jesus' appearance in verses 26–29. Thomas was not present on the occasion of Jesus' appearance to the apostles on the day of his resurrection (vv. 19–23). He did not believe the apostles' report, "We have seen the Lord." One imagines that there was more dialogue involved than John's terse account supplies. They likely reported Jesus' disclosing the scars from the nails and the spear, and they may have included the detail in Luke's account that Jesus invited them to touch his body. Thomas insistently stated the conditions for his belief that Jesus had been raised from the dead; he would believe only if he could *see* the scars and *touch* them. His determination is unmistakeably clear in the most emphatic double negative of the Greek text, "I will *not never* believe"—bad English but perfect Greek! Projecting our knowledge of our own nature into the situation, we can feel certain that the running topic of the entire week was the no of Thomas and the yes of the apostles— perhaps the needling, "Look what you missed by not being at church last Sunday night!" When we call him "doubting Thomas," however, let us remember that he asked for no evidence which had not been available to the others. He asked only for that.

Verse 26 sets the situation as identical with the previous one. "Eight days later" means on the first day of the week, as before. They were again "in the house." That Revised Standard Version translation suggests that it was the same house. It may have been; the Greek text has simply "were inside." "The doors were shut" (locked) as before. There was one major detail which differed, "and Thomas was with them." Just as on the preceding Sunday, Jesus appeared in their midst and said, "Peace be with you."

While all eyes were doubtless on Jesus, all minds were likely on Thomas. Would he believe now? Jesus addressed only Thomas. For the dramatic effect of the highly charged emotional situation, let us use a very literal translation of Jesus' words to Thomas: "Bring your finger right here and explore my hands, and bring your hand and put it firmly upon my side, and stop being an unbeliever but [become] a believer" (v. 27).

Jesus' words interpret themselves. He knew the mind and the need of Thomas. He offered to Thomas the most objective proof possible. "Right here" (hōde) is very specific—bring your finger to the very spot where the nail had been—"see" the scar with your hand. Bring your hand and put it firmly over the scar from the spear. Adjectives are then used as nouns with the imperatives—"Stop being an unbelieving person, but [start] being a believing person."

Did Thomas accept the Lord's invitation to satisfy his mind by the evidence of touch? The text makes no statement to that effect. The impression is that he was convinced by sight just as the others had been. His reverent response has the tone of a creedal confession: "My Lord and My God!" It is the most direct and most emphatic of any of the verbal expressions of acceptance of the risen Lord. The Gospel of John ends as it begins, with an emphatic assertion of the essential deity of Jesus Christ: 1:1, "the Word was God," and 20:28, "My Lord and My God!" That same affirmation runs as a consistent theme through the entire Gospel from beginning to end.

Jesus accepted Thomas' confession of faith and pronounced a blessing upon all of like confession. His words may be a declarative statement, "You have believed because you have seen" (v. 29, KJV and ASV) or a question, "Have you believed because you have seen me?" (RSV and TEV). Interpreters divide, as do the translators, but all recognize the words as an acceptance of the confession. The major thrust of Jesus' response is in the second part, "Blessed are those who have not seen and yet believe" (v.

29). This is not a rebuke to Thomas for requiring sight as a basis for faith. So had all of the other apostles, with the possible exception of the beloved disciple who "believed" when he saw the grave clothes (20:8). Rather, Jesus' blessing was pronounced upon those who would not be privileged to see him in his resurrection form and yet would believe in it. As through Christian history, believers have accepted Jesus' prayer in 17:20 as a prayer for them, so they have accepted his blessing in 20:29 as his blessing upon them: "He prayed for me; he blessed me." Such claim has reality beyond sentimentality. By the time this Gospel was written, thousands had believed though they had not seen. Even with the modern scientific methods of computation, no one could estimate the multiplied millions who since John's day have believed though they have not seen. All of them confess with Thomas, "My Lord and My God!" All of them claim the risen Lord's blessing.

The conclusion to the Gospel of John was penned very appropriately at the point of that confession and blessing (vv. 30–31). There can be no doubt that the writer regarded his Gospel as completed, planned a very fitting conclusion, and intended to add nothing. He looked back over the ministry of Jesus. He made mental note of the many miracles (signs) which Jesus had done. He looked again at the seven which he had used in his "book of signs," chapters 2—11. He framed a conclusion which would explain to all readers (1) why he had written and (2) why he had chosen these particular signs to carry out his purpose.

Jesus had performed "many other signs in the presence of his disciples" (v. 30). We have no way of determining how many he performed. We can read the four Gospels and count thirty-five to thirty-seven depending on one's interpretation. This was discussed in the exposition of 6:1–71. In addition to these, the Gospel writers mention other healing situations in which multiple miracles were performed, but no number is given (Matt. 4:23; 9:35; Mark 6:56; Luke 4:40; 5:15; 6:17–19; 7:21; John 2:23; 3:2;

4:45; 20:30; 21:25). The only safe course seems to be John's reference to "many others."

Under the guidance of the Holy Spirit of whom he had written at length (chs. 14—16), John selected those which he considered best for eliciting the *faith* which leads to *life* (v. 31). In the general introduction to this Gospel we noted that John used the miracles which from the human viewpoint make the greatest demand on credence. John wrote to convince his readers that (1) Jesus was the Christ, the Son of God, and (2) that by believing in him one might have eternal life. His thought was that belief that Jesus had done these miracles led logically to belief that he was the Son of God. Eternal life is God's gift to those who exercise that faith in Jesus Christ. John framed his Gospel to that end, and he felt that he had accomplished that end as he wrote his conclusion.

P.S.: Do You Love Me?
21:1–25

Acceptance by seven disciples stands last in the Gospel of John, but it is not in the main part of the Gospel. It is in a beautiful and dramatic postscript (21:1–25). Since it is not a part of the Gospel as concluded in 20:30–31, it cannot properly be called an epilogue as some interpreters suggest. In subjective appraisal, it deserves a bit more than the prosaic addendum for which other interpreters settle. Postscript accurately describes it, and it will be quickly recognized that the remainder of the title grows out of Jesus' dialogue with Simon Peter in verses 15–19.

All interpreters consulted in this study recognize the nature of the chapter as an addition to the original body of the Gospel. All recognize that it was added before the Gospel went into circulation. There is not one fragment of evidence to suggest that chapters 1—20 were ever circulated without chapter 21. Debate over the chapter is carried on in relation to questions such as: Was it written by the writer of chapters 1—20 or by someone else? Why was it added to the original Gospel? How is this appearance of Jesus to be fitted into those in chapter 20? Then, of course there are many, many questions of how we are to understand the details of action and dialogue in the event. That is a part of all exposition and theological pursuit.

Plummer has the best argument favoring the view that the writer of chapter 21 was the same person who wrote chapters 1—20.[12] His commentary throughout is a strong defense for John the son of Zebedee as the beloved disciple and the author of the Gospel. Barrett [13] and Brown [14] have the best arguments for someone other than the writer of chapters 1—20 as the writer of chapter 21. Neither endorses the apostle John as the writer of either part. Brown refers to the writer of chapters 1—20 as the "evangelist" and the writer of chapter 21 as the "redactor." He views the redactor as thoroughly Johannine in thought and writing and likely of the same community of scholars as the evangelist. All of these scholars, and most others who were consulted, see some vocabulary and stylistic differences between chapters 1—20 and chapter 21, but their thought is that the two sections are enough alike to see chapter 21 as very much at home in the language of chapters 1—20. One thing is certain; there will be no meeting of interpreters' minds on who wrote the chapter. Regardless of who wrote it, and granting the presence of other unanswered questions which will come up in the exposition, it belongs where it is—a part of John, but an added part.

Appearance (vv. 1–14)—The format is a post-resurrection appearance of Jesus which brings about: (1) a miraculous catch of fish, (2) added apostolic faith in Jesus' resurrection, (3) the restoration of Simon Peter as the leader of the believing community, and (4) the clarification of a rumor in the early church that Jesus had said that the beloved disciple would not die but would live until his return. The setting was the familiar scene of one of Jesus' early miracles when he had helped Peter, Andrew, James, and John to catch fish after they had fished all night and had caught nothing. That was when he called them to leave the fishing business and follow him in catching men (Mark 1:16–20; Luke 5:1–11). The participants were seven of Jesus' disciples: Simon Peter; Thomas; Nathanael, of whom no mention has been made since his dialogue with Jesus in 1:45–51; the sons of Zebedee, the only definite reference to them in John though their role in the Synoptics is major; and two unidentified "disciples" (v. 2). Was the writer thinking of these seven as a part of the ten in 20:19–23 and the eleven in 20:24–29? Perhaps so; he states in verse 14 that this was the "third time that Jesus was revealed to the disciples after he was raised." That would pose some problem since Nathanael was not one of the twelve in any of the four listings of their names (Mark 3:16–19; Matt. 10:2–4; Luke 6:14–16; Acts 1:13). The extreme alphabetical manipulation which some have used to equate Bartholomew of those lists with Nathanael in John is very fragile. Some have suggested that the two unidentified disciples were Andrew and Philip. That could be; their homes were nearby and both are very prominent in the Gospel of John. If so, however, it is strange that their names would not be given. Plummer holds that probably the two were not identified because they were not apostles.[15]

Simon Peter, who is named first in all of the above cited lists, took the lead in this event by announcing, "I am going fishing" (v. 3). The others agreed to go with him. Some think he had in mind only a temporary occupation as they waited for Jesus to join them in Galilee as he had promised (Matt. 26:32; 28:7). Others think that Peter was so broken and discouraged by what had happened to Jesus and his own cowardly action in it that he meant to return to his previous business as a fisherman on a permanent basis. The key for unlocking this problem is unavailable. That key is the time of this appearance in relationship to his other appearances. It is unthinkable that Peter would consider giving up his work for the Lord if this came after the other appearances which he had experienced. On the other hand, if this appearance came before the others, how do we explain Thomas' witnessing it and then reacting and acting as he did in reference to the other two appearances in John 20:19–28? There seems to be no way to fit this appearance into the others without leaving some unanswered questions.

The seven spent the night casting their nets and pulling them in empty (v. 3). In the dim light of the early dawn Jesus stood on the beach and called across the water that separated him from the boat, "Boys, you haven't anything to eat, have you?" (v. 5, author's translation). If that literal translation has a sound of levity inappropriate for the risen Lord, note what is in it and what develops from it. "Boys," "Lads," "Fellows"—any of these fit the situation of a stranger talking to strangers better than "Children," the usual translation of *paidia;* to the disciples, the man on the beach was a stranger (v. 4). As asked, the question anticipated a negative answer. The word which is usually translated "fish" meant "anything which one eats with bread"—sometimes a relish, sometimes meat. Fish was so commonly eaten with bread that the word many times was translated "fish." The verb which is usually translated "caught" is the verb *to have.* Fishermen and hunters sometimes used it in reference to catching game. Jesus' question was in the language of everyday use and very pointedly called attention to their plight—they had caught nothing; they had nothing to eat.

Any person who has fished all night and has caught nothing, can appreciate the lack of enthusiasm in the one word answer to Jesus' question, "No." And three of these men, perhaps four, were professionals! The stranger on the beach called back, "Cast the net on the right side of the boat, and you will find some" (v. 6). Professionals do not always welcome suggestions from strangers about how to do their work—especially professional fishermen and professional interpreters of the Scriptures! But fishermen will try anyone's suggestion when no fish are being caught. They cast the net. It enclosed so many fish that they could not get it into the boat. Interesting, isn't it, that these men were professional fishermen, but in the Gospels the only time they caught fish was when Jesus helped them.

Now the man on the beach was no longer a stranger. One betrayed; one denied; nine ran away; only one stayed with Jesus unto the end. That one, the beloved disciple, made a discovery— to Peter he said, "It is the Lord!" or preserving a bit better the emphatic structure of his exclamation, *"The Lord* it is!" Impulsive Simon temporarily lost interest in the fish. Putting on his outer robe which he had put aside for the work of fishing, he leaped overboard and went swimming and wading to the shore leaving the others to follow in the boat dragging the fish-filled nets.

If the next few sentences were in the Synoptics, they would be regarded as simple narration of event. In John, with his love for double meaning, they have strong theological overtones. The disciples who had caught nothing came ashore with the fish which Jesus had helped them to "find" (v. 6) and found their crucified and resurrected Lord with a charcoal fire, with *fish* already cooking, and *bread* to go with it. His invitation was hortatory, "Come on! Break your fast" (v. 12, literal translation). What theological overtones are there? Two of his miracles are recalled. Once before he had miraculously shown them where to catch fish after they had worked at their job all night and had taken nothing (Luke 5:1–11). That miracle could well have been on the very spot of this one. Once before he had provided bread and fish for them and five thousand others with food to spare (Luke 9:10–17). That was all before death on a Roman cross took him from their midst. Now here he was, alive this side of that cross, and again he provided bread and fish for their need. *The cross had not stopped his ability to be with them and to provide for their needs!* All of them were convinced that he was alive again. They were so awestruck, however, that not one of them questioned him, Who are you? They knew he was Jesus of Nazareth, their Teacher and Leader, but they knew more than that—he was the Lamb of God, their sacrificed but triumphant Redeemer.

Commission (vv. 15–23)—Jesus commissioned Simon Peter a second time. On the earlier occasion, the miraculous catch of fish had brought Simon Peter to his knees in confession of his sin and his unworthiness to be in Jesus' presence (Luke 5:8–9). Jesus had calmly quieted his fear and had said, "Henceforth you will be catching men" (v. 10). The four fishermen left their boats and nets to become four fishers of men (v. 11). Three years of association with Jesus and preaching, teaching, and healing by his appointment had brought them to that sad night of his arrest. He warned them of danger and predicted that when the crisis point came they would flee, leaving him alone (John 16:32–33). A bit earlier Peter had said, "I will lay down my life for you" (13:37). He had boasted that even though all the others forsook Jesus, he would not; he was ready to go to prison and to death for Jesus (Mark 14:29; Matt. 26:33; Luke 22:33). But when the crisis came, Peter was so overcome by fear that he denied three times that he was even acquainted with Jesus (John 18:15–27 with parallels in the three Synoptics). Later Peter had wept bitterly over his conduct. He above all of the others who had run away needed assurance of restoration. It was given to him at this appearance of the Lord whom he had denied.

After breakfast, and apparently in the presence of the other disciples, Jesus initiated a question and answer dialogue with Peter. Woven into it was his commission to Peter for the work which ultimately would lead to Peter's martyrdom. Even that prospect was not to turn Peter aside from his service; the two imperatives in verses 19 and 22 are in the present tense, "Keep on following me." The dialogue consisted of three questions from Jesus, three responses from Peter, and three words of commission from Jesus. The form and vocabulary of the dialogue has resulted in fragmentation on the part of interpreters. Two different words are used for love; two different words are used for sheep; two different words are used for caring for the sheep. Are these only stylistic differences for variety of expression just as three different words are used for fish in verses 5, 9, and 11? Or is there a special reason for the use of the different words?

The main area of disagreement among interpreters is the meaning of the two words which are used for love. The two verbs which are used in the Greek New Testament for expressing the emotion of love are *agapaō* and *phileō*. Basically, *agapaō* involves rational good will, priority of value on the part of its object, to put the object first. God put such value upon the world that he gave his Son to redeem it (John 3:16); to love one's enemies is to exercise rational good will for them in evaluating them as persons, after the pattern of God's evaluation and rational good will for them (Matt. 5:44–46). A man puts such value on his wife that he sacrifices his own best interest in order that her best interest may be advanced, after the pattern of Christ's evaluation and sacrifice for the church (Eph. 5:25). In all of these passages the verb is *agapaō*. Basically, *phileō* involves warm, personal affection for its object. Parents and children mutually exercise warm personal affection for one another, but it is not to exceed their warm, personal affection for Jesus (Matt. 10:37). Jesus had warm, personal affection for Lazarus (John 11:3,36) and the beloved disciple (20:2). These passages use *phileō*.

These are basic uses which generally follow a consistent pattern in the New Testament. It must be recognized, however, that there are exceptions to such basic use. It must also be remembered in dealing with this passage that in John the above distinction is not consistently followed. Jesus' disciples love him (16:27*b*), where *phileō* encroaches on the basic use of *agapaō*. The same is true in 16:27*a* of God's love for Jesus' disciples and in 5:20 in God's love for Jesus. Is the basic distinction to be understood in 21:15–17, or does *phileō* so encroach on *agapaō* in the dialogue that the distinction is lost? Here is the position of the interpreters who have been consistently used in this volume. Those who insist that the distinction must be maintained if the real meaning of the passage is understood are: Hendriksen, Hovey, Lenski, Plummer, Temple, and Westcott. Those who think that the distinction is not to be observed are: Barrett, Brown, Bultmann, Hoskyns, Hull, Strachan, and Tasker. All of the New Testament versions which have been consistently used translate "love" for both words, thus leaving the debate to the expositors!

Jesus' first question was, "Do you love me more than these?" He used *agapaō*. Peter answered, "Yes, Lord; you know that I love you," He used *phileō*. If the interpreters who insist on the distinct basic meaning of the two words are right, the thrust of the exchange would be something like: "Simon . . . do you put such value upon me that I come first in your life?" "Yes, Lord; you know that I have warm affection and esteem for you." The difference would be that Peter would not venture to affirm such loyalty as Jesus had proposed in his question. Undoubtedly Peter had understood Jesus' "more than these" reference and he intentionally omitted any response to it. There is a degree of ambiguity in the words. Interpreters find three possible meanings in the construction: (1) Do you love me more than you love these *fishing nets and boat*. In this case "these" should be in the neuter accusative plural case form. It is actually in a genitive plural case form which may be either masculine or neuter. (2) Do you love me more than you love *these other disciples*. In this case "these" would need to be in the masculine plural case form. (3) Do you love me more than *these other disciples love me*. In this case the masculine genitive plural case form which is used is correct; grammarians call it the genitive of comparison.

Interpreters who bother to comment on number (2) leave it out as unthinkable; there seems to be no possibility that Peter could confess to loving his friends more than he loved his Lord. Some interpreters accept number (1) with the view that Jesus was chiding Peter for leaving his work as an apostle to return to his former fisherman's role. By far the majority of the interpreters accept number (3) as Jesus' meaning. They relate it, as Peter must have, to his former boasting that even though all of the others ran away he would not because his love for Jesus was too great for that. Jesus' question would then mean, "Simon . . . do you still profess to love me more than the other disciples do?" The thrust was too painful for a response. Peter sidestepped it to respond that the Lord knew that he loved him—though even the "rock" had stumbled in a testing situation that proved to be too big for him!

Jesus knew Peter's devotion and his character. His response was in words of commission again. Once he had commissioned Peter to be a fisher of men; now he commissioned him as a shepherd, "Feed my lambs" (v. 15). The profession of love calls for the commitment to service. To love Christ is to serve Christ, and he has many "lambs" that need to be fed.

Jesus' second question was the same as the first except that, out of compassion for one who was suffering in his own self-condemnation, he dropped the "More than these" part and asked, "Do you love me?" He still used *agapaō*, and Peter responded with *phileō*, "Yes, Lord; you know that I love you." Jesus' words of commission changed to, "Tend my sheep" (v. 16). The word for "feed" in verse 15 is probably to be restricted to feeding, although in the sense of grazing it could have a larger application. The word for "tend" in verse 16 is much broader in scope. It means to exercise all of the responsibility of a shepherd: to lead to pasture; to protect from wild animals and robbers; to nurture—caring for all needs. That may be the reason for the change from "lambs" of the previous commission to "sheep." Some interpreters suggest that lambs have one main need, feeding, but that sheep have many other needs out in open pasture.

Jesus' third question was the same as his second except that he changed verbs. "Do you love me?" He used *phileō*, changing to Peter's word. The next sentence has been the source of most of the divided opinion on the use of the two verbs for love—"Peter was grieved because he said to him the third time, 'Do you love me?' " (v. 17). Was Peter grieved because in the third question Jesus changed to his verb, hence, questioning if Peter really felt the warm, personal affection of *phileō?* Those interpreters who insist on distinguishing between the two verbs say, yes. Those who hold to no significant distinction between the two verbs in John's Gospel say, no; Peter was grieved because Jesus asked him the same question three times. Peter had denied the Lord three times. The Lord asked "Do you love me?" for every time that Peter had said, essentially, "I do not know him." Peter's emotion mounted each time his Lord questioned his love for him, and the third time was almost too much. His answer was even more emphatic than the first two, "Lord, you know everything; you know that I love you." He was certain that Jesus knew everything that was in his heart, and in his heart he really did love Jesus. Jesus' response was, "Feed my sheep." He used the same word for sheep which he had used in the second case but went back to the first one for "feed." Sheep, no less than lambs, need to be fed. The Lord's sheep never grow so old or mature that they do not need to be fed on the Word.

No final conclusion seems forthcoming on the use of the two verbs for love. One must agree with one group that: (1) the proliferation of synonyms in this passage, multiple words for "fish," "feed," "sheep," and "love," weakens the argument for a sharp distinction between *agapaō* and *phileō* in this case; (2) a thrice-repeated question on so delicate a matter as Peter's love for his Lord was enough to grieve him regardless of the words used; and (3) few interpreters would deny that the dialogue was carried on in Aramaic in which no such distinction is possible. On the other hand one must agree with the other interpreters that: (1) what we have is the Greek text in which the writer was presenting his understanding of what went on in the Aramaic dialogue; and (2) if he did not mean to show a distinction between the two verbs, why would he for stylistic variation use them thus creating almost inevitable confusion of understanding rather than clarity of understanding?

Having given to Simon Peter a clear and dramatic commission as leader of the new Israel, the redeemed community for his countinuing witness, Jesus spoke to him of the fate that would be his in that service. As a young man Simon had been strong, self-willed, self-determining in his life-style as a fish merchant among a strong, self-willed, self-determining people. He went where he wished and did what he wished. Now he was commissioned and committed to a new life which for the years ahead would mean a life of ideological conflict and hostility where the minds and hearts of men meet and clash in the arena of religion. His course would be perilous. Age and conflict would bring him to a situation in which he would not will his own life and conduct. Others would bind his outstretched hands and lead him along the road which he would not choose to go—the road to death as a martyr. He would glorify God in life; then he would glorify God in death, just as his Lord had done (v. 19). Early Christian history speaks to the fulfillment of Jesus' words of prophecy. It reports that Peter died as a martyr and that he died as his Lord had died, by crucifixion. Having spoken those solemn words, Jesus added, "Follow me" (v. 19). The form is the present imperative which carries the force of continuous action, "Keep on following me." There was to be no turning back.

From verses 20–23 it appears that Jesus led Peter away from the group. It could have been for a continuance of his speaking of Peter's service and ultimate martyrdom. As they walked along the beach, Peter's mind was more on the martyrdom than on the service. Glancing back, he saw that the beloved disciple was following them (v. 20). If death as a martyr was to be his fate, he wondered what was in store for that disciple who of all of them seemed to be closest to Jesus. So he asked, "Lord what about this man?" (v. 21). This is a smooth translation of an elliptical expression—"Lord, this man but what?" Words have to be supplied to make the meaning clear. "This man" is in the emphatic position and clearly stands as a contrast to Simon Peter, as if Peter asked, "Lord, if I am to be executed as a martyr, what about this man?" Jesus understood Peter's frame of mind and his question. His answer was, "If it is my will that he remain until I come, what is that to you? Follow me!" (v. 22). The verb "wish" is subjunctive, "If I should wish." The verb "to remain" is used in 1 Corinthians 15:6 to mean "stay alive." "Until I come" can hardly be questioned as a Parousia saying. The rarely expressed subject of the imperative is emphatic, *you* and the imperative as noted above is the present tense of continuing action. Putting all of that together we have, "If I should wish him to stay alive until I come, what concern is that to you? *You,* keep on following me." Verse 23 contains a rumor that circulated widely that Jesus had predicted that the beloved disciple would not die at all but would live until the Lord returned. If one accepts the tradition of the early church that the beloved disciple was John the apostle and that he lived until near the end of the first century (and there is more evidence for accepting both than for rejecting them), it is easy to understand how a rumor got out that John was going to live until the Lord's return. The writer of this Gospel explained that it was a false rumor that grew out of Jesus' words to Simon Peter. Those words were to rivet his attention on his one legitimate concern, that he keep on following his Lord in the service to which he had been commissioned even with the prospect of a martyr's death at the end of the road.

Validation (vv. 24–25)—The author of the Gospel framed his own conclusion in 20:30–31. He may or may not have written verses 1–23 of the postscript. It is clear, however, that he did not write verses 24–25. Their language clearly identifies them as coming from someone other than the writer of the Gospel. These verses form a validation of the Gospel by the Christian community from which the Gospel went out literally to the whole world. By dependable tradition, that Christian community was Ephesus. Their guarantee of the Gospel is stated in three parts: (1) the beloved disciple was the one who brought to Ephesus the record of the words and works of Jesus which make up this Gospel ("This is the disciple" [v. 24] points back to "the disciple whom Jesus loved," [vv. 20–23]); (2) that same disciple was the one who wrote down the things that are in this Gospel (v. 24*b*); [16] (3) the Christian community at Ephesus felt that it was the trustee of this form of Jesus' words and works; they had accepted the witness of it from the beloved disciple and they knew that it was a true witness (v. 24*c*).

The final word as this marvelous Gospel went out from the Ephesian Christians was from an unidentified member of their community. Anonymously he is indicated only by the pronoun "I" in verse 25. His responsibility was to put everything in order and to get the Gospel on its way. We may call him the editor or its more commonly used synonym redactor. What a debt of gratitude Christians of all ages owe to this brother in Christ. Having completed what he must have considered as a labor of love, he penned his own words of wonder: "But there are also many other things which Jesus did; were every one of them to be written, I suppose that the world itself could not contain the books that would be written." Hyperbole? Granted, but most appropriate hyperbole for *"The Lamb of God who takes away the sin of the world!"*

Notes

1. Mark is not listed here because for a hundred years the best of textual opinion has been that 16:9–20 was not a part of the original Mark. That view is currently being challenged by some scholars. The three appearances which are in the long ending (vv. 9–14), while differing radically in details, are also in Matthew, Luke, and John.
2. For more detailed presentation of the resurrection of Jesus, see Summers,

Commentary on Luke, pp. 315–338 and *The Life Beyond,* pp. 32–46.

3. Robertson, *A Harmony of the Four Gospels,* p. 249 including the footnote.
4. Strachan, p. 344.
5. It is difficult to determine exactly where the appearance ends in the Luke account. Does it end with verse 43 or 44 or 49? A subjective opinion is that: (1) it ends with verse 43; (2) verses 44–49 summarize the thrust of Jesus' instructions to the apostles during the forty days; and (3) verses 50–53 parallel the ascension appearance which Luke recounts fully in Acts 1:3–11.
6. After lengthy discussion covering large parts of pages 1018–1045, R. E. Brown presents a very precise statement of this view on pages 1038–1039.
7. Plummer, pp. 343–344.
8. R. E. Brown, pp. 1039–1046.
9. Ibid., p. 1043.
10. Hovey, pp. 404–406.
11. Ibid., p. 405.
12. Plummer, pp. 384–357.
13. Barrett, pp. 479–490.
14. R. E. Brown, p. 1067–1130.
15. Plummer, p. 349.
16. Review the discussion on the authorship of this Gospel in the introduction above.

Bibliography

Commentaries

Barrett, C. K. *The Gospel According to St. John.* London: S.P.C.K., 1958.

Brown, Raymond E. "The Gospel According to John," 2 vols. *The Anchor Bible.* Garden City, N.Y.: Doubleday and Company, Inc., 1966.

Bultmann, R. *The Gospel of John.* Edited by R. W. N. Hoare and J. K. Riches. Translated by G. R. Beasley-Murray. Philadelphia: The Westminster Press, 1971.

Calvin, J. *The Gospel According to St. John,* 2 vols. Translated by T. H. L. Parker. Grand Rapids: Wm. B. Eerdmans Publishing Co., 1959.

Filson, Floyd V. "The Gospel According to John." *The Layman's Bible Commentary,* vol. 19. Richmond: John Knox Press, 1963.

Hendriksen, William. "Exposition of the Gospel According to John," 2 vols. *New Testament Commentary.* Grand Rapids: Baker Book House, 1953.

Hoskyns, E. *The Fourth Gospel.* Edited by F. N. Davey. London: Faber and Faber Limited, 1947.

Hovey, Alvah. "John." *An American Commentary on the New Testament,* vol. 3. Philadelphia: American Baptist Publication Society, 1885.

Howard, Wilbert F. "The Gospel According to St. John." *The Interpreters Bible,* vol. 8. Edited by George A. Buttrick. New

York: Abingdon-Cokesbury Press, 1952.

Hull, William E. "John." *The Broadman Bible Commentary,* vol. 9. Edited by Clifton J. Allen. Nashville: Broadman Press, 1970.

Lenski, R. C. H. *The Interpretation of St. John's Gospel.* Columbus: Lutheran Book Concern, 1942.

Plummer, A. "The Gospel According to St. John." *Cambridge Greek Testament for Schools and Colleges.* Cambridge: University Press, 1905.

Richardson, Alan. "The Gospel According to Saint John." *Torch Bible Commentaries.* London: SCM Press, Ltd., 1959.

Robertson, A. T. *Word Pictures in the New Testament,* vols. 3,5. Nashville: Broadman Press, 1932.

Tasker, R. V. G. "The Gospel According to St. John." *The Tyndale New Testament Commentaries.* Grand Rapids: Wm. B. Eerdmans Publishing Company, 1960.

Westcott, B. F. *The Gospel According to St. John.* London: James Clarke and Co., 1958.

Other Books

Beasley-Murray, G. R. *Baptism in the New Testament.* New York: St. Martin's Press, 1962.

Bultmann, R. *Theology of the New Testament,* vol. 1. Translated by Kendrick Grobel. New York: Charles Scribner's Sons, 1951.

Colwell, E. C. and Titus, E. L. *The Gospel of the Spirit.* New York: Harper and Brothers Publishers, 1953.

Corell, Alf. *Consummatum Est: Eschatology and Church in the Gospel of St. John.* New York: The Macmillan Company, 1958.

Cullmann, Oscar. *Baptism in the New Testament.* Chicago: Henry Regnery Company, 1950.

Culpepper, R. Alan. *The Johannine School.* Missoula, Montana: Scholars Press, 1975.

Dana, H. E. *The Ephesian Tradition.* Kansas City: The Kansas City Press, 1940.

_____. *The Heavenly Guest.* Nashville: Broadman Press, 1943.

Dodd, C. H. *The Fourth Gospel.* Cambridge: At the University Press, 1958.

Fortna, Robert T. *The Gospel of Signs.* Cambridge: Cambridge University Press, 1970.

Glasson, T. F. *Moses in the Fourth Gospel.* Naperville, Ill.: Alec R. Allenson, Inc., 1963.

Headlam, A. C. *The Fourth Gospel as History.* New York: The Macmillan Company, 1948.

Howard, Wilbert F. *The Fourth Gospel in Recent Criticism and Debate.* London: The Epworth Press, 1931.

_____. *Christianity According to St. John.* Philadelphia: The Westminster Press, 1946.

Isaac, Jules. *The Teaching of Contempt.* New York: Holt, Rinehart and Winston, 1964.

Jeremias, Joachim. *The Rediscovery of Bethesda,* "The New Testament Archaelogy Monograph No. 1." Edited by E. Jerry Vardaman. Louisville, Ky.: Southern Baptist Theological Seminary, 1966.

_____. *The Eucharistic Words of Jesus.* New York: The Macmillan Company, 1955.

Josephus, Flavius. *Complete Works of Flavius Josephus,* tran. by William Winston. Grand Rapids: Kregel Publishers, 1960, p. 382—optional reference in *any* edition of Josephus' works: Antiquities XVIII. 5.2.

Morris, Leon. *Studies in the Fourth Gospel.* Grand Rapids: Wm. B. Eerdmans Publishing Company, 1969.

Robertson, A. T. *A Harmony of the Four Gospels.* New York: Harper and Brothers Publishers, 1922.

_____. *Epochs in the Life of the Apostle John.* New York: Fleming H. Revell Company, 1935.

Robinson, J. A. T. *Redating the New Testament.* Philadelphia: The Westminster Press, 1976.

Smith, Dwight Moody, Jr. *The Composition and Order of the Fourth Gospel.* New Haven: Yale University Press, 1965.

Smith, T. C. *Jesus in the Gospel of John.* Nashville: Broadman Press, 1959.

Stewart, James S. *The Wind of the Spirit.* Nashville: Abingdon Press, 1968.

Strachan, R. H. *The Fourth Gospel, Its Significance and Environment.* London: Student Christian Movement Press, Ltd., 1917.

Strack, H. L. and Billerbeck, P. *Kommentar zum Neuen Testament aus Talmud und Midrash,* 6 vols. Munich: Beck, 1963.

Summers, Ray. *Commentary on Luke.* Waco, Texas: Word Books, Publisher, 1972.

_____. *Ephesians: Pattern for Christian Living.* Nashville: Broadman Press, 1960.

_____. *The Life Beyond.* Nashville: Broadman Press, 1959.

_____. *The Secret Sayings of the Living Jesus.* Waco, Texas: Word Books, Publisher, 1968.

_____. *Worthy Is the Lamb.* Nashville: Broadman Press, 1951.

Temple, William. *Readings in St. John's Gospel.* London: Macmillan and Company, Ltd., 1961.

Vardaman, E. Jerry and Garrett, James Leo, Jr., Editors. *The Teachers Yoke: Studies in Memory of Henry Trantham.* Waco, Texas: Baylor University Press, 1964.

Whittier, John Greenleaf. *The Complete Poetical Works of Whittier.* Boston: Houghton Mifflin Company, 1894.

Windisch, Hans. *The Spirit-Paraclete in the Fourth Gospel.* Translated by James W. Cox. Philadelphia: Fortress Press, 1968.

Articles

Barrett, C. K. "The Lamb of God." *New Testament Studies,* Fel ruary 1955.

Bowker, J. W. "The Origin and Purpose of St. John's Gospel." *New Testament Studies,* July 1965.

Brown, Raymond B. "The Distinctives of John's Gospel." *Southwestern Journal of Theology,* October 1965.

_____. "The Prologue of the Gospel of John." *Review and Expositor,* Fall 1965.

Brown, R. E. "The Gospel of Thomas and St. John's Gospel." *New Testament Studies,* January 1963.

_____. "The Paraclete in the Fourth Gospel." *New Testament Studies,* January 1967.

Bruns, J. Edgar. "The Use of Time in the Fourth Gospel." *New Testament Studies,* April 1967.

Bultmann, R. "The Interpretation of the Fourth Gospel." *New Testament Studies,* November 1954.

Caird, G. B. "The Glory of God in the Fourth Gospel." *New Testament Studies,* April 1969.

Cullmann, Oscar. "A New Approach to the Interpretation of the Fourth Gospel." *The Expository Times,* October 1959.

Cribbs, F. Lamar. "A Reassessment of the Date of Origin and the Destination of the Gospel of John." *Journal of Biblical Literature,* March 1970.

Deeks, David. "The Structure of the Fourth Gospel." *New Testament Studies,* October 1968.

Fiorenza, Elizabeth Schussler. "The Quest for the Johannine School: The Apocalypse and the Fourth Gospel." *New Testament Studies,* July 1977.

Fortna, Robert T. "Source and Redaction in the Fourth Gospel's Portrayal of Jesus' Signs." *Journal of Biblical Literature,* June 1970.

Hunt, W. Boyd. "John's Doctrine of the Spirit." *Southwestern Journal of Theology,* October 1965.

Lee, E. K. "St. Mark and the Fourth Gospel." *New Testament Studies,* November 1956.

Parker, P. "Luke and the Fourth Gospel." *New Testament Studies,* July 1963.

Price, James L. "The Search for the Theology of the Fourth Evangelist." *Journal of the American Academy of Religion,* March 1967.

Robinson, J. A. T. "The Destination and Purpose of St. John's Gospel." *New Testament Studies,* January 1960.

_____. "The Relation of the Prologue to the Gospel of St. John." *New Testament Studies,* January 1963.

Smith, T. C. "The Book of Signs." *Review and Expositor,* Fall 1965.

Songer, Harold S. "The Gospel of John in Recent Research." *Review and Expositor,* Fall 1965.

Summers, Ray. "The Death and Resurrection of Jesus, John 18–21." *Review and Expositor,* October 1965.

_____. "The Christ of John's Gospel." *Southwestern Journal of Theology,* October 1965.

Torrey, C. C. "In the Fourth Gospel the Last Supper Was the Paschal Meal." *Jewish Quarterly,* January 1952.

Zeitlin, Solomon. "The Last Supper as an Ordinary Meal in the Fourth Gospel." *Jewish Quarterly,* January 1952.